The Stories We Share

The Stories
We Share

A Guide to PreK–12 Books on the Experience of
Immigrant Children and Teens in the United States

LADISLAVA N. KHAILOVA

ALA
Editions
CHICAGO 2018

Dr. Ladislava Khailova is an associate professor at the Founders Memorial Library, Northern Illinois University, serving as a humanities and social sciences subject specialist and coordinator of library services for persons with disabilities. Born in the Czech Republic, Khailova came to the United States as a Fulbright grantee to study twentieth-century American literature and, subsequently, library and information science. She earned a PhD in English and an MLIS from the University of South Carolina and an MA in Russian and American studies from Charles University in Prague. Khailova's ability to produce quality research studies has been repeatedly recognized, as evidenced by her list of publications and awards. She has published articles on the historical and cultural factors that shape constructions of the social Other (in terms of disability, national origin, race, ethnicity, or gender), including the immigrant Other. She has also been awarded a number of grants in her topic area, including the prestigious ALA Carnegie-Whitney Award in 2015. She lives in the Midwest with her husband and their two children, who are growing up trilingual.

ISBN: 978-0-8389-1651-3 (paper)

Library of Congress Cataloging in Publication Control Number: 2017052427

Book design by Kimberly Thornton in the More Pro, Source Sans, and Adelle typefaces.

♾ This paper meets the requirements of ANSI/NISO Z39.48–1992 (Permanence of Paper).
Printed in the United States of America

22 21 20 19 18   5 4 3 2 1

For Annette and Tommy—may they always feel they belong

*Migration
is the way
of humankind.*

CONTENTS

Acknowledgments ix

PART I   ***The Power of Stories on***   1
Immigrant Children and Teens

       Chapter 1   Why Share Books on Immigrants?.............3

       Chapter 2   Selection and Organization Principles 21

PART II   ***Let's Get Reading!***   31

       Chapter 3   Asia.....................................33

       Chapter 4   Latin America and the Caribbean............93

       Chapter 5   Europe................................147

       Chapter 6   Africa and the Middle East 185

Bibliography 215

Index 223

ACKNOWLEDGMENTS

THIS BOOK WOULD NOT HAVE BEEN POSSIBLE WITHOUT THE HELP OF many people. My first thanks go to Jamie Santoro, the ALA Editions acquisitions editor, who firmly believed in the project from its earliest stages, helping me navigate the complex terrain of the publishing process as well as offering indispensable feedback on all chapters and encouraging me to "always keep writing." Similarly, Gail Jacky, the director of the Northern Illinois University (NIU) Writing Center, read all of the material as it was gradually drafted and provided her expert advice on how to make the writing more polished. My special thanks also go to Lynne Smith and the entire unit of the NIU Libraries' User Services, who made sure I had continuous access to all the books I needed for the purposes of this guide. Multiple colleagues, especially Beth McGowan, then provided invaluable emotional and intellectual support by always finding the time to listen to me talk about the project's highs and lows, while offering helpful suggestions along the way. Others stepped in during my sabbatical leave, for which I am forever grateful to NIU, to relieve me of my regular work responsibilities so that I could focus on this project. Additionally, multiple professors at the University of South Carolina, whom I had the pleasure to meet during my graduate studies, equipped me with the apparatus of knowledge and work ethic necessary for conducting this type of scholarly work.

Last but perhaps most importantly, my deepest thanks go to my family and friends, particularly my husband, Seangchan Ryu, who has always kept his confidence in me, listened to my ideas, relentlessly provided feedback, and offered his love and care throughout the joyful but also rather lengthy process of putting the manuscript together. Our young children, Annette and Tommy, helped as well: they agreed to serve as my test preK–3 population, reading and patiently listening to me read quite a few of the narratives within their grade level and answering the related discussion questions I drafted. Likewise, my parents, siblings, and many friends helped tremendously by offering encouraging words that kept reigniting both my passion for the project and my faith that I would complete it one day. In many ways, this project is thus a product of a community effort that is simply anchored in my name.

PART I

The Power of Stories on Immigrant Children and Teens

Chapter 1

Why Share Books
on Immigrants?

I MMIGRATION IS PART OF AMERICA'S BLOODSTREAM. SINCE ITS very inception, the United States has served as a powerful magnet for migrants from all parts of the world. Given nicknames such as the Land of the Free, the Promised Land, the Land of Opportunity, and the Melting Pot, America has unceasingly attracted asylum seekers, fortune seekers, and adventurers, as well as those who have simply wanted a fresh start in a new environment, hoping for a better life. The flow of immigrants into the country has continued in the twenty-first century. According to the U.S. Census Bureau, between 2000 and 2009 the number of foreign-born individuals residing in the country increased from 31,107,889 (11.1 percent of the total population)[1] to 38,517,234 (12.5 percent).[2] By 2013 the number had risen even more—to 40,106,000 (12.9 percent of the total population).[3] To put it in another perspective, one in five persons currently living in the United States is a first- or second-generation immigrant.[4] Children significantly contribute to these numbers. In 2010, 24.1 percent of children under eighteen residing in the country lived with at least one non-native parent, implying their first- or second-generation immigrant status.[5]

However, as history shows, the persistent allure of the United States for migrants does not necessarily mean they have always been welcomed with open arms. Traditionally, strong tensions have existed between the earlier settlers and recent newcomers,[6] with every new wave of immigrants greeted by the Statue of Liberty's pro-inclusive symbolism but also by manifestations of resentment by nativism-endorsing factions of the more established population. As historian Paul A. Kramer puts it, America's "xenophobic impulses and loftiest ideals have been in conflict since the founding."[7] Recent developments under the Trump administration only attest to the country's clashing attitudes toward immigration. The 45th president's first weeks in office resulted in a series of executive orders mandating the construction of a wall on the U.S.-Mexico border,[8] the barring of citizens from seven Muslim-majority countries from entry for 90 days, suspension of the U.S. refugee program for 120 days, and the shutting down of the Syrian refugee program indefinitely,[9] but it also led to widespread public protests and the judicial branch's opposition to such executive decisions.

This book represents a response to the rising sociopolitical anxiety surrounding immigration. Specifically, it aims to help librarians, teachers, and other professionals involved in the psychosocial development of preschool, elementary school, middle school, and secondary school students to quickly navigate the vast terrain of multicultural literature in search of vetted preK–12 immigrant youth-centered titles that inspire informed discussions on the controversial topic of migration. While such conversations may be challenging, avoiding them or addressing them superficially can contribute to children and teens growing up with intercultural misunderstandings that lead to unsubstantiated bias.[10] The thoughtful, active incorporation of carefully selected intercultural literary works in educational settings has the potential to produce a much more optimal effect. As developmental psychology and childhood education research documents, readings of immigrant-focused texts and related discussions can promote empathy and self-reflection, thus helping young readers learn to distinguish between primal fears of difference and realistic economic, security, and cultural threats. Such pro-pluralistic educational efforts also help professionals respond more adequately to first- and second-generation immigrant youth's currently intensified need for inclusion. They make young newcomers feel welcome in the United States while also enabling them to see their non-mainstream experience reflected in the experience of literary others—a prerequisite for their positive self-image and balanced cultural identity development.

Theories of Discrimination Against the Immigrant Other

Historical examples of the ostracism of immigrants in the United States deserve a closer look because they provide important insight into the psychosocial principles behind the current attitudes. In general, exclusionary sentiments tend to revolve around the ethnic/racial, religious, and class/economic preferences of the nationalistic facets of the mainstream population. For instance, during the large waves of immigration in the nineteenth and early twentieth centuries, the Chinese represented the first group to be demonized to the extent that they were programmatically excluded from entry into the United States, with the infamous 1882 Chinese Exclusion Act rooted in economically and racially motivated fears of "labor competition and civilization decline."[11] Other ethnic groups immigrating during the era, such as the Irish Catholics escaping famine, and later, Jews fleeing the persecution of tsarist Russia, were subjected to prejudice primarily based on the religious fervor of Protestant nativist groups,[12] but the racial and class/economic subtext played a significant role in their case as well. The nineteenth-century portrayals of the Irish illustrate the mechanics of the discriminatory process very clearly. While contemporary America would be very unlikely to question the whiteness of the Irish, Topp documents the mid-nineteenth-century tendency to associate them racially with African Americans, correlating such typology with perceptions of the Irish as low-class alcoholics prone to criminal behavior.[13] Southern and Eastern European immigrants, arriving mostly after 1880 and assuming the hierarchically unfavorable place of the Irish (who by then had moved closer to the mainstream), had their whiteness similarly challenged, with such views likewise predicated on their perceived lower-class characteristics and the desire of the earlier European-descent immigrant groups to biologically separate themselves from the new settlers. Accordingly, sociologist Edward A. Ross describes the non-Anglo-Saxon European settlers in his 1914 *The Old World in the New* as "low-browed, big-faced persons of obviously low mentality" and "sub-common" blood,[14] accusing them of invasive overbreeding and bad hygiene.[15] As Ross, quoting a physician, asserts, Slavs especially were "immune to certain kinds of dirt [that] . . . would kill a white man."[16] Ross's matter-of-fact characterization of the Slavs as located outside of the white race reflects the historical period's increasingly narrow definition of whiteness that was used to justify new quota-based restrictions on immigration, culminating in the 1924 Immigration Act.[17] Examples like these, while far from exhaustive, illustrate the tendency of pro-nativist factions to construct the immigrant Other, who was perceived as economically, religiously, or ethnically undesirable, as inherently inferior and/or dangerous, and therefore as deserving to be barred from entry.

Research grounded in political economy and social psychology indicates that there has been a recent shift in critical thinking as to which elements of the triangle of economic, racial/ethnic, and religious concerns contribute more significantly to the social production of anti-immigrant attitudes. Traditionally, studies have associated the tendency to ostracize newcomers primarily with economic concerns such as competition in the labor market and the potential financial burden on public services posed by immigrants.[18] However, lately, these economic self-interest theories have been found lacking in substantial empirical grounding, with researchers advocating instead the further development of existing socio-psychological arguments that move beyond individuals' material interests to concerns related to immigration's ethnic and cultural impact.[19] A synthesis of the last twenty years of such research is provided by Hainmueller and Hopkins, who mention that antipathy to immigration is often driven by "symbolic concerns about the nation as a whole,"[20] with native-born populations fearing the loss of a national identity and, correspondingly, emphasizing the need for immigrant assimilation and English language acquisition.[21]

Psychoanalytic theory adds an important dimension to the discussion on the correlation between anti-immigrant views and concerns about national identity. It implicitly links exclusionary immigrant stereotypes to the self's primal fear of difference as a potential threat to the self's integrity. A thorough description of the psychological mechanisms that punish difference through stereotyping is offered in Sander Gilman's seminal study *Difference and Pathology.*[22] Describing the process of individuation, Gilman argues that stereotypes are our universal means of coping with anxieties engendered by our inability to control the world. As a child begins to distinguish more and more between the outside world and the self, she experiences anxiety from a perceived loss of control over her environment. The child fights this anxiety by dividing the objects and people around her into stereotypical images of the "good" and "bad," generally perceiving the "bad" as her antithetical image—the Other.[23] In this way, stereotypes, defined by Gilman as "a crude set of mental representations of the world," are a necessary component of human psychology[24]—they arise whenever "self-integration is threatened."[25] As Gilman adds, the Other constructed in this way is very fluid. In his words, "As any image is shifted, all stereotypes shift. Thus, stereotypes are inherently protean rather than rigid."[26] In view of Gilman's theory, the creation of immigrant stereotypes can be ascribed to the American national self's psychological need to define its boundaries in opposition to the cultural Other who appears potentially uncontrollable. When a large group of immigrants, such as the Irish, arrives, it tends to be shunned for its difference from the national self. As the group becomes more familiar and acculturated and thus more integrated into the American national self, a more recent group of newcomers, such as Eastern and Southern Europeans, assumes the unfavorable social position. This process gets repeated with slight variations to match the evolving hierarchy of social concerns about the national self's well-being.

Given the crucial role of the construct of the immigrant Other in the preservation of the national self, the question presents itself as to how we as a society can move further away from harmful stereotypes and attempt to embrace diversity more decisively. In other words, how do we ensure that the desire for a national self with clear boundaries does not result in violent rejections of the immigrant Other but rather in its comparative acceptance, with its specific differences? The scholarly and education processes seem to point to the answer. According to Gilman, stereotypes will never be completely thwarted, and worse, will never be converted to purely harmless ideations. Nevertheless, as Gilman adds, research and education present ways to mediate stereotypes' negative impact, with his book taking on the goal of putting his readers in the habit of self-reflection by exposing the ideologies they use to structure their world.[27] In his words, "We cannot eradicate images of difference, but we can make ourselves aware of the patterns inherent in these images."[28] His idea is indirectly endorsed by the socio-psychological strand of research that associates education with increased levels of support of cultural diversity and, correspondingly, with less restrictive views on immigration.[29]

Books as Tolerance-Promoting Windows into the Worlds of Young Immigrants

Authentic literature featuring immigrants represents a powerful tool that teachers, librarians, and other professionals can use in Gilman-advocated education efforts. With guidance, such literature can assist youths of all social groups in acquiring the habit of self-reflection regarding their attitudes toward the non-native Other. The need for the curricular integration of carefully selected titles to create learning communities that encourage diversity and respect for all is emphasized by many scholars who discuss multicultural literature as a larger category encompassing immigrant-centered works.[30] In her seminal piece, Bishop introduces the metaphor of multicultural books as windows into the ethnic complexity of the contemporary world, warning about the negative effect of the absence of such windows from educational and other settings. In her words, "If [children from dominant social groups] see only reflections of themselves [in books], they will grow up with an exaggerated sense of their own importance and value in the world—a dangerous ethnocentrism."[31] Other theorists similarly argue for the active incorporation of texts featuring minority ethnic groups, including immigrants, in the curriculum in order to help all children develop a better understanding of the peoples around the world.[32] There is also agreement that it is especially in instances when such texts feature themes of social justice, survival, coming of age, and friendship that children can begin making connections between their lives and those of others[33]—which is a vital step toward their beginning to critically self-reflect on their potentially stereotypical views of minorities.[34] In relation to the non-native cultural Other, a textual focus on first- and second-generation immigrant peers is especially significant, with young readers being able to identify the particular struggles faced by newcomers to the country more easily than if the text focused on multiculturalism in general.

Current empirical research in psychology and childhood education provides evidence for the theoretically outlined interrelation between young readers' engagement with purposely chosen intercultural texts and the decreased likelihood of them adopting a hostile attitude toward Other-culture groups, such as immigrants. Several studies analyze the broader link between fiction reading on any topic and empathy, which is defined as the ability to perceive and respect the emotions of the Other—a powerful catalyst for diversity acceptance. Mar, Oatley, and Peterson's high-impact replication of an earlier study by Mar et al.[35] on human subjects ranging in age from teenage years to the mid-thirties confirms that readers of fiction generally have a better ability for empathy even after variables such as the character trait of openness and the tendency to become immersed in fiction are controlled for.[36] Bal and Veltkamp present similar findings by using young adult participants, while also pointing out that the positive change in subjects through reading is conditional on their emotional transportation into the story.[37] In other words, readers need to be able to identify with the text and become emotionally involved with it for the reading experience to result in the enhancement of their empathic skills. Should the emotional transportation not occur, readers' empathy could be lowered due to disengagement.[38]

School-age children represent ideal candidates for such needed emotional transportation into a story so that their empathy can be enhanced through the reading experience. As Manderson observes, the younger the reader, the more absolute is her transportation by narratives. As he explains, "The story has a power over the very young that it may never have again."[39] In the eyes of the young, the narrative possesses almost a sacred quality, with the young also perceiving stories as an integral part of their lives as they are just learning to distinguish between realities of different kinds.[40] For intervention purposes, young readers' predisposition to be deeply affected by narratives pairs well with their rapidly developing capability to be empathic. Cress and Holm, who are childhood education theorists and advocates of using realistic literature with children to enhance their empathy, refer to prior research to assert that children "become aware that others might have feelings . . . different from their own" as early as two to three years of age, with the ability to empathize becoming stronger especially as their language skills improve.[41] By the time they leave primary school, children will have acquired the ability to empathize with those not physically present. In late childhood, this ability will have further broadened to include entire groups of people or society as a whole.[42] In view of these psychosocial developments, school age is a perfect time for introducing books relaying the experience of immigrants in order to foster feelings of empathy for and understanding of the non-native Other.

The potentially transformative effect of empathy-provoking intercultural literary texts on school-age children's attitudes toward immigrants has been tested directly. For instance, Cameron et al. evaluate the effectiveness of using story reading to alter 5- to 11-year-old white British children's views on refugees.[43] The stories selected for the experiment were based on existing children's books and focused on friendships between refugee and English children, with the readings followed by group discussions.[44] The intervention resulted in the reduction of the English children's negative attitudes toward refugees.[45] Similar results were achieved by Vezzali, Stathi, and Giovannini, who moved beyond the early through mid-childhood age to focus on secondary-school Italian students.[46] Confirming the findings of previous research on the topic, they concluded that, by reading books on intercultural themes as a means of indirect social contact with people from different cultures, the students experienced a reduction of their prejudice against immigrants. Students also "displayed less bias in behavioral intentions, and were more willing to engage in future contact compared to participants in the control conditions."[47] Such results attest to the possibility of successfully using pre-selected preK–12 immigrant-focused books to encourage students to embrace immigration as a form of social diversity, thus increasing the likelihood for positive intergroup relations.

The use of discussion plays a special role in these attempted interventions. As mentioned above, Cameron et al. followed each empathy-provoking reading session by a small group conversation led by one of the study's authors and shaped by theories of intergroup contact.[48] Their choice of discussion as an intervention medium was not accidental. According to Graseck, educator-facilitated dialogue on controversial topics helps prepare students for their upcoming full citizenship in a democratic society.[49] In her words, structured conversations on contentious current issues, including immigration, provide "a powerful vehicle for developing civic skills," deepening student knowledge on the topic, encouraging analysis and reflection, and promoting the understanding of different perspectives.[50] Graseck also offers anecdotal evidence of students with initially strong anti-immigrant views becoming more receptive to less oppositional attitudes following the reading-inspired classroom discussions.[51] In fact, empirical studies posit that student attitudinal change is more likely to occur if readings are followed by issue-oriented discussions than if students are exposed to readings alone. Gall and Gillett, referring to prior research, show such a hypothesis confirmed by an experimental testing of fifth-grade student attitudes toward Native Americans as an example of an ethnic/cultural minority group, linking the favorable effect of post-reading discussions to the students being compelled to clarify their positions in front of others.[52] In view of the documented significance of post-reading discussions, this book accompanies each annotation of an award-winning preK–12 title on immigrant youth experience with a series of grade-level-appropriate discussion questions and emotionally charged quotations for collective interpretation.

Books on Child and Teen Immigration as Confidence-Boosting Mirrors

If the readings and subsequent discussions of empathy-provoking immigrant-centered literary works can promote the habit of attitudinal self-reflection in all readers, they also carry the important potential of contributing to young immigrants' positive concept of self. More specifically, as a pro-diversity initiative, the active use of intercultural texts in educational settings sends the message to immigrants that they are welcome here. By allowing them to see their own experiences reflected in the experiences of literary characters deemed worthwhile, such use enhances their sense of being valued and represented in the culture. First- and second-generation immigrant youth are perceived to have a relatively high need for such psychological reassurance, since they can be at risk of experiencing an identity crisis as well as low self-concept due to the stressful experience of migration-triggered cultural clashes and the need for significant adjustments. Children who immigrated and/or were born to immigrant parents are usually confronted with the demands of at least two cultures—one (or two) at home, depending on their parents' origin, and one outside of it. In addition, for many first- and second-generation child and teen immigrants, being a minority in the host country often goes hand in hand with being subjected to racial and ethnic stereotypes, having a comparatively low economic status accompanied by an assignment to an underprivileged segment of the society, and being isolated from extended family members who stayed in the home country.[53] The need for linguistic adaptation presents yet another issue, especially if the immigrant children live in non-English-speaking neighborhoods—a circumstance that can potentially delay their English language proficiency.[54] In view of these and similar socioeconomic and cultural challenges, Aronowitz observes that immigrant youth are often considered to be "particularly vulnerable and at psychological risk."[55] As he clarifies, immigrant children are not necessarily diagnosed with a greater number of psychological disorders than their native peers, but when these disorders do occur, they tend to revolve around an identity conflict, self-depreciation, and corresponding behavioral issues.[56]

Unfortunately, immigrant children and teens frequently cannot rely on their parents to help them mediate the identity confusion or the lack of self-worth they may experience. Rather, the intergenerational clashes at home exacerbate the problem. As the APA Presidential Task Force on Immigration points out, young immigrants live in an increasingly different cultural world from the role-model figures in their family because they "acculturate in different ways and at different rates."[57] Generally, first- and second-generation immigrant children and teens become Americanized at a rate the parents cannot keep up with.[58] In fact, in many cases they act as interpreters for their parents, a role inversion that can undermine their parents' authority in the household.[59] These factors often contribute to the children concluding that their parents cannot help them with their acculturation-related questions or concerns.[60] As Hwang observes, such "Acculturative Family Distancing" in terms of communication and cultural values places the families at risk for dysfunction or even mental illness.[61]

Literary works on immigrant experience, when properly selected, can help affected youth navigate the clashes between the multiple cultural worlds they inhabit. Children's books have a long tradition of being used by educators and parents alike to support children's psychosocial development and maturation, aiding young readers in conflict resolution and self-regulation by conveying what is perceived as right and wrong by the society.[62] Along these lines, texts authentically portraying the young first- or second-generation immigrant readers' multiple cultural environments can assist these readers in successfully negotiating the conflicting social norms they are subjected to, while affirming their place in their respective societies and increasing their sense of self-worth. In other words, the literary characters that immigrant readers encounter through such texts can help them see options for finding one's place within the majority culture without losing sight of the minority culture, thus providing readers with the role models they may have been missing in their families due to intergenerational and intercultural conflicts. As a result, immigrant readers exposed to authentic texts featuring children or teens like them can be expected not only to develop their moral attitudes, values, and concepts about the world in general, but also to experience reinforcement of their own multiple identities, including cultural identities, while overcoming their potential feeling of isolation.[63] As Lifshitz puts it, "Seeing yourself reflected in a book is one way to believe you matter, you are worthy, and you belong. It is one of the easiest ways to feel connected to others and to see you are not alone."[64]

Education and library science scholarship further explore the multilayered significance of immigrant children and other minority youth being able to find themselves reflected in literary texts.[65] Perhaps most tellingly, Bishop accompanies her seminal discussion of books as metaphorical windows into the lives of diverse others with the complementary image of books as powerful mirrors, explaining that when young readers see their lives and experiences reflected "as part of the larger human experience," reading "becomes a means of self-affirmation" for them.[66] In minority readers, such self-validation through reading is shown to directly correlate with their positive cultural identity development. Al-Hazza and Bucher, focusing on Arab American students born in the Middle East but attending elementary schools in the United States, posit that texts accurately reflecting the immigrant students' cultural group validate their cultural heritage, a prerequisite for their positive view of their multiple environments as well as their adequate self-esteem and cultural sense of self.[67] In other words, by being exposed to their ancestors' achievements, lifestyles, customs, and traditions through literary works, immigrant students are more likely to form positive ethnic identification with their minority culture.[68] This sense of inclusion and balanced cultural identity affirmation through texts also enhances the diverse readers' literacy skills, promoting their love of reading.[69] In fact, readers provided with culturally accessible images and topics are reported to generally perform at higher academic levels.[70]

Conversely, diverse young readers, including immigrants, who cannot relate to the characters, lives, and problems of the books presented to them in educational settings because the portrayals are nothing like them or appear distorted or negative, are in danger of having their sense of cultural belonging and self-value undermined. In Bishop's words, "they learn a powerful lesson about how they are devalued in the society of which they are a part."[71] Accordingly, the reading experience, and, more broadly, the educational experience is likely to seem frustrating rather than enjoyable to them.[72] It is in this context that Grace Lin, an acclaimed children's writer and illustrator, laments the unavailability of relevant textual mirrors to her during her childhood. As a second-generation Taiwanese immigrant growing up in a predominantly white American neighborhood, the author experienced a dire absence of culturally authentic literary characters she could identify with, prompting her to suppress her Taiwanese heritage and to doubt her ability to participate fully in American society.[73]

Limited Availability of Literary Texts Featuring Child and Teen Immigrants

Unfortunately, Grace Lin's experience of cultural exclusion through available literary texts is not unique. As Tschida, Ryan, and Ticknor assert, many readers "do not see reflections of themselves in children's literature."[74] The reasons for this reside in a combination of authorial and publishing choices, library collection development practices, and educator decisions. As for the publishing market, multiple studies focusing on the representation of nonwhite children, including nonwhite immigrants, mention the discrepancy between the progressive diversification of American society and the number of children's books on ethnic and racial minorities published in the country each year.[75] Accordingly, while the U.S. Census Bureau data indicates that more than half of the children ready to enter the country's educational system in 2016 were members of a racial minority, only 14.8 percent of the children's books appearing on the market in 2015 portrayed the experiences of such children.[76] Moreover, where present, the portrayals do not necessarily tend to be at the book's center or to be culturally authentic, making Lempke conclude her informal survey of 216 picture books with the observation that we "don't [yet] have much to offer" to ethnic minority youth, including foreign-born children, who, like everybody else, "want to see something that reminds them of their own lives, at least occasionally."[77] Libraries' varying commitment to collecting preK–12 books promoting diversity often further intensifies the problem, with researchers suggesting that racial/ethnic minority children tend to remain underrepresented in the youth library collections that are available to them.[78] Budget limitations are not necessarily the cause of such library choices, since Williams and Deyoe report that "more than one-third of libraries spending over $100,000 per year on materials did not achieve the minimal level for representations of racial/ethnic diversity."[79] To make matters worse, the comparative unavailability of diversity literature through publishing venues and libraries is occasionally reinforced by educator choices, resulting in the near absence of titles portraying areas of marginalization, including immigration, from some classrooms.[80]

In the current political climate of the nationalistic faction's increased antipathy toward immigrant groups, especially those of Latino origin and/or Muslim faith, the comparative shortage of authentic literary texts representing their experiences is particularly troublesome. Now more than ever, librarians and teachers need to be able to expose school-age children to works that serve both as windows into and mirrors of the struggles of the immigrant Other, thus promoting a habit of student attitudinal self-reflection while simultaneously increasing young immigrants' sense of belonging. This book addresses the situation by aiming to make it easier for librarians and teachers to quickly locate relevant quality titles within the limitations of their proportionate scarcity. Unlike existing guides to the broader field of multicultural literature, this publication zooms in on critically–vetted authentic and engaging preK–12 books that directly contribute to young readers' understanding of the immigrant question. Correspondingly, it focuses on recently published award-winning preK–12 fictional and nonfictional titles featuring a first- or second-generation immigrant child or teen in the central position of a narrator or main character, thereby encouraging readers' emotional transportation into the story through character identification. The hope is that, in accordance with the ALA's renewed commitment to diversity,[81] this focused guide will aid libraries and schools in their efforts to make their collections and instruction truly culturally responsive. After all, as Bishop poignantly puts it, it is only when "there are enough books available that can act as both mirrors and windows for all our children [that] they will see that we can celebrate both our differences and our similarities, because together they are what make us all human."[82]

Notes

1. U.S. Census Bureau, "Nativity, Citizenship, Year of Entry, and Region of Birth: 2000," https://factfinder.census.gov/faces/tableservices/jsf/pages/productview.xhtml?pid=DEC_00_SF3_QTP14&prodType=table.

2. U.S. Census Bureau, "Selected Social Characteristics in the United States: 2009," http://factfinder2.census.gov/faces/tableservices/jsf/pages/productview.xhtml?pid=ACS_09_1YR_CP2&prodType=table.

3. U.S. Census Bureau, "Table 1.1: Population by Sex, Age, Nativity, and U.S. Citizenship Status: 2013," www.census.gov/data/tables/2013/demo/foreign-born/cps-2013.html.

4. APA Presidential Task Force on Immigration, "Crossroads: The Psychology of Immigration in the New Century," *Journal of Latino/a Psychology* 1, no. 3 (2013): 133.

5. U.S. Census Bureau, "The Foreign-Born Population in the United States," www.census.gov/newsroom/pdf/cspan_fb_slides.pdf.

6. Jim Murphy, *Pick & Shovel Poet: The Journeys of Pascal D'Angelo* (New York: Clarion Books, 2000), 61–62.

7. Paul A. Kramer, "Not Who We Are," *Slate*, February 3, 2017, www.slate.com/articles/news_and_politics/history/2017/02/trump_s_muslim_ban_and_the_long_history_of_american_nativism.html.

8. White House Office of the Press Secretary, "Executive Order: Border Security and Immigration Enforcement Improvements," last modified January 25, 2017, https://www.whitehouse.gov/the-press-office/2017/01/25/executive-order-border-security-and-immigration-enforcement-improvements.

9. White House Office of the Press Secretary, "Executive Order: Protecting the Nation from Foreign Terrorist Entry into the United States," last modified January 27, 2017, https://www.whitehouse.gov/the-press-office/2017/01/27/executive-order-protecting-nation-foreign-terrorist-entry-united-states.

10. Luz Carime Bersh, "The Curricular Value of Teaching about Immigration through Picture Book Thematic Text Sets," *Social Studies* 104, no. 2 (2013): 47.

11. Kramer, "Not Who We Are."

12. Ibid.

13. Michael Miller Topp, "Racial and Ethnic Identity in the United States, 1837–1877," in *Race and Ethnicity in America: A Concise History*, ed. Ronald H. Bayor (New York: Columbia University Press, 2003), 66.

14. Edward Alsworth Ross, *The Old World in the New: The Significance of Past and Present Immigration to the American People* (New York: Century, 1914), 285.

15. Ibid., 287–300.

16. Ibid., 291.

17. Karel D. Bicha, "Hunkies: Stereotyping the Slavic Immigrants, 1890–1920," *Journal of American Ethnic History* 2, no. 1 (1982): 30; Andrew R. Heinze, "The Critical Period: Ethnic Emergence and Reaction, 1901–1929," in *Race and Ethnicity in America: A Concise History,* ed. Ronald H. Bayor (New York: Columbia University Press, 2003), 139; Kramer, "Not Who We Are."

18. Jens Hainmueller and Michael J. Hiscox, "Attitudes toward Highly Skilled and Low-Skilled Immigration: Evidence from a Survey Experiment," *American Political Science Review* 104, no. 1 (2010): 61–84.

19. Ibid.

20. Jens Hainmueller and Daniel J. Hopkins, "Public Attitudes toward Immigration," *Annual Review of Political Science* 17 (2014): 227.

21. Ibid., 226.

22. Sander L. Gilman, *Difference and Pathology: Stereotypes of Sexuality, Race, and Madness* (Ithaca, NY: Cornell University Press, 1985).

23. Ibid., 17–19.

24. Ibid., 17.

25. Ibid., 18.

26. Ibid.

27. Ibid., 240–42.

28. Ibid., 240.

29. Hainmueller and Hiscox, "Attitudes toward Highly Skilled and Low-Skilled Immigration," 79; Hainmueller and Hopkins, "Public Attitudes toward Immigration," 241.

30. Tami Craft Al-Hazza, "Motivating Disengaged Readers through Multicultural Children's Literature," *New England Reading Association Journal* 45, no. 2 (2010): 63–68; Tami Craft Al-Hazza and Katherine T. Bucher, "Building Arab Americans' Cultural Identity and Acceptance with Children's Literature," *The Reading Teacher* 62, no. 3 (2008): 210–19; Rudine Sims Bishop, "Mirrors, Windows, and Sliding Glass Doors," *Perspectives: Choosing and Using Books for the Classroom* 6, no. 3 (1990), https://scenicregional.org/wp-content/uploads/2017/08/Mirrors-Windows-and-Sliding-Glass-Doors.pdf; Susan A. Colby and Anna F. Lyon, "Heightening Awarness [sic] about the Importance of Using Multicultural Literature," *Multicultural Education* 11, no. 3 (2004): 24–28; Qiaoya Huang, "Multicultural Children's Literature: Through the Eyes of Many Children," *International Journal of Bilingual Education and Bilingualism* 17, no. 6 (2014): 748–52; Fran

Levin, "Encouraging Ethical Respect through Multicultural Literature," *Reading Teacher* 61, no. 1 (2007): 101–4; Christina M. Tschida, Caitlin L. Ryan, and Anne Swenson Ticknor, "Building on Windows and Mirrors: Encouraging the Disruption of 'Single Stories' through Children's Literature," *Journal of Children's Literature* 40, no. 1 (2014): 28.

31. Bishop, "Mirrors, Windows, and Sliding Doors."

32. Al-Hazza and Bucher, "Building Arab Americans' Cultural Identity," 211; Colby and Lyon, "Heightening Awareness," 24.

33. Al-Hazza, "Motivating Disengaged Readers," 64; Al-Hazza and Bucher, "Building Arab Americans' Cultural Identity," 210–12; Levin, "Encouraging Ethical Respect," 101.

34. Colby and Lyon point out that not only students, but also the educators themselves can benefit from the integration of multicultural texts in classroom-like settings because it allows them to reflect on their own mainstream-privilege biases or blindness toward the cultural and racial Other. Colby and Lyon, "Heightening Awareness," 24–28.

35. Raymond A. Mar et al., "Self-Liking and Self-Competence Separate Self-Evaluation from Self-Deception: Associations with Personality, Ability, and Achievement," *Journal of Personality* 74, no. 4 (2006): 1047–78.

36. Raymond A. Mar, Keith Oatley, and Jordan B. Peterson, "Exploring the Link between Reading Fiction and Empathy: Ruling Out Individual Differences and Examining Outcomes," *Communications* 34, no. 4 (2009): 407–28.

37. P. Matthijs Bal and Martijn Veltkamp, "How Does Fiction Reading Influence Empathy? An Experimental Investigation on the Role of Emotional Transportation," *PLoS ONE* 8, no. 1 (2013): 1–12.

38. Ibid., 8.

39. Desmond Manderson, "From Hunger to Love: Myths of the Source, Interpretation, and Constitution of Law in Children's Literature," *Law and Literature* 15, no. 1 (2003): 91.

40. Ibid., 92.

41. Susan W. Cress and Daniel T. Holm, "Developing Empathy through Children's Literature," *ERIC Document 427 316* (1998): 4.

42. Ibid.

43. Lindsey Cameron et al., "Changing Children's Intergroup Attitudes toward Refugees: Testing Different Models of Extended Contact," *Child Development* 77, no. 5 (2006): 1208–19.

44. Ibid., 1211.

45. Ibid., 1216.

46. Loris Vezzali, Sofia Stathi, and Dino Giovannini, "Indirect Contact through Book Reading: Improving Adolescents' Attitudes and Behavioral Intentions toward Immigrants," *Psychology in the Schools* 49, no. 2 (2012): 148–62.

47. Ibid., 158.

48. Cameron et al., "Changing Children's Intergroup Attitudes toward Refugees," 1211–12.

49. Susan Graseck, "Teaching with Controversy," *Educational Leadership* 67, no. 1 (2009): 45–49.

50. Ibid., 48.

51. Ibid., 46.

52. Meredith Damien Gall and Maxwell Gillett, "The Discussion Method in Classroom Teaching," *Theory into Practice* 19, no. 2 (1980): 99–100.

53. Min Zhou, "Growing Up American: The Challenge Confronting Immigrant Children and Children of Immigrants," *Annual Review of Sociology* 23 (1997): 76–81.

54. Ibid., 86–87.

55. Michael Aronowitz, "The Social and Emotional Adjustment of Immigrant Children: A Review of the Literature," *International Migration Review* 18, no. 2 (1984): 240.

56. Ibid., 243–45.

57. APA Presidential Task Force on Immigration, "Crossroads," 137.

58. Zhou, "Growing Up American," 83.

59. Ibid., 83–84.

60. APA Presidential Task Force on Immigration, "Crossroads," 137.

61. Wei-Chin Hwang, "Acculturative Family Distancing: Theory, Research, and Clinical Practice," *Psychotherapy: Theory, Research, Practice, Training* 43, no. 4 (2006): 397.

62. Al-Hazza, "Motivating Disengaged Readers," 63–64; Patricia M. Cooper, "Teaching Young Children Self-Regulation through Children's Books," *Early Childhood Education Journal* 34, no. 5 (2007): 315.

63. Al-Hazza, "Motivating Disengaged Readers," 63–68.

64. Jessica Lifshitz, "Curating Empathy," *Literacy Today* 33, no. 6 (2016): 25.

65. Bishop, "Mirrors, Windows, and Sliding Doors"; Levin, "Encouraging Ethical Respect," 101; Lifshitz, "Curating Empathy," 24–26; Tschida, Ryan, and Ticknor, "Building on Windows and Mirrors," 29; Eva Zygmunt et al., "Books like Me: Engaging the Community in the Intentional Selection of Culturally Relevant Children's Literature," *Childhood Education* 91, no. 1 (2015): 26.

66. Bishop, "Mirrors, Windows, and Sliding Doors."

67. Al-Hazza and Bucher, "Building Arab Americans' Cultural Identity," 210–19.

68. Al-Hazza, "Motivating Disengaged Readers," 64.

69. Al-Hazza, "Motivating Disengaged Readers," 63; Bena R. Hefflin and Mary Alice Barksdale-Ladd, "African American Children's Literature That Helps Students Find Themselves: Selection Guidelines for Grades K-3," *The Reading Teacher* 54, no. 8 (2001): 810; Zygmunt et al., "Books like Me," 25–26.

70. Al-Hazza and Bucher, "Building Arab Americans' Cultural Identity," 210.

71. Bishop, "Mirrors, Windows, and Sliding Doors."

72. Colby and Lyon, "Heightening Awarness," 26; Hefflin and Barksdale-Ladd, "African American Children's Literature That Helps Students Find Themselves," 810.

73. Grace Lin, "The Windows and Mirrors of Your Child's Bookshelf: TEDx Talk," filmed January 2016, Natick, MA, http://mirrorswindowsdoors.org/wp/ted-talk -by-grace-lin/.

74. Tschida, Ryan, and Ticknor, "Building on Windows and Mirrors," 29.

75. Bishop, "Mirrors, Windows, and Sliding Doors"; Susan Dove Lempke, "The Faces in the Picture Books," *Horn Book Magazine* 75, no. 2 (1999): 141–47; Brooke Manross Guilfoyle, "Colorblind Ideology Expressed through Children's Picture Books: A Social Justice Issue," *Jesuit Higher Education: A Journal* 4, no. 2 (2015): 37–56; Renee I. Ting, "Accessibility of Diverse Literature for Children in Librar-ies: A Literature Review," *SLIS Student Research Journal* 6, no. 2 (2017): 1–8.

76. Ting, "Accessibility of Diverse Literature," 3–4.

77. Lempke, "The Faces in the Picture Books," 146.

78. Ting, "Accessibility of Diverse Literature," 1–8; Williams and Deyoe, "Diverse Population, Diverse Collection? Youth Collections in the United States," *Technical Services Quarterly* 31, no. 2 (2014): 97–121.

79. Williams and Deyoe, "Diverse Population, Diverse Collection," 116.

80. Tschida, Ryan, and Ticknor, "Building on Windows and Mirrors," 28.

81. See, for instance, the ALA's statement from January 30, 2017: "ALA believes that the struggle against racism, prejudice, stereotyping and discrimination is central to our mission. We will continue to speak out and support efforts to abolish intol-erance and cultural invisibility, stand up for all the members of the communities we serve, and promote understanding and inclusion through our work." Ameri-can Library Association, "ALA News: ALA Opposes New Administration Policies That Contradict Core Values," last modified January 30, 2017, www.ala.org/news/ press-releases/2017/01/ala-opposes-new-administration-policies-contradict-core -values.

82. Bishop, "Mirrors, Windows, and Sliding Doors."

Chapter 2

Selection and Organization Principles

CREATING A GUIDE TO VETTED PREK–12 LITERARY WORKS that serve both as authentic windows into and mirrors of young immigrant experience presents intrinsic challenges. The vastness of the field of multicultural literature from which to select the texts, the need to cater to students of a wide range of reading grade levels and demographic backgrounds, and political disputes about country borders and geographical affiliations are just a few examples of issues that require careful planning and occasional compromises. This chapter outlines the choices that shaped the writing of this guide. Accordingly, the criteria for text inclusion, the process of drafting annotations and age-appropriate discussion-provoking curricular material, suggestions for using the material in educational settings, and the structural arrangement of the content into chapters are all addressed.

Selection of Literary Texts

The field of multicultural literature may appear overwhelmingly broad. Thankfully, indexers have created tools that are instrumental in conducting preliminary searches for recent multicultural books that focus closely on immigrant experience. Lisa R. Bartle's *Database of Award-Winning Children's Literature*,[1] a massive, publicly accessible resource, as well as the Children's Literature

Comprehensive Database,[2] a subscription-based tool, proved particularly useful for the selection of monographic titles for this guide. Utilizing their keyword search functions, embedded filtering options, and brief title summaries, the goal was to identify literary works that allow the preK–12 reader an ease of identification with the characters and theme and, consequently, her emotional transportation into the story,[3] with the works portraying immigrant generations impacted by the migration most directly. Therefore, books featuring primarily a first- and second-generation immigrant child or teen as a lead character and/or narrator en route to or residing in the United States were considered for inclusion.

Additionally, every effort was made to cover a broad scope of identity-impacting immigrant experiences, reading grade levels, genres, and immigrant world areas of origin. Correspondingly, works centered on issues such as the perilous immigration journey, immigrant cultural and linguistic adjustment, homesickness, intergenerational conflicts, and subjection to ethnic/racial, religious, and class prejudice in American society were sought out for incorporation. As for the grade reading levels, the guide aimed to include texts representing all categories within the preK–12 range, namely grades preK–2, 3–5, 6–8, and 9–12, with some texts falling within more than one category. Similar selection principles applied to genres, with both fictional and nonfictional works and their specific subgenres represented. Likewise, texts reflecting immigration from diverse world regions as identified in the U.S. Bureau of Census's "World Region of Birth of Foreign Born" rubric (Europe, Asia, Africa, Oceania, Latin America, and non-U.S. Northern America)[4] were sought out.

The preliminary selection process also involved closely considering the publication place, date, and portrayed time period of the multicultural books on immigration. To increase the likelihood of librarians and teachers acquiring the presented works relatively effortlessly, the decision was made to focus on texts published and/or distributed in the United States and Canada between 1990 and 2015. At the same time, the guide deliberately features narrative representations of both historical and contemporary migration issues, with portrayed periods roughly spanning the large waves of immigration that occurred at the turn of the century (i.e., the late nineteenth and early twentieth centuries) and the early twenty-first-century migration. The purpose behind this relatively broad historical scope is to allow educators to initiate important empathy-

provoking discussions on the similarities and differences between the experiences of earlier immigrants to the United States and their more recent counterparts.

Once the initial phase of selecting was complete, all titles were subjected
to a rigorous quality analysis to further narrow the choices. Specifically, each
work's authenticity, thematic relevance and depth, plot construction, character development, use of language, and quality of illustrations were examined.
Similar to checklists in other resources on literary texts featuring minorities,[5]
questions for evaluation included some of the following: Does the theme promote young readers' emotional transportation into the story? Along the same
lines, is the plot engaging and reflective of the struggles that young immigrants
face, particularly as these relate to their cultural identity-building in American
society? Are the immigrant child and teen characters memorable and persuasively drawn, while authentically embodying their respective cultures? Are
the characters free from stereotypes endorsed by the narrative? Equally, are
they presented as resourceful individuals capable of addressing the challenges
they face without having to rely excessively on the benevolence of people from
the host culture? Is the book's language vivid and authentic, and appropriate
for the narrative's time period and locale? When present, are the illustrations
of high artistic quality, and fully supportive of the immigration theme? The
answers to questions like these served as a basis for the final decision to include
or not to include the initially selected work.

The issue of cultural authenticity reflected in many of the questions proved
especially challenging. While I as the guide's author am a first-generation
immigrant, my racial/ethnic identification as a white female of Czech descent
represented a limitation. Research documents the difficulty that individuals
encounter when assessing cultural authenticity or attempting to identify stereotypes "in books about racial or ethnic groups to which they do not belong."[6]
A potential solution to this problem is offered by Williams and Deyoe, who suggest that the selector consult book reviews and booklists produced in conjunction with pro-diversity literary awards and honors.[7] Correspondingly, I opted
to only include those preK–12 titles on immigration whose authenticity has
been positively evaluated by reviewers. Similarly, only books critically recognized through at least one significant literary award or honor were included.
Within the approximately 135 awards and honors consulted,[8] special attention

was given to those that celebrate literary texts on immigration within the scope of their interest.[9]

Reviewing Style, Discussion-Promoting Curricular Material, and Recommendations for Use

As a result of the in-depth evaluation process, 101 award-winning preK–12 books centered primarily on first- and second-generation child or teen immigrants to the United States were selected for the guide.[10] All titles were carefully annotated and paired with discussion-provoking material in the form of direct questions and quotations for interpretation. The annotations were drafted with the goal of being summative as well as evaluative in order to help librarians and teachers quickly identify literary works representing the best match for their project needs, including the building of concentrated library book collections and the preparation of diversity-promoting storytime, workshop, or lesson plans. Accordingly, the summaries touch on key parts of the plot development while also describing the immigrant generation of the featured character, his or her age, birth country affiliation, the book's setting, and audience, with the material generally erring in the direction of breadth rather than omission. The evaluative elements of the annotations are then a product of the quality analysis addressed in the "Selection of Literary Texts" section above, revolving around issues of cultural authenticity as well as the work's literary and artistic merit as confirmed by the work's critical reception. Given the overarching purpose of the guide, special focus is often also on the potential of each text to be used in support of the immigrant child and teen's positive self-concept building, as well as the development of the student's habit of attitudinal self-reflection as it relates to the immigrant Other.

The discussion-provoking material, which follows each annotation under the headings "Discussion Starters" and "Quotes for Interpretation," aims to further advance the goals of the guide through active student involvement in librarian- or teacher-facilitated debates on immigration-related issues. Such involvement increases the likelihood of student attitudinal change[11] while helping to prepare the students for their upcoming full citizenship in a democratic society.[12] More specifically, the "Discussion Starters" section usually consists of four to five direct questions crafted to linguistically and cognitively correspond to the grade reading levels of the featured literary texts. Students should always be prompted to support their answers by referring to specific passages from the text. For example, educators can ask them to provide the following information: "How do you know that?" "Where in the book does it say that?" As for the "Quotes for Interpretation" segment, it is comprised of one to three quotations selected in view of their potentially high emotional impact on the young reader, and it generally expands on the topics addressed within the direct discussion questions. Correspondingly, students can be encouraged to identify the immigration-related issues that the individual quotations highlight, while also describing their emotional response to the quotations. For instance, questions like the following come to mind and should be modified based on the meaning of a particular quotation and student grade level: "What is the character/narrator trying to say in this quotation?" "What prompted the character/narrator to say that?" "Why did the characters behave in this way?" "What does this quotation indicate about the challenges that immigrants face?" "What do we learn about the position of immigrants in the United States from the quotation?" "How does this quotation make you feel and why?" or "Can you relate to this quotation in any way? Why/why not?" Embedding the post-reading quotations and questions into the educational experience helps librarians and teachers encourage young readers of all demographic backgrounds to reflect on their belief system concerning the immigrant Other, while guiding them to relate to the specific cultural, socioeconomic, and intergenerational challenges that such an Other encounters—a marginalized position that quite a few of the readers may directly identify with. Given the related sensitivity of the topics addressed, it is worth considering dividing larger heterogeneous classes and workshops into smaller groups so that recent immigrants, other minority students, and introverted individuals are more likely to contribute to the debate. When utilized, the smaller-group conversations become even more effective if followed by a whole-group debriefing, with every participant keeping in mind that the discussion material is intentionally drafted as open-ended. In other words, there are no correct answers and interpretations implied here, a circumstance promoting a genuine dialogue among the students and the educator in order to mimic the mechanics of the democratic process.

Chapter Organization

To help educators quickly identify books on immigrant groups that best reflect the needs of the student body, the featured preK–12 texts are arranged based on the world region of origin of the portrayed immigrant character/narrator. Proportionately, the guide's representations of the world regions roughly correspond to existing immigration trends. According to the APA Presidential Task Force on Immigration, while immigrants have come to the United States "from all over the world, in the last 3 decades migration has primarily originated from Latin America, the Caribbean, and Asia."[13] Correspondingly, the largest set of the included books highlights the experience of immigrants from Asia (37 titles covered in chapter 3), followed closely by Latin America[14] and the Caribbean (31 titles presented in chapter 4), with books in both chapters focusing primarily on contemporary immigration. In contrast, chapter 5, covering 20 literary texts on European-born immigrants, focuses largely on historical immigration, which matches the steadily decreasing share of Europeans among the total U.S. foreign-born population.[15] Geographic areas with the least robust representation include Africa (8 titles) and the Middle East (5 titles), with the decision made to combine them into chapter 6 to create a more balanced segment and to account for the transcontinental character of the Middle East.[16] Oceania and non-Hispanic Northern America are not represented in any of the 101 selected titles.

Chapters 3 through 6 each open with a brief overview of immigration from the specific world region into the United States, with a related concise list of additional scholarly resources also offered. Following this contextualizing material, every chapter is subdivided into alphabetically arranged countries. Such segmentation occasionally proved challenging due to ongoing sociopolitical disputes about borders, as well as the lack of explicit identification of the main immigrant character's/narrator's origin in some works, and the presence of multiple characters of nonidentical background in others. In relation to the first listed challenge, countries such as Afghanistan, Egypt, Armenia, Taiwan, and the Republic of Kosovo required a closer look. Due to Afghanistan's geopolitical affiliations,[17] the country was listed within the Middle Eastern bloc (chapter 6). Similar logic was applied to the classification of Egypt as part of the Middle East (chapter 6). Armenia, classified interchangeably as a European and Middle Eastern country in scholarly sources, is included in chapter 5 in respect of Armenia's self-definition.[18] Taiwan, whose independence from China is questioned by many,[19] including the U.S. government,[20] is listed under the combinatory heading "China and Taiwan" in chapter 3. In contrast, the Republic of Kosovo, given the increasingly wide recognition of it as a sovereign state,[21] including by the U.S. government,[22] is featured under the independent heading "Kosovo" in chapter 5. Also of note are works that do not explicitly identify the lead character's/narrator's national origin. Whenever possible, textual clues were used to assign a specific country to the character/narrator, but in cases where such efforts seemed purely speculative, the work was listed under the heading "Unidentified" with the appropriate continental affiliation. Finally, for texts featuring multiple immigrant characters of varying origins, the level of the characters' prominence in the narrative was assessed, with the most visibly represented region of birth used for the listings. For characters of nonidentical background and comparatively equal narrative significance, the heading "Multiple" with the relevant continental denominator was created.

Additional Resource: *The Stories We Share* Database

While this guide aims to offer an authoritative map of the field of award-winning preK–12 immigrant-focused literary texts, publishing costs and continuing contributions to the literary body result in the guide not possibly being fully comprehensive. Librarians and teachers wishing to consult an additional resource on the topic can consider looking at *The Stories We Share: Database of PreK-12 Books on the Experience of Immigrant Children/Teens in the U.S.*, which was created by me based on funding received through the 2015 ALA Carnegie-Whitney Grant.[23] While lacking the present guide's discussion-provoking material and the contextualizing overviews of group immigration patterns, the database contains bibliographic information and annotations of several additional works. The hope is that, in conjunction with the database, this guide will make it easy for educators to locate vetted titles that have the potential of inspiring informed discussions on the contentious topic of migration, thus helping to dismantle the metaphorical walls between established Americans and more recent newcomers to the United States.

NOTES

1. Lisa R. Bartle, Database of Award-Winning Children's Literature, www.dawcl .com/.

2. Children's Literature Comprehensive Database, www.clcd.com.

3. The necessity of a reader's emotional transportation into a literary text to encourage attitudinal change and self-reflective behavior, outlined in chapter 1 of this book, is discussed in detail by P. Matthijs Bal and Martijn Veltkamp, "How Does Fiction Reading Influence Empathy? An Experimental Investigation on the Role of Emotional Transportation," *PLoS ONE* 8, no. 1 (2013): 1–12.

4. U.S. Census Bureau, "Selected Social Characteristics in the United States: 2009– 2013 American Community Survey 5-Year Estimates," https://factfinder.census .gov/bkmk/table/1.0/en/ACS/13_5YR/DP02/330M200US422.

5. See, for example, Tami Craft Al-Hazza and Katherine T. Bucher, "Building Arab Americans' Cultural Identity and Acceptance with Children's Literature," *The Reading Teacher* 62, no. 3 (2008): 214; and Bena R. Hefflin and Mary Alice Barksdale-Ladd, "African American Children's Literature That Helps Students Find Themselves: Selection Guidelines for Grades K-3," *The Reading Teacher* 54, no. 8 (2001): 815–16.

6. Brooke Manross Guilfoyle, "Colorblind Ideology Expressed through Children's Picture Books: A Social Justice Issue," *Jesuit Higher Education: A Journal* 4, no. 2 (2015): 40.

7. Virginia Kay Williams and Nancy Deyoe, "Diverse Population, Diverse Collection? Youth Collections in the United States," *Technical Services Quarterly* 31, no. 2 (2014): 105.

8. See Bartle, *Database of Award-Winning Children's Literature.*

9. For instance, the following awards represent some of those consulted most diligently: the Américas Award for Children's and Young Adult Literature, recognizing works authentically portraying Latin America, the Caribbean, and/or Latinos in the United States; the Arab American National Museum Book Award, highlighting titles contributing to the authentic portrayal of the Arab American community and its cultural heritage; the Asian/Pacific American Award for Literature, honoring books about Asian/Pacific Americans and their heritage; the Jane Addams Children's Book Award, identifying texts that successfully engage children in thinking about social justice, peace, and equality; the Middle East Book Award, honoring children's and young adult books that encourage the understanding of the Middle East; Notable Social Studies Trade Books for Young People, celebrating works representing a diversity of groups and a broad range of cultural experiences; the Pura Belpré Award, highlighting children and teen literary works that celebrate the Latino cultural experience; the Sydney Taylor Book Award, repre-

senting the best in literature authentically portraying the Jewish experience; and the Tomás Rivera Mexican American Children's Book Award, identifying works that authentically depict the experience of Mexican Americans.

10. The targeted number of 101 literary works was largely determined by the estimated publishing cost of this guide.

11. Meredith Damien Gall and Maxwell Gillett, "The Discussion Method in Classroom Teaching," *Theory into Practice* 19, no. 2 (1980): 99–100.

12. Susan Graseck, "Teaching with Controversy," *Educational Leadership* 67, no. 1 (2009): 45–49.

13. APA Presidential Task Force on Immigration, "Crossroads: The Psychology of Immigration in the New Century," *Journal of Latino/a Psychology* 1, no. 3 (2013): 135.

14. Latin America is defined here as territories in the Americas where the Spanish and Portuguese languages prevail.

15. Jie Zong and Jeanne Batalova, "European Immigrants in the United States," *Migration Information Source*, December 1, 2015, www.migrationpolicy.org/article/european-immigrants-united-states.

16. The implicit limitation of such area combination is that it may seem to underplay the ethnic, religious, and cultural diversity of Africa and the Middle East. The annotations of individual titles attempt to revise any such possible impression.

17. "Middle East," in *Encyclopedia Britannica*, last modified August 20, 2014, https://www.britannica.com/place/Middle-East.

18. Central Intelligence Agency, "Armenia," in *The World Factbook 2017* (Washington, DC: Central Intelligence Agency, 2017), https://www.cia.gov/library/publications/the-world-factbook/geos/am.html.

19. Central Intelligence Agency, "Taiwan," in *The World Factbook 2017* (Washington, DC: Central Intelligence Agency, 2017), https://www.cia.gov/library/publications/the-world-factbook/geos/tw.html.

20. U.S. Department of State, "U.S. Relations with Taiwan," last modified September 13, 2016, https://www.state.gov/r/pa/ei/bgn/35855.htm.

21. Central Intelligence Agency, "Kosovo," in *The World Factbook 2017* (Washington, DC: Central Intelligence Agency, 2017), https://www.cia.gov/library/publications/the-world-factbook/geos/kv.html.

22. U.S. Department of State, "U.S. Relations with Kosovo," last modified March 17, 2016, https://www.state.gov/r/pa/ei/bgn/100931.htm.

23. Ladislava Khailova, *The Stories We Share: Database of PreK-12 Books on the Experience of Immigrant Children/Teens in the U.S.*, http://library.niu.edu/ulib/projects/stories/index.html.

PART II

Let's Get Reading!

Chapter 3

Asia

Overview of Asian Immigration to the United States

A S SCHOLARS WARN, ANY "CONGLOMERATE IMAGE OF 'ASIAN Americans,'" including their immigration patterns, "is an illusion"[1] because of the diversity among the subgroups in terms of their culture, time, and conditions of entry into the United States, and their area of settlement.[2] Yet, in view of existing research, valid observations can be made about the group's overall numerical representation and evolving reception in the United States. More specifically, in terms of numbers, studies persuasively show that Americans of Asian origin or descent currently represent the fastest-growing racial minority in the United States, with 18.2 million foreign- and U.S.-born Asian Americans reported to reside in the country in 2011.[3] In fact, according to Zong and Batalova, Asia is the second-largest world region of birth of U.S. immigrants after Latin America, with the projection of them becoming the most numerous foreign-born group by 2055.[4] Such a prognosis is supported by Asians recently surpassing Hispanics in the number of new immigrants to America by year,[5] with immigration from Southeast and East Asia particularly continuing to grow exponentially.[6] At present, the top six countries of origin for Asian immigrants are China, India, Japan, Korea, the Philippines, and Vietnam.[7]

The rapidly increasing group of Asian immigrants exhibits substantial success regarding their educational and professional endeavors, which correlates with the group's generally positive reception by contemporary America. For example, Zong and Batalova describe Asian immigrants as "significantly more educated, more likely to be employed in management occupations, and hav[ing] higher household incomes" than the overall immigrant or native-born U.S. population.[8] They also tend to have a higher level of English proficiency than the overall foreign-born population, while simultaneously being less likely to use English at home.[9] The Pew Research Center confirms such a portrayal, adding that Asian immigrants correspondingly tend to exhibit higher levels of satisfaction with their lives and personal finances than the general public. Along the same lines, they largely do not tend to feel discriminated against by the mainstream society,[10] even though they continue to experience a certain degree of cultural separation from it.[11]

The documented overall success and feeling of acceptance that current generations of Asian immigrants experience is in stark contrast with the cultural and racial Otherness imposed on them in the not-so-distant U.S. past, as reflected in the history of legally sanctioned discrimination against them. The Chinese, as the first Asian group to immigrate to the country in significant numbers,[12] serve as a prime example of the biased treatment. Starting to arrive just before the mid-nineteenth-century California Gold Rush, the mostly male Chinese newcomers of lower-class background found employment as miners, farmers, railroad-builders, and restaurant and laundry operators.[13] For a very brief period, they appeared to be relatively well received, and were viewed as "objects of curiosity" who offered supplementary services not competing with those provided by the mainstream.[14] However, racially charged anti-Chinese sentiments did not take long to develop, with the hostility taking on a verbal as well as a physical form and accompanied by consistent pressure on politicians to bar Chinese immigration.[15] This pressure resulted in the passing of several ostracizing pieces of legislation. In 1875 the Page Law banned Chinese prostitutes from entering the United States, and simultaneously discouraged the immigration of all Chinese women, since the laws allowed for an invasive examination of their personal lives.[16] The year 1882 saw the passing of a much more aggressive ban in the form of the Chinese Exclusion Act, described by Daniels as "the hinge on which all of American immigration policy turned."[17] Forbidding the entry of Chinese laborers for ten years and confirming that Chinese immigrants were ineligible for citizenship, it represented the first wide-reaching restriction of free immigration to the country, and was renewed for another decade in 1892 and then made permanent in 1902.[18] The notorious act remained in effect until 1943, when China was given a miniscule quota of 105 immigrants per year in conjunction with its being the United States' ally during World War II.[19]

Other Asian groups experienced similar officially endorsed discrimination. The Immigration Acts of 1917 and 1924 that continued to serve as the basis for U.S. immigration policy for decades extended the immigration ban to virtually all Asians, with slight exceptions made for Filipinos and the Japanese.[20] As for the Filipinos, they were considered American nationals—but not citizens—as long as the Philippines remained an American colony, and thus they were not barred from entry. However, when in the 1930s laws promised independence to the territory, the United States introduced only a small quota for Filipino immigrants while simultaneously confirming their ineligibility for naturalization.[21] The Japanese, who began to arrive in substantial numbers in the latter half of the nineteenth century mainly to work on the Hawaiian plantations,[22] were also initially allowed to continue entering in minor numbers as a result of the 1907–1908 Gentlemen's Agreement signed in view of Japan's rising military power.[23] Nevertheless, the 1924 legislation banned their entrance. Subsequently, they came into negative prominence, especially after the attack on Pearl Harbor in 1941, when, as Kitano puts it, the "cumulative effect of many decisions, past feelings and actions of prejudice, discrimination, segregation, panic, racism, and the wartime atmosphere" resulted in the evacuation and internment of the entire Japanese American population on the West Coast, both citizens and aliens.[24] In total, approximately 120,000 Americans of Japanese ancestry,[25] defined as any individuals with "as little as one-eighth Japanese blood,"[26] were forcibly incarcerated until a 1944 legal action ended the practice.[27]

In spite of the closing of the internment camps and the repeal of the Chinese Exclusion Act in the 1940s, it was not until the 1950s and, more significantly, the 1960s that the racially motivated targeting of Asians through severe immigration restrictions and other measures began to taper off more visibly. In 1952, a new act gave a quota to every nation in the world, including all Asian countries, and while the Asian admission numbers remained small, the immigrants from the region were now eligible for naturalization.[28] The resulting trend of steadily growing Asian immigration was considerably reinforced in 1965, when the Johnson administration introduced the landmark Immigration and Nationality Act.[29] With its basic premise to replace nationality quotas with hemispheric limits to redress "the wrong done to those 'from southern and eastern Europe'" under previous acts, the legislation was not originally expected to noticeably enlarge the Asian presence in the country.[30] This assumption was soon proven incorrect. By the 1980s, more than four-fifths of immigrants were Asia- or Latin America-born.[31] To put it in another perspective, while in 1965, less than 1 percent of the U.S. population was of Asian origin and/or descent, by 2011 the number had risen to 5.8 percent,[32] with violence and political unrest in numerous Asian countries, especially Vietnam, Cambodia, Laos, Bhutan, Burma, Nepal, and Thailand, continuing to contribute refugees to the increasing number of newcomers.[33]

Such a dramatic rise in the Asian American population, linked closely to immigration reforms, points to the real possibility of a largely positive attitudinal change of the mainstream towards the immigrant Other. In the era following the civil rights movement of the 1960s, Asian immigrants who were once dismissed by white Americans "as the product of a decaying culture"[34] and barred from entry now enjoy a relatively favorable position in the United States, with the society's official norms supporting inclusive institutions mandating their equality.[35] As a result, today's Asian Americans for the most part report not having experienced "the sting of racial discrimination or the burden of culturally imposed 'otherness'" that their nineteenth- and early twentieth-century predecessors were so familiar with.[36] The brief section below offers additional scholarly resources that shed light on this demographic group's painful, yet ultimately also hope-filled, history of immigration to the United States.

Additional Scholarly Resources

Chang, Iris. *The Chinese in America: A Narrative History.* New York: Penguin, 2004.

Choy, Catherine Ceniza. *Global Families: A History of Asian International Adoption in America.* New York: New York University Press, 2013.

Lee, Erika. *The Making of Asian America: A History.* New York: Simon & Schuster, 2015.

Okihiro, Gary Y. *The Columbia Guide to Asian American History.* New York: Columbia University Press, 2001.

Pfaelzer, Jean. *Driven Out: The Forgotten War against Chinese Americans.* Berkeley: University of California Press, 2008.

Reeves, Richard. *Infamy: The Shocking Story of the Japanese American Internment in World War II.* New York: Picador, 2016.

Takaki, Ronald T. *Strangers from a Different Shore: A History of Asian Americans.* Boston: Little, Brown, 1998.

Vo, Nghia M. *The Vietnamese Boat People, 1954 and 1975–1992.* Jefferson, NC: McFarland, 2006.

Yang, Philip Q. *Asian Immigration to the United States.* Cambridge: Polity, 2011.

Zia, Helen. *Asian American Dreams: The Emergence of an American People.* New York: Farrar, Straus and Giroux, 2001.

Recommended Children's and Young Adult Books

BANGLADESH

***Ask Me No Questions.* Marina Budhos. Atheneum Books for Young Readers, 2006. 978-1-4169-0351-2. 162 pp. Fiction. Gr. 7–10.**

Selected Awards: ALA Best Books for Young Adults 2007; ALA Notable Children's Books 2007; Notable Social Studies Trade Books for Young People 2007.

This suspenseful coming-of-age story follows the desperate efforts of Aisha and Nadira, two Bangladeshi Muslim teenage sisters who are illegal immigrants, to earn U.S. citizenship. In the aftermath of 9/11, the family attempts to seek asylum in Canada, but is turned down. As a consequence, the father is detained and the mother stays in a nearby shelter. After the sisters travel back alone to New York

(Queens) to continue school, the readers watch the A-plus overachiever Aisha plunge into depression that causes her to miss classes, while Nadira blossoms from a rather naive, insecure girl into a confident, resourceful young woman. The ending of this moving story feels a little too optimistic, but not completely unrealistic. Nadira makes a surprising appearance in court, making the jury aware that the accusations against her father were based on a misspelled surname and securing the family an appeal for residency with the Immigration and Naturalization Service. The book closes with a helpful endnote explaining the harsh realities of the crackdown on illegal Muslim immigrants after 9/11. The characters and their thought processes are believable, promoting a reader's transportation into the story. Child and teen immigrants who have been subjected to a similar plight because of their immigrant status or religious affiliation will find it particularly easy to identify with the characters.

Discussion Starters

1. Why is the book titled *Ask Me No Questions?*
2. How does the family's Muslim affiliation affect their immigration journey? Link your answer to the events of 9/11. Would their situation be likely to be any different now? Why/why not?
3. Describe how each of the sisters changes because of the family's hardships. Do you see their individual transformations as positive or negative? Why?
4. Where does the book seem to stand on the controversial issue of illegal immigration? How does its stance compare to your personal opinion on the matter?

Quotes for Interpretation

1. "You forget. You forget you don't really exist here, that this really isn't your home" (8).
2. "When we came to America, though, we didn't know what the right thing was. Here we lived with no map" (57).
3. "'I think, Aisha, that you're always thinking about doing or saying the right thing. Wearing the right clothes. Blending in. But some-

times . . . sometimes you have to tell them who you are. What you really think. You have to make them see us'" (147).

CAMBODIA

A Path of Stars. **Anne Sibley O'Brien. Ill. by the author. Charlesbridge, 2012. 978-1-57091-735-6. 1 volume (unpaged). Picture Book/ Fiction. K–Gr. 3.**

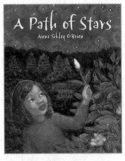

Selected Awards: Asian/Pacific American Award for Literature (Honor) 2012–2013.

This deeply moving picture book, sponsored by the Maine Humanities Council in order to preserve the experiences of Maine's refugee community, explores the strong bond between a grandmother (addressed as Lok Yeay) and her granddaughter Dara. Dara, a second-generation Cambodian immigrant, spends hours listening to Lok Yeay's nostalgic stories about Cambodia—the sweet smell of the warm air, evenings spent in the coconut tree eating fruits, and the family pastime of star-watching and storytelling. As the story progresses, the images of a native country's bliss are replaced by those of war-induced suffering, loss, and the desperate escape of Lok Yeay, her only surviving brother (Lok Ta), and her young daughter (Dara's mother) from Cambodia in the 1970's. Guided by "the light of the stars," they travel to a Thai-Cambodian border refugee camp with Lok Yeay and Dava mother, and later relocate to the United States. When Dara's family receives the news of Lok Ta's death, Lok Yeay sinks into depression. Initially at a loss about how to help, Dara draws on the cultural paradigms she infers from her grandmother's stories to lead her out of grief like the star that her name stands for. Remembering how Lok Yeay and her brother coped during the war, she helps her grandmother set up an altar for Buddha with the picture of the deceased brother. She also gives her grandmother hope for a future trip to the "house by the river" of her Cambodian childhood. Breathtakingly beautiful double-page oil paintings with oil crayon accents accompany this authentic story of intergenerational and intercultural love and understanding.

Discussion Starters

1. Where is Cambodia? Why did Dara's grandmother and mother leave it for the United States?

2. Do you think that people like Dara's grandmother and mother, who are refugees, should be allowed to come to America and stay here? Why/why not? What have you heard on the news about other refugees recently?

3. Why is Dara's grandmother so sad when her brother dies? Why was their relationship so special?

4. It seems that only Dara is able to make her grandmother feel better. How does she do that? Think of a time when you made someone who was very sad feel better.

Quotes for Interpretation

1. "Lok Yeay curves her hand along my cheek. 'My Dara,' she says. 'My star.'"

CHINA AND TAIWAN

American Born Chinese. **Gene Luen Yang. Ill. by the author and colored by Lark Pien. First Second, 2006. 978-159643-152-2. 233 pp. Graphic Novel/Fiction. Gr. 6–12.**

Selected Awards: ALA Best Books for Young Adults 2007; ALA Top Ten Best Books for Young Adults 2007; Michael L. Printz Award for Excellence in Young Adult Literature 2007; National Book Award for Young People's Literature (Honor) 2006.

In this masterful graphic novel consisting of three closely interrelated narratives, indie comics icon Gene Luen Yang provides a complex commentary on a minority member's identity confusion when subjected to hurtful stereotypes. The first story features the Chinese mythological Monkey King as he attempts to leave behind his stigmatized origin and achieve a divine status, only to ultimately realize "how good it is to be a monkey" (223). His experience is paralleled by that of a second-generation Chinese immigrant named Jin Wang, who, isolated and bullied in his overwhelmingly white school, aspires to suppress the visible signs of his difference and to win the affection of the dominant culture's female ideal—a blond, blue-eyed classmate. Having failed, he dissociates himself from his only friend, a recent Taiwanese immigrant, and is magically transformed into an all-American white teenager, Danny, the novel's third lead character. Danny's story, unique in its distinct sitcom character, follows the same imperative of having to come to terms with one's identity in spite of painful racial stereotypes, represented here by Danny's cousin Chin-Kee. In a cleverly engineered plot resolution, the three stories converge into one, with Chin-Kee proving to be the disguised Monkey King guiding Jin in finding self-acceptance. The empowering fable, conveyed in comic panels of clean lines and short captions, demonstrates the harmful effects of stereotyping, and is likely to resonate with all readers who have struggled with establishing a sense of belonging without abandoning their non-mainstream heritage.

Discussion Starters

1. Why does Jin have difficulty fitting in even though he was born in the United States?
2. What do Jin and the Monkey King have in common? Discuss their psychological development.
3. What racial stereotypes does Chin-Kee embody? Why is his story told as a TV sitcom?
4. In your opinion, do immigrants have to "transform" themselves to be part of America? Why/why not? Discuss a time when you changed in an attempt to fit in.

Quotes for Interpretation

1. "'It's easy to become anything you wish ... so long as you're willing to forfeit your soul'" (29).
2. "'My momma says Chinese people eat dogs.'
   'Now be nice, Timmy! I'm sure Jin doesn't do that! In fact, Jin's family probably stopped that sort of thing as soon as they came to the United States'" (31).

Good Fortune: My Journey to Gold Mountain.
   Li Keng Wong. Peachtree, 2006. 978-1-56145-367-2. 136 pp. Autobiography/Nonfiction. Gr. 4–7.

Selected Awards: Notable Social Studies Trade Books for Young People 2007.

In this fast-paced memoir, the retired elementary school teacher Li Keng Wong (née Gee) describes her Chinese family's immigration and acculturation in the United States in the 1930s. The uniqueness of the narrative lies in its honesty. In a matter-of-fact manner, it reveals the clever scheme the family used for the Gee women to be granted entry to Gold Mountain (a metaphor for the United States) under the discriminatory Chinese Exclusion Act of 1882 that barred the wives of Chinese American men from immigrating: while detained and interrogated at Angel Island, the Gee sisters pretended that their mother was their aunt. Similar openness is applied to passages on the father's illegal gambling store in Oakland's Chinatown. The resulting ramifications, including police raids, the family's increasing poverty, and the father being shot by a lender are also discussed. Nevertheless, the overall tone of the narrative remains optimistic, with the author highlighting the "good fortune" the new country brought to her family: the book closes with them developing a sense of belonging by gaining citizenship, running a profitable restaurant, and the children succeeding educationally and professionally. Young readers are likely to find the narrative's simple language very accessible, but they may have questions about some of the Chinese cultural practices described in the book, including arranged marriages and the strong preference for male children.

Discussion Starters

1. What were the reasons behind the Chinese Exclusion Act? How did the Gee family women manage to enter the United States under its strict rules? What is your opinion on the strategy they used, given the character of the Exclusion Act?

2. What were some of the most difficult challenges the family faced after immigration? How did they cope?

3. Discuss the tone of the book. Why does the author continue to view their immigration as positive in spite of the family's hardships?

4. Why do the narrator's parents keep trying to have a boy? How does it influence the female narrator's concept of self? Do you see any signs of such valuing of males over females in today's American or Chinese societies? Use specific examples to support your answer.

Quotes for Interpretation

1. "'Gold Mountain has laws which make it hard for Chinese people to go there. One of those laws says a Chinese laborer can't bring his wife to the United States'" (17).

2. "'A good education is a must if you want to leave Chinatown and find a good job in the white world'" (96).

Hannah Is My Name. **Belle Yang. Ill. by the author. Candlewick Press, 2004. 0-7636-2223-0. 1 volume (unpaged). Picture Book/Fiction. K–Gr. 3.**

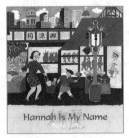

Hannah Is My Name

Selected Awards: Notable Social Studies Trade Books for Young People 2005.

In this multilayered story of immigration set in San Francisco in the 1960s, Belle Yang introduces young readers to the complexity of the issue of illegal employment. The narrative focus is on a newly arrived Taiwanese family that has selected the United States as their new home because of its grounding in freedom. However, as the book conveys through the eyes of the family's young daughter Na-Li/Hannah, they cannot fully participate in the country's liberties until they secure their green cards—a task that proves quite difficult, with agonizingly long wait times, causing the immigrant family to work illegally at meagre wages in the interim. The narrative presents this risky decision in a matter-of-fact manner, linking it simply to a lack of alternative choices. While the book's ending is optimistic, with the newcomers finally receiving their permits and not having "to stay quiet and make [themselves] small" any more, the book shows that others are not necessarily so lucky—the plot references the family of Na-Li/Hannah's friend being deported from the country. An underlying theme of the young narrator's identity change, which is epitomized by her adopting a new American name, is explored as well, drawing a direct correlation between the status of the family's pursuit of legalization and the daughter's level of comfort with her new, Americanized self. The author's beautiful and vivid illustrations in gouache make this generally optimistic immigration narrative a great read-aloud for lower-level elementary school children.

Discussion Starters

1. What does Na-Li/Hannah's family like about America? In your opinion, what are the advantages of living in the United States?
2. What is a green card? Why do Na-Li/Hannah and her parents worry so much about being able to get one? Why do they risk working without a green card, which is illegal, for some time?
3. How does the main character feel about her new American name at the beginning of the book? How and why do her feelings change?
4. Why do you think some immigrants change their names after coming to the United States? Would you do or have you done the same thing? Why/why not?

Quotes for Interpretation

1. "It feels strange to become Hannah all of a sudden."
2. " . . . it is not easy to become an American if you are not born here."

Landed. Milly Lee. Ill. by Yangsook Choi. Farrar, Straus and Giroux, 2006. 978-0-374-34314-9. 1 volume (unpaged). Picture Book/Fiction. Gr. 3–6.

Selected Awards: Notable Social Studies Trade Books for Young People 2007.

Based on a true story of the author's father-in-law, *Landed* illustrates the difficulties that Chinese immigrants faced following the discriminatory 1882 Chinese Exclusion Act. While Sun, the book's twelve-year-old main character, enjoys a relatively comfortable transoceanic passage because of his family's ability to afford the ship's second-class quarters, he experiences hardships once they arrive at San Francisco Bay's Angel Island. His father, classified as a returning merchant, is allowed to enter the United States immediately; however, the boy, as a potential new immigrant from an unwelcome group, is shockingly separated from him and detained for the purposes of a humiliating medical exam and intense interrogation aimed at verifying his eligibility for immigration. Having befriended other detainees, Sun finds out that children are often prevented from entering the country for an extended period of time. With his four-week waiting period, he proves comparatively lucky, and, in spite of his initial difficulties answering questions relating to directionality, manages to prove that he is his father's legitimate son in order to finally get "landed." Lee's prose is quite restrained, softening the emotional implications of the story, but Choi's sepia-toned full-page paintings spell out the main character's fears and frustration resulting from his being subjected to profiling based on his national origin. This highly informative book on a problematic aspect of U.S. immigration history closes with the author's note offering additional detail about the Exclusion Act.

Discussion Starters

1. List some of the questions the immigration officers ask Sun. Try to answer them as they relate to your family. How easy or difficult is the task?
2. What is a "paper son"? Why do Sun's two friends hide their true identity in order to be allowed to enter the United States? Do you agree with their behavior? Why/why not?
3. How does Sun's race/national origin influence his immigration experience? What other immigrant groups have a history of being less welcome in America because of their race or national origin?
4. What led to the passing of the 1882 Chinese Exclusion Act? Do you find the Exclusion Act reasonable? Why/why not?

Quotes for Interpretation

1. "'BaBa, are there really gold nuggets on the streets of Gum Saan for anyone to pick up?' asked Sun.
   'No, that's a myth. We all work hard in Gum Saan,' said Father. 'But with hard work there are many ways to succeed in America.'"
2. "The windows had bars. The door was locked behind them. Angel Island was like a prison."

***Mommy Far, Mommy Near: An Adoption Story.* Carol Antoinette Peacock. Ill. by Shawn Costello Brownell. Albert Whitman, 2000. 0-8075-5234-8. 1 volume (unpaged). Picture Book/Fiction. K–Gr. 3.**

Selected Awards: Notable Social Studies Trade Books for Young People 2001.

Dedicated to the author's adoptive daughters, this touching story explores a young child's identity confusion triggered by her status as an international adoptee. The narrator, Elizabeth, has always known that she and her younger sister Katherine were brought over to America from China as infants—Elizabeth's white American mother created a photo book of the adoption story that they like to read together. However, when Elizabeth realizes that China is not a universal place of birth and that she and her sister in fact have two mothers—one far and one near—she experiences an emotional crisis. The narrative outlines parental options in helping the child successfully navigate the sense of abandonment that such a crisis is predicated on. Through a series of games ("Look," calling "China mommy," and "Adopt Me"), Elizabeth and her adoptive mother manage to further deepen their significant bond, with Elizabeth beginning to understand that her biological mother cared about her but had to give her up because of China's strict one-child policy. Brownell's broad-brushstroke illustrations expand on the text, portraying the range of emotions Elizabeth experiences as she moves toward self-acceptance. This is an excellent resource for parents and educators wishing to start a conversation with an internationally adopted child who may not feel fully loved.

Discussion Starters

1. What is adoption? Why do some American families choose to adopt children from other countries like China?
2. Why is Elizabeth so sad when she sees an Asian mother with her daughter walk by the playground?
3. What games does Elizabeth like to play with her American mother and sister? How do these games help her feel more accepted and loved?
4. What makes someone a mother? What are some of the things that make your mother (or female caregiver) special to you? Do you think Elizabeth's American mommy is a true mother?

Quotes for Interpretation

1. "'I thought all babies came from my China.'"
2. "She was too far away to have a name. Far like the moon, or the first star for wishing."

My Chinatown: One Year in Poems. Kam Mak. Ill. by the author. HarperCollins, 2002. 0-06-029191-5. 1 volume (unpaged). Picture Book/Poetry/Fiction. Gr. 1–4.

Selected Awards: ALA Notable Children's Books 2003; Notable Social Studies Trade Books for Young People 2003.

Mak's visually stunning picture book written in free verse traces the year of a school-age boy as he grows to accept New York's Chinatown as his new home after relocating there from Hong Kong. Compared to other immigrant children who have to navigate the demands of two cultures, the boy's transition is made somewhat easier by Chinatown being a cultural hybrid in itself. The simply worded poems, chronologically and thematically structured around the year's four seasons, show that the narrator gradually establishes a feeling of being at home in America largely through seeing and actively connecting to signs of the culturally familiar in his new neighborhood: the smells of delicious Chinese foods, the sounds of songbirds he knows from Hong Kong, and the bright colors of paper dragons and butterflies that are just like those in his place of origin. Empowered by these connections, the boy also slowly embraces elements of the more mainstream America, such as its games. Accordingly, when winter returns, his deep nostalgia for Hong Kong is replaced by his joyful participation in Chinatown's New Year's Day festivities. The extremely detailed, photograph-like illustrations further assist young readers in understanding the emotional struggles of an immigrant child as he successfully revises his views of his new community.

Discussion Starters

1. In your opinion, what are some good and bad things about immigrating to the United States?
2. How does the main character feel about his new home at the book's beginning? How do his feelings change by the book's end and why?
3. What do we learn about Chinatown from the book? How does living there help the narrator get used to his new home faster than if he lived in an all-American neighborhood?
4. What does the main character miss the most about Hong Kong? If/when leaving your home country, what would you/did you hate to leave behind the most?

Quotes for Interpretation

1. "Mama says it will be just like home.
   But it isn't home ..."
2. "So many things got left behind—
   a country
   a language
   a grandmother
   and my animal chess game."

Ruby Lu, Brave and True. **Lenore Look. Ill. by Anne Wilsdorf. Atheneum Books for Young Readers, 2004. 0-689-84907-9. 105 pp. Fiction. Gr. 1–3.**

Selected Awards: ALA Notable Children's Books 2005; Notable Children's Books in the English Language Arts 2005.

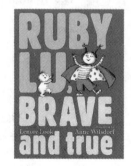

This short chapter book focuses on the daily life of Ruby Lu, the almost eight-year-old energetic daughter of "an A.B.C. (American-born Chinese)" father and a Chinese immigrant mother (40). Each chapter offers an episode about Ruby's adventures, including her attempts to teach her younger brother Oscar how to talk, her well-attended backyard magic shows, her taking classes at Chinese school on Saturdays, driving a car by herself, and, most importantly, adjusting to a life with her newly arrived Chinese cousin. Wilsdorf's lively, whimsical black-and-white illustrations help bring the episodes to life. The value of this quick-read book is enhanced by its ability to challenge stereotypes pertaining to Chinese culture and the immigrant population in general. Ruby, a second/third-generation immigrant herself, transforms her negative opinions on Chinese school and her cousin after getting to experience them firsthand. Also, Chinese customs and language are made less "foreign" to the reader through the use of terms in Cantonese and Taishanese dialects, transcribed into the Latin alphabet and explained in a glossary.

Discussion Starters

1. How does Ruby Lu react when her mother asks her to attend Chinese school? Why? How does her opinion of the school change once she actually starts attending?

2. How does Ruby feel about her Chinese cousin coming over from China and sharing her room? How would you respond in her situation?

3. What does Ruby think of her cousin after meeting her in person and spending some time with her?

4. Describe a situation when your view of something or someone unfamiliar changed once you got to know it or them better.

Quotes for Interpretation

1. "Ruby had heard about immigrant relatives. They are noisy and loud. They talk too fast in a language you have trouble understanding even when it's spoken slowly. They sleep when it's light and wake when it's dark. They don't laugh at your jokes, but they laugh at everything else. They eat cloud ears and bird spit. They get lost. They dress funny" (81–82).

2. "Then Ruby wondered what it would feel like to leave her home, like Flying Duck was doing. . . . There would be so many things Ruby would miss" (90–91).

Ruby Lu, Empress of Everything. Lenore Look. Ill. by Anne Wilsdorf. Atheneum Books for Young Readers, 2006. 978-0-689-86460-5. 164 pp. Fiction. Gr. 1–3.

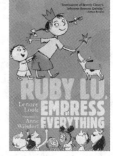

Selected Awards: ALA Notable Children's Books 2007; Gryphon Award (Honor) 2007.

This sequel to *Ruby Lu, Brave and True* (2004) focuses on the challenges a child, herself a second/third-generation immigrant, can face when living with a newly arrived immigrant relative. After Ruby's deaf cousin, Flying Duck, emigrates from China, Ruby's feelings range from exhilaration and acceptance to frustration and rejection. While her life is now more exciting and she achieves her dream of becoming a Smile Buddy as Flying Duck's helper at school, she resents having to use chopsticks and not being able to understand the sign language suddenly spoken at home. She also takes her role of her cousin's school aide so seriously that she begins to neglect her own schoolwork, and they both have to attend summer remedial school. Ruby's summer ends up being a success regardless and includes such adventures as scary swimming lessons, a stray dog adoption, and a rocky relationship with her friend Emma. The sentence structure of the narrative is simple, but beginning readers may find the length of the book a little daunting. They receive help with potentially challenging terminology through the book's "Glossary and Guide to Important Words." Sample Chinese sign language signs are also included.

Discussion Starters

1. How does Ruby's life change after the immigration of her Chinese cousin? Do you consider the changes good or bad? Why?
2. Does it surprise you how little Ruby seems to know about China even though she is Chinese American? Why/why not?

3. Flying Duck is not only a new immigrant; she is also deaf. How does she communicate with other children? Do they seem to accept her?

4. Emma describes Flying Duck as a dangerous alien (58). How does Ruby respond? How would you react if your friend or family member was described negatively because of being different?

Quotes for Interpretation

1. "Before Flying Duck arrived, Ruby's father had told her that immigrants do many things differently ... Different didn't mean wrong. It just meant not the same.

   Ruby liked different.

   She even liked weird.

   But Ruby didn't like having her life turned upside down" (14).

2. "But the truly best thing about summer school was this: Flying Duck got to meet other immigrant children ... Together, they felt less homesick.

   Immigration became less scary.

   Even for Ruby" (114–16).

***Split Image: A Story in Poems*. Mel Glenn. Harper Tempest, 2002. 0-06-000481-9. 153 pp. Poetry/ Fiction. Gr. 8–12.**

Selected Awards: ALA Best Books for Young Adults 2001.

Penned by a veteran Brooklyn high school teacher, this young-adult novel in verse focuses on the problem of teen suicide as linked to the intergenerational gap between immigrant parents and their children. The story is told in voices anchored in varying ethnic and religious backgrounds, and it provides a multi-perspective portrait of the seventeen-year-old Chinese emigre Laura Li, who struggles with the clash between her family's traditional gendered demands for her and her aspirations fueled by mainstream American culture. On the outside, Laura seems to represent a model teenager: labeled "the most popular girl in school" by both her admirers and contesters at Tower High (69, 70), she is intelligent, hard-working, beautiful, and well-connected. However, Laura also proves to be quite unhappy, trying to escape the stifling situation in her somewhat stereo-typically portrayed Chinese American household: with her successful businessman father always absent, Laura's overbearing, emotionally unavailable mother controls the home, expecting Laura to obediently put her disabled older brother's needs above her own. Using late-night dance club visits as a rebellious and risky outlet, Laura is crushed when her mother puts a stop to the practice, and her desperation culminates in her taking her own life in the library's peaceful setting where most of the story's voices intersect. The book's poems are quite accessible, providing a song-like rhythm to the story, and young readers of all back-grounds are likely to relate to the featured dichotomy between the inter-nal and external aspects of a troubled immigrant teen's personality.

Discussion Starters
1. Why is the book titled *Split Image?*
2. In your opinion, why do the younger and older generations often disagree on values? How does the Li family's immigrant background intensify the intergenerational conflict between Laura and her mother? Relate this discussion to Laura's gender and age.
3. Discuss the Sam Adamson section (72–73). What does it suggest about the social position of immigrants who do not become U.S. citi-zens?
4. What ethnicities are given voice in the book? What do they seem to have in common in spite of their relative cultural separation?

Quotes for Interpretation
1. "Yes, Mother, I will do anything you ask,
   To prove that a second-born
   Can take first place in your heart" (19).
2. "Nobody thinks I ever do anything wrong,
   Part of the image, part of the stereotype" (100).

Yang the Youngest and His Terrible Ear. **Lensey Namioka. Ill. by Kees de Kiefte. Little, Brown and Company, 1992. 0-316-59701-5. 134 pp. Fiction. Gr. 3–6.**

Selected Awards: Horn Book Fanfare 1992.

The plot of Namioka's humorous chapter book revolves around nine-year-old Yingtao Yang's immigration-triggered journey to self-acceptance. While both of his parents are professional musicians and his three older siblings have inherited their musical talents, Yingtao is tone-deaf and no amount of violin practice can bring his skills up to the family's standards. The family's move from China to Seattle has only increased the pressure on Yingtao to perform well, interfering with his American-born desire to spend time playing baseball, his real natural talent. In preparations for a recital that is to culminate in the performance of the four Yang children in the hope that their mastery will attract more students for their music-teacher father, Yingtao has to stop baseball practice. Desperate, Yingtao arranges for a lip-syncing violin switch with his new best friend Matthew, who is a talented violinist and faces the opposite problem of being barred from playing the instrument by his parents out of fear that he does not dedicate enough time to baseball. Due to a staged mishap, the scheme is uncovered, leading both families to the appreciation of their children. In the end, the immigration, with its explicit challenges, thus proves to have its benefits for Yingtao, allowing him to see that his parents' preferences are culturally conditioned.

Discussion Starters
1. What are some of the main differences between the American and Chinese cultures that Yingtao notices?
2. In your opinion, do the Yangs as Chinese immigrants feel accepted by American society? Why/why not?
3. Why do Yingtao's parents want him to stay away from baseball? And why do Matthew's parents discourage their son from playing the violin? Explain these different attitudes.

4. What are some of your talents? How does your family support them?

Quotes for Interpretation

1. "At first [Father] didn't get many students. Parents didn't want to bring their children to a music teacher who spoke so little English and had such a strong Chinese accent" (6).

2. "I laughed, too. This was not like Jake and the others laughing at me for standing at attention when the teacher came in. We were laughing together because we were sharing a joke" (32).

The Year of the Dog: A Novel. Grace Lin. Ill. by the author. Little, Brown and Company, 2006. 0-316-06000-3. 134 pp. Fiction. Gr. 3–5.

Selected Awards: ALA Notable Children's Books 2007; Asian/Pacific American Award for Literature (Honor) 2006–2007; Notable Children's Books in the English Language Arts 2007.

Written by Grace Lin in response to her childhood experience of not being able to find "a book that had someone like [her] in it," this narrative features a young Taiwanese American girl who attempts to navigate the demands of her two conflicting cultures. Modeled loosely on the author-illustrator, the English-only-speaking narrator Pacy/Grace decides to use the Chinese Year of the Dog in accordance with its zodiac meaning—as an opportunity to find herself. The individual chapters, told in a lighthearted tone, follow her on this quest, detailing the progress she makes on the way as she makes a new close friend with the same dual cultural background, reflects on having two first names, secures a confidence-boosting part in a school play, attends a summer camp for Taiwanese Americans, and, most importantly, wins fourth place at a national young authors/illustrators competition for her book about growing visually unappealing Chinese vegetables that taste delicious. The prestige of the award results in Pacy/Grace making an early decision on her future career and feeling more at peace with her uniqueness. Captioned, childlike black-and-white illustrations accompany the text, accentuating the whimsical feel of a book that addresses relatively serious identity issues experienced by many second-generation immigrant children. Young readers, especially those of related backgrounds, are likely to welcome the empowering message of this coming-of-age narrative.

Discussion Starters

1. Why do Pacy/Grace and Melody become such good friends? Describe what makes you feel close to your best friend.
2. Why does Pacy/Grace decide not to compete for the part of Dorothy? Was that a good decision? Why/why not?
3. Why do the girls at the Taiwanese American camp make fun of Pacy/Grace? What do you think about their behavior?
4. How does the Lins' being Taiwanese American influence the way they celebrate holidays? Which of your family's traditions may be different from those of other families?

Quotes for Interpretation

1. "'My mother says she would never let me become Americanized. She said that when you're Americanized you don't have any culture'" (100).
2. "'To Americans, I'm too Chinese, and to Chinese people, I'm too American. So which one am I supposed to be?'" (105).

INDIA

***Born Confused.* Tanuja Desai Hidier. Scholastic, 2003. 0-439-97862-9. 413 pp. Fiction. Gr. 9–12.**

Selected Awards: ALA Best Books for Young Adults 2003; Asian/Pacific American Award for Literature (Honor) 2001–2003.

Tanuja Desai Hidier's acclaimed debut novel traces an Indian American teen's journey toward self-discovery as she learns to embrace her hybrid cultural identity. Describing herself as "born turned around

. . . backwards and clueless" (1), the seventeen-year-old gifted, curvy narrator Dimple Lala struggles to belong in New Jersey suburbia while subjected to the expectations of her Indian immigrant parents. She tends to focus her artistic photographs on a single subject—her charismatic, blond, blue-eyed, all-American best friend Gwyn, whom she would rather be. As the novel reveals in a series of captivating and often humorous plot twists, Dimple's desire to suppress her non-mainstream characteristics is ironically paralleled by Gwyn's attempt to adopt Dimple's Indian ones. When Gwyn actively tries to achieve mastery of Indian cuisine, fashion, and customs to win over Karsh, a "suitable boy" whom Dimple's parents preselected for their daughter (91), she indirectly prompts Dimple to become more knowledgeable and receptive of her ethnic heritage. The narrator's identity transformation is reflected in her camera increasingly zooming in on New York's Indian cultural scene—and with Dimple desperately falling in love with Karsh herself. While the resolution of the Dimple-Gwyn-Karsh love triangle comes off as a little too convenient, the author's ability to infuse the narrative with poetry and to non-didactically introduce readers to the particularities of Indian culture add to the authenticity of the book, making it an important addition to any young-adult book collection on second-generation immigrants' identity struggles.

Discussion Starters

1. Analyze Dimple's near-obsession with Gwyn. What is the basis of their friendship?

2. Gwyn sees Dimple's quest for identity as typical for all teenagers (327). Do you agree with her? Why/why not? What role does Dimple's ABCD ("American Born Confused Desi" (89)) status play in this quest?

3. What strategies does Dimple use to find out more about her heritage? What ultimately helps her the most in this regard?

4. How do the changes in Dimple's photography reflect her evolving relationship to her Indian roots?

5. Can culture be learned? Could Gwyn ever succeed in becoming Indian? Support your answer.

Quotes for Interpretation

1. "—... At least we have a culture to share. The poor girl—what does she have? Pokémon and McDonald's and Survivor.
   —But that's what I have, too, Mom" (234–35).
2. "—... I guess I'm just not Indian enough for the Indians or American enough for the Americans, depending on who's looking.
   —What if you are looking" (316)?

Monsoon Summer. Mitali Perkins. Delacorte Press, 2004. 0-385-73123-X. 257 pp. Fiction. Gr. 7–12.

Selected Awards: Notable Social Studies Trade Books for Young People 2005.

Written by an author committed to "fiction for young people caught between cultures," this engaging narrative explores the positive outcome of a dual-heritage teen's connecting directly with her immigrant mother's culture. Fifteen-year-old Jasmine (Jazz) Gardner, the book's narrator who owns a successful Berkeley photo-postcard business with her best friend (and secret crush) Steve, is initially quite unhappy about the prospect of spending her entire summer in Pune, India, to help her mother set up a women's clinic at the orphanage the mother was adopted from at the age of four. However, acknowledging the Gardner code of "Stick[ing] Together, no matter what" (24), Jazz joins the rest of her family on the philanthropic mission, only to blossom under the magic of India's monsoon summer into a confident young woman. Following her father's and younger brother's lead of ceasing to play it safe, she leaves the preppy Pune academy she initially opted for, choosing to help the talented orphan Danita start her fashion design business instead. In the process, Jazz internalizes India's reinterpretation of her large athletic build as desirable, if not noble, gaining enough confidence to disclose her romantic feelings to Steve. The pro-philanthropic messages scattered throughout this coming-of-age novel may seem somewhat didactic at times, but the references to India's caste system-bred inequalities are likely to provoke interesting discussions.

Discussion Starters

1. Why is Jazz initially reluctant to spend the summer in her mother's homeland, even though she seems to have embraced being half Indian? Along the same lines, why does she resist the request to help in the orphanage?

2. Discuss Jazz's observation that all family members are "doing things that are out of character" while in Pune (241). What drives their transformation?

3. How and why does Jazz's interpretation of her appearance change while in India? What does it suggest about any culture's "ideal" body?

4. How does Jazz's mom's success as a social activist influence Jazz? Think of the most generous thing you have ever done to help someone in need.

Quotes for Interpretation

1. "What kind of system divided people up based on who their ancestors were? It seemed to narrow your whole life before you had a chance to widen it" (120–21).

2. "India was my mother's birthplace ... 'It's a wonderful country,' I answered firmly. 'I'm glad I'm half Indian'" (131).

Motherland: A Novel. **Vineeta Vijayaraghavan. Chicken House, 2003. 1-903434-93-9. 231 pp. Fiction. Gr. 9–12.**

Selected Awards: ALA Best Books for Young Adults 2002.

Leisurely paced yet engaging, Vineeta Vijayaraghavan's debut novel portrays the coming-of-age transformation of a culturally torn Indian American teen during her visit with her extended family in southern India. Though Indian-born, fifteen-year-old Maya appears quite at home in suburban New York, thriving academically and socially. To remind her of "where [she] had come from" (5)—a decision triggered by Maya's frowned-upon involvement with her American semi-boy-friend—her mother sends her off to their affluent relatives' residence in the Coimbatore area of India for the summer. It is under their care that Maya's identity conflicts come to full light, with the teen constantly pondering the differences between the two cultural systems, especially as these pertain to dominant gender and class paradigms. The passages describing her frequent indecision regarding these issues occasionally lack dramatic development, but the narrative is propelled forward through the event of Maya's accidental head injury. In the whirlwind of changes that ensue, the teen reestablishes closeness to her grandmother (Ammamma), learning an important family secret from her and renegotiating her troubled relationship with her mother as a result. While losing Ammamma to illness shortly afterward, Maya finds a sense of stability, believing she now possesses an inner map "of the heart" that enables her to "take root anywhere" (231). An additional subplot, albeit a less successfully developed one, evolves around the manhunt following Prime Minister Rajiv Gandhi's assassination. The novel is likely to speak to all teens of complex backgrounds who have experienced similar identity struggles.

Discussion Starters

1. What makes a country one's home? How does Maya come to terms with being affiliated with two cultures?
2. What social rules does Maya as an Indian American struggle with the most in India? What does she learn when trying to oppose them?
3. Discuss Maya's opinion on the advantages and disadvantages of dating as compared to arranged marriages. Where do you stand on the issue?
4. How and why does Maya's relationship to her mother change throughout the novel?

Quotes for Interpretation

1. "'If I try to make Maya live in America the way we would have lived here, I'll lose her'" (230).
2. "Usually when Sanjay uncle said something was American, it was

something I didn't want to be. This time I wasn't sure. Even if trying to have that kind of friendship—the kind that made you see the other person's humanity—wasn't very realistic, it surely was better than not trying" (228).

Shine, Coconut Moon. Neesha Meminger. Margaret K. McElderry Books, 2009. 978-1-4169-5495-8. 253 pp. Fiction. Gr. 8–12.

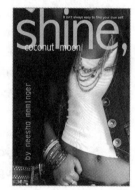

Selected Awards: Notable Social Studies Trade Books for Young People 2010.

Meminger's acclaimed debut novel focuses on the transformative power that reconnecting with an extended family of an immigrant background can have on one's identity. Samar (Sam), an Indian American teen in New Jersey, has always been trained to erase signs of her difference by her single mother in efforts to prevent ostracism. Consequently, Sam blends in well, living a relatively uncomplicated life of not having to negotiate between multiple cultures. However, this arrangement comes to an end when her estranged uncle Sandeep, a turban-wearing Sikh, shows up on the doorstep of Samar's house shortly after 9/11. Samar's mother had cut ties with her well-to-do but culturally and religiously rigid family years ago; yet her brother feels that the tragic events of the terrorist attack demand they reconnect. As a result, Samar begins to understand how important her Indian Sikh heritage is to her self-knowledge, and she makes daring changes in her life that reflect her renegotiated affiliations—including breaking up with her conventionally American boyfriend. Meminger's narrative is honest and bold, showing the full implications of Sam's coming-out culturally in an environment of hate crimes against anyone who seems to bear any resemblance to the terrorists, even when they do not share the same religion.

Discussion Starters

1. Discuss the relationship between Samar and Mike. Why does it fall apart?

2. Why does the Indian Sikh community, including Samar's uncle and the gurdwara (Sikh place of worship), become the target of violence after 9/11? Think of a situation when you may have applied stereotypes to someone based solely on their appearance.

3. Why does Samar's mom insist on Samar trying to hide her Indianness and being simply an American (24)? What do you think about such a parental decision?

4. What are some of the challenges that Indian Sikh women—Samar, her mother, Balvir—face growing up in the mainstream American culture?

5. How does the book's title capture Samar's identity development?

Quotes for Interpretation

1. "It dawns on me . . . how wrapping a turban, speaking the language of your parents' parents' parents, and celebrating the same holidays that everyone before you celebrated are all like little thank-yous to those who survived" (87).

2. "'Do you even know who you are? You need to learn about more than just your Sikhness; you need to learn about your American-ness, too!'" (109).

3. "'But the coconut is also a symbol of resilience, Samar'" (203).

JAPAN

***Full Cicada Moon.* Marilyn Hilton. Dial Books for Young Readers, 2015. 978-0-525-42875-6. 389 pp. Poetry/Historical Fiction. Gr. 5–8.**

Selected Awards: ALA Notable Children's Books 2016; Asian/Pacific American Award for Literature 2015–2016; Jane Addams Children's Book Award (Honor) 2016; Notable Social Studies Trade Books for Young People 2016.

Inspired by the story of Mimi Yoshiko Oliver, "a sensitive, intelligent, determined, and courageous girl" (383), this moving novel in verse illuminates the discrimination and related sense of isolation experienced by a biracial teen of immigrant background in a homogeneous 1960s community. As the daughter of a Japanese mother and an African American father, the book's seventh-grade narrator straddles multiple identity categories, which conflicts with the preferences of Hillsborough, the all-white small town in Vermont to which her family has just moved from the comparatively multicultural Berkeley, California. Mimi is repeatedly subjected to suspicion and ostracism in her new school and neighborhood, an issue only exacerbated by her defiance of traditional gender expectations. While other girls are content to attend a home economics class, she insists on taking shop and aspires to become an astronaut. The narrative demonstrates the redeeming value of close relationships in these potentially disempowering situations. Supported by close friends and guided by her loving parents, Mimi faces the discriminatory practices with grace, and persists in following her dreams and establishing a sense of belonging. The novel's optimistic message is enhanced by its structure: many of Mimi's initially negative social experiences are later overwritten by more positive encounters in the same settings once the community learns to be more accepting of her. A detailed glossary of Japanese terms accompanies this empathy-inducing lyrical narrative.

Discussion Starters

1. Discuss the differences between 1960s Berkeley and Hillsborough. Where does Mimi feel more comfortable and why?

2. What helps Mimi gradually become more accepted in her new community? What does this change suggest about the nature of stereotypes?

3. Why does Mimi return to the store after being accused of trying to shoplift (340–42, 350–52)? Would you have done the same in her situation? Why/why not?

4. What impact does Mimi's mother's Japanese origin have on the life of the family, both within and outside of it?

5. At school Mimi boldly mentions the existence of internment camps for Japanese Americans (116). Discuss the class's responses to what she shared. How would you have reacted and why?

Quotes for Interpretation

1. "I am
   half Mama,
   half Papa,
   and all me.
   Isn't that all anyone needs to know?" (2).
2. "I'm the girl all alone at the center
   of attention,
   not because of what I can do
   but because of what I am" (90).

Under the Blood-Red Sun. Graham Salisbury. Delacorte Press, 1994. 0-385-32099-X. 246 pp. Historical Fiction. Gr. 6–9.

Selected Awards: ALA Best Books for Young Adults 1995; ALA Notable Children's Books 1995; Phoenix Award (Honor) 2014; Scott O'Dell Award for Historical Fiction 1995.

Set in 1941 Hawaii, this suspenseful historical novel traces the identity shift of a second-generation Japanese immigrant teen due to the post-Pearl Harbor persecution of Japanese Americans. Tomikazu (Tomi) Nakaji, the book's teenage, baseball-loving narrator, has experienced anti-Japanese sentiments prior to the war: his Japanese-born family members cannot become American citizens because of discriminatory immigration laws, and his white landlord's son consistently bullies him for having Japanese roots. Straddled between the two cultures, Tomi often has trouble identifying the appropriate response to such mistreatment. While his traditional Japanese father urges for patient acceptance to preserve family honor, Tomi would rather opt for American-like direct confrontation. After the bombings, his inner identity conflict intensifies. While ashamed of the Japanese aggression, he is shocked by the U.S. armed forces' arrests of Papa and his rather eccentric Grampa based on fears of conspiracy. Only when he is appointed as the struggling family's head is Tomi shown to gradually move toward a

more balanced bicultural selfhood, continuing to assert his American-
ness but also embracing his role of the custodian of the Nakajis' Japanese
heritage. The open-ended narrative manages to avoid an overgeneral-
izing view of the discriminatory climate in which Tomi's maturation
occurs, highlighting that not all Hawaiian whites were susceptible to the
anti-Japanese hysteria. Additional data on the treatment of Japanese-
Americans during World War II is included in the book's epilogue.

Discussion Starters

1. Discuss Tomi's reaction to Grampa's hanging out the Japanese flag
   after washing it (2). What does this suggest about attitudes towards
   Japanese immigrants before the attack on Pearl Harbor?
2. How do the bombings change the life of Tomi's family? Analyze the
   impact of these changes on Tomi's relationship to his Japanese heritage.
3. Find examples of Tomi's friends coming to his defense when subjected to racially fueled harassment. Why is it important not to
   remain a passive onlooker in such situations?
4. Why is Grampa attached to the katana? Think of an object that has
   been cherished in your family for similar reasons.
5. How did Mama get to immigrate to Hawaii? What is your opinion of
   such a practice?

Quotes for Interpretation

1. "Grampa narrowed his eyes and clenched his fists ... 'You Japanee!'
   he said. 'Japanee!'
   'American,' I said" (3).
2. "... the law wouldn't allow Grampa [to be an American citizen]. Or
   Mama and Papa. Papa said the haoles wanted Japanese to come work,
   but not stay around afterward" (76).

Weedflower. Cynthia Kadohata. Atheneum Books for Young Readers, 2006. 978-0-689-86574-9. 260 pp. Historical Fiction. Gr. 5–8.

Selected Awards: Jane Addams Children's Book Award 2007; Notable Social Studies Trade Books for Young People 2007.

Kadohata's heart-wrenching narrative details the experience of Japanese Americans during World War II, particularly the deep social prejudice against them that resulted in the placement of most of the group's Pacific Coast residents in internment camps. The book's events center on the sixth-grader Sumiko, who is being raised in California by the family of her Japanese-born uncle and grandfather following the tragic death of her and her younger brother's parents. In spite of being subjected to much ostracism by her white classmates and being occasionally torn between her Japanese and American cultural affiliations, Sumiko is content on the family's flower farm, joining them in their hard work and dreaming about her future as a flower shop owner. However, after the attack on Pearl Harbor, the family is forced to evacuate the area. Having sold their property at a fraction of its actual value, they are sent to an internment center in the Arizona desert. Fighting despair, Sumiko uses her uncle's special strain of weedflowers to establish a garden that reminds her of home. She also befriends a Mojave boy, forming a tender relationship with him based on the limited access to America's democratic rights that both Japanese Americans and Native Americans suffer from. The narrative's combination of an acute sense of social injustice with impressive research and plausible character development is sure to capture the attention of many readers, especially those from similarly ostracized populations.

Discussion Starters

1. How were Japanese immigrants treated in the United States before the attack on Pearl Harbor?

2. What is an internment camp, and why were many Japanese Americans sent there after Pearl Harbor? How and why do Sumiko's feelings about the Poston internment center develop throughout the narrative?

3. What experiences do the Japanese Americans and the Mojaves share that help Sumiko and Frank bond?

4. Describe the differences between the Japanese and American cultures as portrayed in the book. In what ways is Sumiko part of both cultures?

5. Discuss the image of America as a land of freedom. In view of the book, how does it compare to reality?

Quotes for Interpretation

1. "Sumiko figured that hakujin thought they were better than the Japanese and the Indians; the Indians didn't seem to particularly like whites or Japanese; and Japanese didn't want to socialize with the Indians and resented the whites" (178).

2. "...she realized that it had not been freedom that Jiichan came to America for, but the future. And not his future, but hers—the future of his unborn grandchild. That's why he had left Japan" (250).

KOREA

Dear Juno. Soyung Pak. Ill. by Susan Kathleen Hartung. Viking, 1999. 978-0-670-88252-6. 1 volume (unpaged). Picture Book/Fiction. PreK–Gr. 2.

Selected Awards: Notable Children's Books in the English Language Arts 2000.

In this tender tale, the multicultural boy Juno and his Korean grandmother find a way to communicate and discover many similarities in their lives in spite of the linguistic, geographical, and generational distances that potentially separate them. When Juno's grandmother sends him a letter from Korea, Juno figures out how to read it even though he is unfamiliar with the Korean alphabet. He infers that the cat on the enclosed photograph is his grandmother's new pet and that the dried flower is from her garden. He responds by drawing pictures and including objects that represent important aspects of his life while also connecting to hers: he draws his dog and encloses a leaf from a tree in his yard. The picture of an airplane tells the grandmother that he wants her to visit; she answers by sending a toy airplane indicating she is coming. As the seasons in Hartung's beautiful, warm illustrations change, readers watch the connection between the boy and his grandmother grow deeper, until he is able to envision her initially unfamiliar life in his dreams. This is a noteworthy book that convincingly portrays the possibility of immigrant children developing wholehearted relationships with relatives who stayed in the home country.

Discussion Starters

1. Juno finds a way to "read" his grandmother's letters and to "write" back without knowing Korean letters. How does he do that?
2. What are some of the things Juno's grandmother puts in her letters? What do they tell Juno about her life? What does he send in his letters, and what do these tell his grandmother about his life?
3. Have you ever tried to talk to or write to someone who did not speak the same language or use the same alphabet? How did you/would you go about that?
4. Juno and his grandmother live in different countries. What do they have in common?

Quotes for Interpretation

1. "'Just like you read [the letter] yourself,' Juno's father said.
   'I did read it,' Juno said.
   'Yes, you did,' said his mother."
2. "Juno looked at the letter pinned to the board. Did his grandmother like getting letters, too? Yes, Juno thought. She likes getting letters just like I do. So Juno decided to write one."

Halmoni's Day. **Edna Coe Bercaw. Ill. by Robert Hunt. Dial Books for Young Readers, 2000. 0-8037-2444-6. 1 volume (unpaged). Picture Book/Fiction. Gr. 1–3.**

Selected Awards: Notable Children's Books in the English Language Arts 2001; Notable Social Studies Trade Books for Young People 2001.

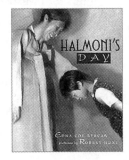

Bercaw's affectionate tale communicates the mixed feelings that Jennifer, a Korean American, experiences when her maternal grandmother (Halmoni) comes to visit from Korea just one day before the Grandparents' Day celebration at school. Jennifer is excited to see her grandmother, but also worries about how her non-English-speaking Halmoni, dressed in a traditional Korean silk hanbok, will be received by a room full of her American classmates and their culturally more predictable relatives. However, Halmoni skillfully manages to find her way to Jennifer's heart by sharing a family memory of hardship and separation during the Korean War (as translated by Jennifer's mother) and by expressing the sense of pride she feels for her Korean American granddaughter. Hunt's soft-hued, photograph-like paintings capture the emotional interactions between the characters perfectly. This is an interesting book that portrays not only the deep sense of cultural estrangement between immigrant children and their non-American relatives, but also the possibilities for bridging that estrangement.

Discussion Starters

1. Why is Jennifer worried about taking Halmoni to the Grandparents' Day celebration at school? Do you think it is understandable for her to feel that way? Why or why not?
2. Think of a situation when you felt embarrassed by someone in your family. How did you deal with those emotions?
3. What are some of the ways Halmoni uses to communicate with her English-speaking granddaughter?
4. Why does the story that Halmoni shares in Jennifer's class make Jennifer more accepting of her?

Quotes for Interpretation

1. "Jennifer wondered what her classmates would think of this tiny woman in strange clothes. Halmoni didn't even speak English!"
2. "'Today is your day, Halmoni,' [Jennifer] whispered. 'Thank you for making it mine too.'"

My Name Is Yoon. Helen Recorvits. Ill. by Gabi Swiatkowska. Frances Foster Books, 2003. 0-374-35114-7. 1 volume (unpaged). Picture Book/Fiction. K–Gr. 2.

Selected Awards: ALA Notable Children's Books 2004.

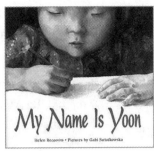

Recorvits's poetic story focuses on the issue of naming in order to document the identity confusion and sense of isolation that many new immigrant children experience when trying to adjust to their life in America. Yoon, having recently arrived from Korea, resists her father's and teacher's prompts to transliterate her name using the English alphabet. As Yoon explains, in English the letters each stand alone, while in Korean, they dance happily together—a statement evocative of the dominant emotions she associates with each cultural space. To overcome her immense sense of loneliness, Yoon decides to substitute other words for her "English" name. Thus, she calls herself CAT, wishing to hide in a corner until found by her affectionate mother. As BIRD, she imagines flying back to Korea, nesting safely. She also takes on the identity of CUPCAKE, dreaming of acceptance by her classmates. Gradually, Yoon connects emotionally with her teacher and one classmate, which leads her to finally embrace the transliterated name that is symbolic of her new, hybrid identity: she concludes that the name still means Shining Wisdom, even when written in English. Swiatkowska's stunning illustrations enhance the story's message, moving between sparsely furnished living quarters signaling isolation and rich landscapes and populated rooms evoking abundance and connectedness.

Discussion Starters

1. Do you know what your name means? How did your parents choose it? Would you be willing/have you had to change it in any way, like Yoon did?

2. What is immigration? Have you ever moved to a very different area? If so, how did you like that? How does Yoon feel about immigrating to America?

3. Why does Yoon choose to write CAT, BIRD, and CUPCAKE instead of her "English" name? What do these choices tell us about her wishes?
4. What helps Yoon feel more at home in America?

Quotes for Interpretation

1. "I did not like YOON. Lines. Circles. Each standing alone. 'My name looks happy in Korean,' I said. 'The symbols dance together.'"
2. "I did not want to learn the new way. I wanted to go back home to Korea. I did not like America. Everything was different here."
3. "I write my name in English now. It still means Shining Wisdom."

Necessary Roughness. **Marie G. Lee. HarperCollins, 1996. 0-06-025124-7. 228 pp. Fiction. Gr. 7–10.**

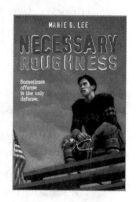

Selected Awards: ALA Best Books for Young Adults 1998.

This first-person coming-of-age story explores the maturation of a Korean American teen as his family relocates from a multicultural Los Angeles to an ethnically homogenous, provincial town called Iron River in Minnesota. Initially feeling isolated in his new "complete whiteout" high school (40), eleventh-grader Chan Kim establishes a sense of connectedness to his classmates by joining the esteemed varsity football team. However, as emotionally charged yet witty passages in the book illustrate, football does not solve all of Chan's problems. His involvement on the team fails to protect him from the area's racism: the slurs he is subjected to by his teammates escalate on one occasion into a violent attack on him in the locker room. Additionally, the sport reignites his long-term conflict with his convenience store-owner father, who considers football practice an unwelcome distraction from studies. The intergenerational clash of values is explored quite extensively in the novel, with Chan and his twin sister Young, having immigrated at a very young age, pulled strongly towards the American lifestyle while their parents demand attachment to traditional Korean principles. Through a rather unnecessarily melodramatic plot twist, Young surprisingly dies in a car accident, with the tragedy contributing to the mending of the father-son bond and prompting Chan to finally disclose the locker-room incident to his coach. Given the text's close attention to the immigrant family dynamics as well as to U.S. regional differences in Asian immigrant experience, the book represents a worthwhile addition to any young-adult reading list or collection on diversity.

Discussion Starters

1. What are the advantages and disadvantages of the Kims moving to a small Midwestern town?
2. Why doesn't Chan initially mention the locker-room incident to anybody? Do you consider this a wise decision? Why/why not?
3. Discuss the differences between the twins' and their parents' opinions on matters such as football and dating. To what extent does the family's immigrant status contribute to this conflict? Think of a similar clash between you and your parents or caregivers.
4. Why does Stover Houses refuse to rent to the Kims (25)? What would you have done if facing similar rejection?

Quotes for Interpretation

1. "Abogee almost didn't let me play soccer. He thought . . . it wasn't something smart college-bound Korean boys did, only dumb wetback Latinos who ended up working in Korean stores for peanuts" (12).
2. "'Chink!' I heard, this time from the stands. 'Chingchong!' The whole town of Moose Creek seemed to be drooling for my blood" (176).

Sixteen Years in Sixteen Seconds: The Sammy Lee Story. **Paula Yoo. Ill. by Dom Lee. Lee & Low Books, 2005. 1-58430-247-X. 1 volume (unpaged). Picture Book/Biography/Nonfiction. Gr. 1–4.**

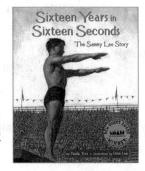

Selected Awards: Asian/Pacific American Award for Literature (Honor) 2005–2006; Notable Social Studies Trade Books for Young People 2006.

In this inspirational picture-book biography, Paula Yoo focuses on Dr. Sammy Lee's ability to achieve his dream of winning an Olympic gold medal in diving in spite of the prejudice directed at him as a second-generation Korean immigrant. Written in simple language but carrying a rather bold message, the narrative shows young Sammy, growing up in 1930s California, persistently subjected to the mainstream society's blatant racism, which interferes with his ability to train—he is only allowed to access the public pool once a week. The discrimination also contributes significantly to the intergenerational conflict between him and his father, steering him further away from his dream. His father insists that Sammy become a doctor rather than an athlete in hopes that the prestige associated with the medical profession will enable his son to overcome the pro-white society's essentialist hierarchies. When Sammy matures enough to understand his father's position, he vows to fulfill both generations' aspirations. Dom Lee's detailed acrylic-and-wax illustrations in sepia tones document the young man's indestructible determination, supporting the text's promise that "in America, you can [ultimately] achieve anything if you set your heart to it"—in spite of external obstacles. Many readers are likely to be shocked by prewar American society's open discrimination against Asian immigrants, as well as relate to the difference in opinions between the two generations.

Discussion Starters

1. Why was twelve-year-old Sammy only allowed to go to the public pool on Wednesdays in the 1930s? What other groups of people were affected by this policy? What is your opinion of such rules?
2. What do you want to be when you grow up? Are your parents supportive of that? Why does Sammy's Korean immigrant father insist that Sammy become a doctor rather than an athlete?
3. How does the main character resolve the conflict with his father? Think of a situation when you were able to meet your parent or caregiver midway during a disagreement.
4. What is discrimination? How did Sammy Lee suffer from it? Do you think immigrants are still discriminated against today? Support your answer.

Quotes for Interpretation

1. "How could his father insist that Sammy could achieve anything in America when he wasn't even allowed to attend his own prom?"
2. "He no longer wanted to win just for himself. He wanted to win to prove that no one should be judged by the color of his or her skin."

A Step from Heaven. An Na. Front Street, 2001. 1-886910-58-8. 156 pp. Fiction. Gr. 8–12.

Selected Awards: ALA Best Books for Young Adults 2002; ALA Notable Children's Books 2002; Asian/ Pacific American Award for Literature 2001–2003; Horn Book Fanfare 2001; Michael L. Printz Award for Excellence in Young Adult Literature 2002; National Book Award for Young People's Literature (Honor) 2001; Notable Children's Books in the English Language Arts 2002.

Through a series of interconnected vignettes, this touching authorial debut traces the acculturation-related identity development of Young Ju Park, a Korean immigrant, from her early childhood to the beginning of her college career. Having left her home country with her parents at a very young age, the narrator initially identifies the United States with heaven, only to witness her vision dissolve as they encounter profound linguistic and financial challenges. The disempowering Korean gender hierarchies that her family continues to impose on her in the new cultural environment are explored with honesty as well. Young Ju is reminded repeatedly that her despotic father's hopes reside in his son because she is merely "a girl" (40), and she is ordered not to associate with her American friend out of fear that the relationship will undermine her prescribed dutifulness. As a result, Young Ju grows increasingly defiant. Her decision to seek liberation from the oppressive structures culminates in her requesting help from the authorities when her father (Apa), having spiraled into alcoholism, cruelly beats her and her mother in one of his violent outbursts. Emerging as a strong, determined young woman out of the culturally fueled immigrant family conflict, Young Ju is ready to follow her dreams of succeeding in her adopted society—without abandoning her heritage. This absorbing immigrant tale is beautifully written, with its lyricism transcending its scenes of heartbreak and domestic abuse.

Discussion Starters

1. What does the family hope for as they plan to immigrate to America? To what extent do their hopes materialize?
2. Discuss the gender structure of the Park household. How does it compare to mainstream American views of women? How successfully does Young Ju navigate this cultural clash?
3. Apa accuses Young Ju of "becoming too American" (112). Is he right? Does she give up her Korean heritage in favor of the American culture? Why/why not?
4. To what extent can the father's descent into alcoholism be blamed on the family's post-immigration struggles? Is Young Ju's decision to call the police justified? What would you do in her situation?

Quotes for Interpretation

1. "Uhmma and Apa do not like it that my best friend is an American, a girl who might influence me in the wrong ways" (105).
2. "Your life can be different, Young Ju. Study and be strong. In America, women have choices.

   I stand up. Stare straight at Uhmma. You have choices, Uhmma" (131).

Wait for Me. **An Na. Putnam, 2006. 0-399-24275-9. 172 pp. Fiction. Gr. 8–11.**

Selected Awards: ALA Best Books for Young Adults 2007.

In this praiseworthy successor to Na's award-winning novel *A Step from Heaven* (2001), the second-generation Korean immigrant Mina struggles to break free from her domineering mother's unrealistic expectations and find her own self. Mina's mother (Uhmma), who considers her own life a failure largely due to the sacrifices she claims to have made for her oldest daughter, nurtures the somewhat stereotypically Asian American parent dream of Mina maintaining academic excellence and getting into Harvard. With the assistance of her Stanford-bound family friend Jonathon, whose physical advances Mina detests, Mina develops a complicated web of lies that make Uhmma believe she is the desired model daughter, but the web begins to unravel the summer before her high school senior year. While working in her parents' California small-town dry cleaning business, Mina meets and falls in love with the young Mexican immigrant Ysrael, a gifted musician, who prompts her to seek her own dreams. However, her choices are complicated by the responsibility she feels for her emotionally deprived and hearing-impaired sister Suna. Na's narrative is poetic and carefully crafted, alternating in perspectives between Mina's first-person past-tense chapters and Suna's third-person present-tense sections, and is sure to capture the interest of young adult readers who are often quite familiar with the conflict between their own desires and their parents' demands.

Discussion Starters

1. Why does Mina fall in love with Ysrael and not Jonathon? What does each of them represent to her?

2. What ethnic stereotypes does Uhmma apply to Ysrael? What does it indicate about hierarchies within immigrant communities?

3. Discuss Uhmma's obsession with Harvard University. How does her immigrant background help fuel her dream of her daughter getting accepted there?

4. To what extent does Mina internalize Uhmma's definition of success? What impact (positive or negative) can parents' high demands have on their children?

5. In your opinion, does the book promote stereotypes of Korean Americans in any way? Why/why not?

Quotes for Interpretation

1. "Since the fourth grade . . . Uhmma had been making plans for me. And it all hinged on the best college. Which led to the best job and husband. The best family. The best life" (53).

2. "No, you stop, Uhmma. Suna is as much your daughter as I am" (109).

3. "'You're the only other person who knows how it is. The way they expect us to bring them the world. How much they need us to be perfect'" (137).

Yoon and the Jade Bracelet. Helen Recorvits. Ill. by Gabi Swiatkowska. Frances Foster Books, 2008. 978-0-374-38689-4. 1 volume (unpaged). Picture Book/Fiction. K–Gr. 2.

Selected Awards: Society of School Librarians International Book Award (Honor) 2008.

Yoon, a young newcomer from Korea previously featured in *My Name Is Yoon* (2003) and *Yoon and the Christmas Mitten* (2006), returns to tell a story about bullying. As an immigrant child, she appears to be an easy target because of her culturally based isolation and corresponding vulnerability. On her birthday, Yoon longs for a jump rope so that she can play with other girls at school, but instead she receives a beautiful heirloom jade bracelet and a Korean book about a little girl tricked by a tiger. An older girl, like the folkloristic tale's tiger, notices Yoon's loneliness and decides to capitalize on it. Pretending to try to befriend and enculturate the recently arrived immigrant, the older girl uses the narrative of sharing as an American token of friendship to trick Yoon out of her bracelet. Yoon ultimately lives up to the meaning of her name—Shining Wisdom—and gathers the courage to tell the teacher about the incident in order to recover her treasure. Swiatkowska's vivid, broad-brush-stroke illustrations enliven this story of empowerment.

Discussion Starters

1. How do we know that Yoon is new and different in her school?

2. The older girl notices that Yoon is from another country. How does she use that to trick her?

3. Why is the bracelet so special to Yoon? What does jade stand for in her culture? Think of something you have that tells the story of your family and/or culture.

4. What does Yoon's name mean? How does she show she deserves that name when dealing with the bully?

5. Mention ways to act if a bully takes something from you.

Quotes for Interpretation

1. "I wanted so much to jump and sing with them, but I was still the new girl. I had not been invited yet."

2. "'In America friends share things. If we are going to be friends, you should share your bracelet with me.'"

3. "I was just like the silly girl in my storybook. I had been tricked by a tiger."

VIETNAM

***All the Broken Pieces: A Novel in Verse.* Ann E. Burg. Scholastic, 2009. 978-0-545-08092-7. 219 pp. Poetry/Historical Fiction. Gr. 5–8.**

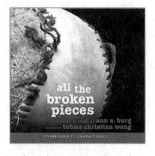

Selected Awards: ALA Best Books for Young Adults 2010; Notable Books for a Global Society 2010.

Ann E. Burg's poetic debut traces the psychological journey of a Vietnamese refugee as he struggles to overcome his war-induced trauma, learning to accept his parallel identities and families in the process. Airlifted from war-torn Saigon and adopted into a loving American household, the book's twelve-year-old Amerasian narrator, Matt Pin, suffers from an acute identity crisis. Subjected to racial slurs and bullied on his middle-school baseball team, Matt is not allowed to feel quite like an American. However, he proves equally unable to anchor his identity in the Vietnam of his past. While his adoption agency's educational program chooses to represent Vietnam through its colorful holidays, foods, and folk tales, all Matt can remember are the sights, smells, and sounds of destruction. His relationship to his homeland is further complicated by his biological brother's post air-raid mutilation, which Matt blames himself for and keeps secret out of fear of being rejected by his adoptive family. Through touching passages, the novel illustrates the importance of bonding among war victims in order for the healing process to take place: only after Matt begins attending Vietnam War veterans' meetings does he move toward self-forgiveness and the corresponding realization that the acceptance of his new self does not entail his betrayal of the world he was born into. The novel's theme of the biracial refugee attempting to construct meaning out of "a pocketful / of broken pieces" (23) is communicated through highly accessible, prose-like verse.

Discussion Starters

1. Why does Matt keep the story of his Vietnamese brother's mutilation secret? Would you do the same if you were him? Why/why not?
2. Discuss Matt's treatment by Rob, his antagonist. Does Rob have the right to bully him? What ultimately changes the way they view each other?
3. What is the reason behind Matt's feeling strange when referred to as "a Vietnamese kid" by his piano teacher? (153).
4. How does Matt remember Vietnam? What helps him revise his attitude towards his homeland by the end of the book?

Quotes for Interpretation

1. "For two years,
   I learned about Vietnam,
   but it wasn't any
   Vietnam I remembered.

   . . .

   My Vietnam is
   only
   a pocketful
   of broken pieces
   I carry
   inside me" (21, 23).
2. "You can love us both,
   Matt. It won't mean
   you've forgotten her
   or that you didn't care" (208).

***Dogtag Summer.* Elizabeth Partridge. Bloomsbury Books for Young Readers, 2011. 978-1-59990-183-1. 229 pp. Historical Fiction. Gr. 6–8.**

Selected Awards: Notable Social Studies Trade Books for Young People 2012.

In this gripping coming-of-age story that incorporates historical research, a biracial tweenager desperately tries to bridge the gap between her current life in a coastal California town and her haunted past as a targeted Amerasian in war-torn Vietnam. Although adopted by an American couple several years ago, Tracy has very limited memories of her early life in her biological grandmother's Vietnamese countryside house, with occasional visits from her single mother employed at a U.S. military base laundromat. When Tracy and her friend Stargazer accidentally discover an old ammunition container in her family's garage and force it open to find a soldier's dogtag, the ghosts of her violent past come alive, trickling through the narrative in italicized flashbacks. The opening of the symbolic Pandora's box begins to torment Tracy's adoptive father Bob, a Vietnam war veteran exhibiting signs of post-traumatic stress disorder, as well. It is only when they confront their harrowing memories together, with Bob identifying the owner of the dogtag as Tracy's American GI birth father killed in combat in Vietnam, that they can begin healing and moving forward as a family. The narrative closes with Tracy gaining enough understanding and acceptance of her Vietnamese heritage to reclaim her name Tuyet as the basis of her newly born, truly hybrid identity.

Discussion Starters

1. Tracy/Tuyet often mentions her inner feeling of emptiness. What causes it and how does she gradually fill the hollowness?
2. What does *con lai* mean? Discuss how attitudes towards Amerasian children in Vietnam in the 1970s impact Tracy/Tuyet's life.
3. How is Tracy/Tuyet viewed in the 1980s United States as a foreign-born biracial adoptee?

4. Why does the main character ask Stargazer to call her Tuyet? What do you think about that decision?

5. If the book were to continue, how do you think the story would go? How would the family's life likely change?

Quotes for Interpretation

1. "Later I realized it began much earlier. Opening the ammo box just let out the ghosts that had been trapped in there for years, waiting" (1).

2. "They'd probably ask me stupid questions, like are you an Indian, or Chinese, or what? Or the question I hated the most: do you speak English?" (5).

3. "'You're acting like this was just your war,' I said softly. 'But it wasn't. It was my war too'" (178).

Escape from Saigon: How a Vietnam War Orphan Became an American Boy. **Andrea Warren. Farrar, Straus and Giroux, 2004. 0-374-32224-4. 110 pp. Biography/Nonfiction. Gr. 5–9.**

Selected Awards: Notable Social Studies Trade Books for Young People 2005.

Based on documented historical facts and interviews with witnesses, this stirring biography chronicles the immigration journey of the eight-year-old South Vietnamese orphan Long to West Liberty, Ohio, to become the adoptive son Matt of the loving Steiner family. Growing up amidst the chaos of the Vietnam War, Long is subjected to a series of heartbreaks. His American father is gone, his Vietnamese mother takes her own life, and his aging grandmother, Ba, leaves him in a Saigon orphanage operated by Holt International Children's Services because she cannot support both of them and fears discrimination against Amerasians. Long recalls his mixed feelings of fear, sorrow, joy, and hope when, during the fall of Saigon, he is chosen to be transported to America as part of the dangerous Operation Babylift that, according to the book, saved 2,242 children. Long's transition to his new identity as the midwesterner Matt Steiner is also emotional and not free from racial prejudice, but the book emphasizes that his new home enables him to thrive. The narrative closes with his moving trip to Vietnam in 1995 to finally achieve an understanding of the sacrifices his biological mother and grandmother made when seemingly abandoning him. Warren provides ample documentation in the form of black-and-white photographs and includes an informative afterword discussing Operation Babylift, international adoptions, and Amerasian children.

Discussion Starters

1. Research U.S. involvement in the Vietnam War. Why did the United States decide to withdraw its forces from Vietnam in 1973?
2. Discuss social attitudes toward Amerasian children in Vietnam during the 1970s. What impact do these attitudes have on Long's/Matt's life?
3. What types of prejudice does Long/Matt encounter as an immigrant and how do they affect him?
4. Why does Long/Matt intentionally avoid anything related to his Vietnamese past for years?
5. How does Long/Matt finally come to terms with being both American and Vietnamese?

Quotes for Interpretation

1. "More than anything, Matt wished to be a real American boy" (78).
2. " . . . an old friend, called out, 'Hey, Chink, good play!' . . . 'I've never forgotten it. When other kids called me names, it made me angry. But a friend . . . well, that really hurt'" (80–81).
3. "'I love my adopted country and I'm proud to be an American. But I will never forget that my American heart is half Vietnamese'" (92).

Inside Out & Back Again. **Thanhha Lai. Harper, 2011. 978-0-06-196278-3. 262 pp. Poetry/Historical Fiction. Gr. 5–9.**

Selected Awards: ALA Notable Children's Books 2012; Jane Addams Children's Book Award (Honor) 2012; National Book Award for Young People's Literature 2011; Newbery Medal (Honor) 2012; Notable Children's Books in the English Language Arts 2012; Notable Social Studies Trade Books for Young People 2012.

Inspired by the author's experience of fleeing the Vietnam War and immigrating to Alabama, this captivating free-verse first-person narrative focuses on the emotional and physical journey of ten-year-old Hà as circumstances force her to change continents and cultures. With her father missing in action, food prices skyrocketing, and bombing moving closer to Saigon, Hà must abandon everything she ever knew—including her beloved papaya tree. Fortunate to get aboard a navy ship with her mother and three older brothers, she experiences a mixture of hope and desperation en route to the refugee camp in Guam, where the family chooses the United States over Canada and France because it provides *more opportunities* and *scholarships* (106). However, once sponsored by an Alabama "cowboy" after a stay in another tent city in Florida (115), the refugees realize that these opportunities come at a price. With rare honesty and detail, the narrative depicts the family's acculturation challenges, which are exacerbated by the community's blatant racism. Descriptions of Hà eating lunches alone in the school's bathroom, running away from bullies calling her a pancake face and mocking her Buddhist religion, as well as her witnessing their rental property being vandalized, are sure to touch the hearts of many readers. Occasional acts of kindness, particularly those by a retired teacher who lost her son in the Vietnam War, are also portrayed. The melancholic narrative in accessible verse closes on a hopeful note as the family celebrates a peaceful Vietnamese New Year in 1976, planning their future.

Discussion Starters

1. Why did the United States aid refugees from South Vietnam? What does Hà think about related acts of generosity?
2. How is Hà treated at her Alabama school? In your opinion, would the American community be more receptive of her and her family these days? Why/why not?
3. Why does Hà no longer feel smart in the new culture?
4. How do Hà and her family move closer to finding their place in the United States? How would you cope in their situation?
5. Explain the title of the book.

Quotes for Interpretation

1. *We must consider the shame*
   of abandoning our own country
   and begging toward the unknown
   where we will all begin again
   at the lowest level
   on the social scale (79).

2. "No one would believe me
   but at times
   I would choose
   wartime in Saigon
   over
   peacetime in Alabama" (195).

Rebecca's Journey Home. **Brynn Olenberg Sugarman. Ill. by Michelle Shapiro. Kar-Ben Publishing, 2006. 978-1-58013-157-5. 1 volume (unpaged). Picture Book/Fiction. K–Gr. 4.**

Selected Awards: Sydney Taylor Book Award (Honor) 2007.

In this endearing picture book written in simple language, Sugarman draws on her personal experience of adopting a Vietnamese baby to educate children about the rationale, the somewhat complicated process, and the joyful outcomes of an international adoption, which is a growing trend among Jewish Americans. While the book's Mrs. Stein and her husband have been blessed with two boys, Jacob (eight) and Gabriel (four), they decide to share their home and love with a girl from a Vietnamese orphanage. When the observant Jewish family finally receives the long-awaited phone call, the mother flies to Vietnam to bring baby Le Thi Hong home. Once in the United States, the new member of the Stein family becomes Rebecca Rose, an American citizen who retains her Vietnamese background while also immersed in the Jewish culture. When she is almost one year old, the adoptee is brought to the *mikvah* (ritual bath) and given the Hebrew name of Rivka Shoshanah. Colorful snippets of Vietnamese culture as well as brief descriptions of Jewish ritualistic traditions are offered throughout the narrative, with an emphasis on the possibility of multiple cultural heritages being "all rolled into one" in an immigrant child's identity. Warm, graphic-style illustrations by Shapiro accompany the text, making it a perfect read-aloud piece.

Discussion Starters

1. What is an adoption? Why do the Steins decide to adopt a girl from Vietnam, even though they have two children of their own?
2. Find Vietnam on a map. What do we learn about this country from the book?
3 Why is the book titled *Rebecca's Journey Home?* If the baby was born in Vietnam, can her real home be in the United States with the Jewish family? Why/why not? What does a home mean to you?
4. How does the baby become American and Jewish, in addition to being Vietnamese? What makes someone part of a certain culture or religion?

Quotes for Interpretation

1. "There were so many babies and children in the world whose parents had loved them but could not take care of them."
2. "'Soon Baby Rebecca won't be Vietnamese anymore. She'll be Jewish,' Gabe had said. . . . 'No! She'll be Vietnamese and Jewish,' said Jacob who was almost eight."
3. "'You can be as many things as you want to be. Or at least you can try.'"

Shadow of the Dragon. Sherry Garland. Harcourt Brace, 1993. 0-15-273530-5. 314 pp. Fiction. Gr. 8–12.

Selected Awards: ALA Best Books for Young Adults 1994.

Combining thriller and romance, Sherry Garland's coming-of-age narrative portrays the identity struggles of Danny Vo (Vo Van Duong), a Vietnamese American high-school sophomore in Houston. Having escaped his home country's communist oppression as a young child, Danny has experienced acculturation difficulties and has vowed that no one will "ever have a reason to make fun of him again" (10). He painstakingly dresses, talks, and eats "like the American kids" (10). His quest to join the American mainstream is also reflected in his desire to win over his blond, blue-eyed schoolmate Tiffany—the book's symbol of an unattainable white female. However, given his refugee family's insistence that he follow established Vietnamese cultural paradigms, Danny feels uncomfortably suspended between the two worlds. As the swift-paced narrative illustrates, his identity confusion intensifies after his adolescent cousin Sang Le, released from a Vietnamese reeducation camp, comes to live with them. Through Sang Le, Danny is exposed to young ethnic pride and is forced to refocus on his family in efforts to save his frustrated cousin from associating with the dangerous Cobra gang. The book's ending is raw and honest, with Sang Le beaten to death by a white supremacist group that includes Tiffany's brother and Danny reembracing his Vietnamese heritage as a result. The deftly drawn inter-cultural and intergenerational conflicts are likely to inspire important classroom discussions.

Discussion Starters

1. How does Danny feel about his Vietnamese heritage at the novel's begin-ning? How and why does his attitude change by the narrative's end?
2. What role does Tiffany's ethnicity play in Danny's love for her?
3. Analyze the intergenerational tensions in the Vu family. What fuels these conflicts? How does the situation compare to intergenerational relationships in your household?
4. Why does Sang Le join the Cobra gang? If not killed, how likely would he be to succeed in fully separating from it? Link your argu-ment to what you know and/or can find out about gang involvement in your geographic area.

Quotes for Interpretation

1. "... he pretended to be Chinese just so kids and even adults wouldn't ask him about the war, or about being a Vietcong, or living in a grass hut, or accuse him of having dogmeat in his lunchbox" (10).

2. "[Danny] didn't want to remember anything about Vietnam . . . He wanted to be an American now, yet he didn't feel part of the world of the children, either. They spoke perfect English and played popular music and American games" (76).

MULTIPLE ASIAN (AND OTHER) COUNTRIES

First Crossing: Stories about Teen Immigrants.
Edited by Donald R. Gallo. Candlewick Press, 2004. 978-0-7636-2249-7. 224 pp. Short Stories/ Fiction. Gr. 7–10.

Selected Awards: Notable Social Studies Trade Books for Young People 2005.

In this collection of well-selected stories on the contemporary experiences of first-generation immigrant teens, acclaimed authors explore a variety of themes related to the newcomers' need to establish a sense of belonging in an unfamiliar cultural space. The strategies that individuals employ in the process are portrayed as often conflicting, with some characters painstakingly attempting to uncover or preserve their first-culture heritage (Marie G. Lee's "The Rose of Sharon," Minfong Ho's "The Green Armchair," and Dian Curtis Regan's "Second Culture Kids") and others trying instead to distance themselves from all possible manifestations of their otherness (Rita Williams-Garcia's "Make Maddie Mad"). The acculturation-related intergenerational clashes within families are addressed as well (Jean Davies Okimoto's "My Favorite Chaperone"). As the narratives show, immigration is also associated with serious dangers, such as the newcomer becoming the community's scapegoat for recent tragedies (Elsa Marston's "Lines of Scrimmage" and Alden R. Carter's "The Swede") or risking his life to cross the border illegally (Pam Muñoz Ryan's "First Crossing"). The inclusion of these solemn-tone stories is balanced by the presence of more lighthearted pieces in the form of Lensey Namioka's "They Don't Mean It!" on country-based differences in communication etiquettes and David Lubar's "Pulling Up Stakes" on a Transylvanian immigrant mistaken for a vampire. Out of the ten cultural affiliations explored,

Asian immigrants receive the largest representation, with characters of Cambodian, Chinese, Kazakh, and Korean heritage included. Immigrants with Haitian, Mexican, Palestinian, Romanian, Swedish, and Venezuelan roots are also present in this empathy-inspiring collection.

Discussion Starters

1. List the various reasons behind the characters' immigration. Which of these can be perceived as traditional? Which are a product of more modern circumstances?
2. Discuss the parent-child relationships in "My Favorite Chaperone." How does immigration change the Alazova family's hierarchies?
3. In "The Rose of Sharon," what impact does Soo-Mi's finding her biological parents have on her identity?
4. How does Sopeap in "The Green Armchair" decide to keep her grandmother's memory alive? Think of additional ways to preserve one's cultural heritage.

Quotes for Interpretation

1. "Mother stopped complimenting people here on how old and fat they looked" (81).
2. "It was strange to think that the people in this tiny, wary group had all been born in one country, and now they were in another, alternately clueless about their lives, both American and Korean" (178).

Yell-Oh Girls!: Emerging Voices Explore Culture, Identity, and Growing Up Asian American. Edited by Vickie Nam. Harper, 2001. 0-06-095944-4. 297 pp. Poetry/Nonfiction. Gr. 9–12.

Selected Awards: ALA Best Books for Young Adults 2002.

Defined in its foreword as "the first anthology of Asian American teenage girls' writings" (xix), this collection represents a passionate attempt of dual heritage high school- and college-age females from across the country to transcend harmful gender and racial stereotypes by defining themselves on their own terms. Selected from hundreds of submissions, the more than eighty short poems, essays, and personal narratives included in this book are structured around five overlapping themes: the bicultural authors struggling to establish a sense of belonging, facing related intergenerational clashes within their immigrant families, experiencing anger and frustration at being subjected to oppressive paradigms, utilizing writing to actively shape their hybrid identities, and, finally, deciding to use their creative energy to "YELL like hell" in order to fight discrimination (xxxi). Vickie Nam, the anthology's editor, carefully contextualizes each theme by including brief quotes by prominent Asian American thinkers and her own reflective passages on feeling estranged both in predominately white Rochester (New York) and in Korea, where she has consistently been labeled a foreigner. Mentor pieces by those who "have, in some way, demonstrated a strong commitment toward nurturing young women and infusing our imagination with colorful possibilities" (xxxi) conclude each chapter. While the anthology reflects the collective consciousness of young women of Asian American background specifically, its topics carry the potential to resonate with all adolescents who are facing conflicts associated with coming of age.

Discussion Starters

1. What makes a place home? According to the anthology, how is the process of finding home more difficult for young American women of Asian immigrant background?

2. What are some of the discriminatory definitions that the featured Asian American girls struggle with? How do they cope?

3. In your opinion, why do people tend to resort to stereotypes when dealing with the immigrant/cultural/racial Other? Can stereotypes be avoided? Why/why not?

4. Discuss the portrayed clashes between the Asian American adolescents and their parents. How does their biculturalism contribute to these conflicts?

Quotes for Interpretation

1. "'Asian America' is a frame of mind, a spiritual place that is located neither in Asia nor America, but hovering somewhere above, between and around the hearts and souls of the people who belong to it" (30).
2. "There are two reasons why I absolutely must be vocal, stubborn, and aggressive: I'm Asian American and I'm female" (261).

UNIDENTIFIED ASIAN COUNTRY

One Green Apple. **Eve Bunting. Ill. by Ted Lewin. Clarion Books, 2006. 978-0-618-43477-0. 32 pp. Picture Book/Fiction. Gr. 1–4.**

Selected Awards: Arab American National Museum Book Award 2007.

In this story of empowerment through newly established connections, Farah, on her "second day in the new school in the new country," ventures out on a field trip to an apple orchard (5). Farah's country of origin is not specified, but the references to a *dupatta* and the way she wears it in illustrations allude to a Muslim South Asia. The book cleverly details the visual and auditory processing a new immigrant engages in to make sense of a space that seems linguistically and culturally inaccessible to her. Moving beyond differences to notice that the children's belches, sneezes, and the dogs' crunching sounds are the same as in her home country, the narrator is able to instill the experience with some familiarity, and, after lending her hand at the cider press, she overcomes her initial inner withdrawal. The cider is used as the book's central metaphor for cultural blending. Watching her little green apple from a tree that "does not seem to belong" mix seamlessly with her classmates' red apples, the narrator gains the confidence that she too will one day become an integral part of the group (14). The narrative closes with the empowered Farah's losing her shyness and using her newly acquired English word ("apple") in front of her classmates-turned-friends. Lewin's sun-filled illustrations that capture the range of Farah's emotions make this a perfect read-aloud story.

Discussion Starters

1. What makes Farah different? Why don't some of her classmates like her?
2. A few classmates try to include Farah. How do they do that? Describe ways to make someone new to the country who does not speak English feel welcome.
3. How does Farah change throughout the story? What small actions point to this change?
4. Why is the book titled *One Green Apple*?
5. Think of a situation when you felt like you were not part of the group. How did you deal with that?

Quotes for Interpretation

1. "I want to say, 'I understand. It's not that I am stupid. It is just that I am lost in this new place'" (12).
2. "... soon I will know their words. I will blend with the others the way my apple blended with the cider" (28).
3. "It is my first outside-myself word. There will be more" (32).

Notes

1. Roger Daniels, "United States Policy towards Asian Immigrants: Contemporary Developments in Historical Perspective," *International Journal* 48, no. 2 (1993): 334.
2. Harry H. L. Kitano, *Race Relations* (Upper Saddle River, NJ: Prentice Hall, 1997), 226.
3. Pew Research Center, "The Rise of Asian Americans," last modified April 4, 2013, www.pewsocialtrends.org/2012/06/19/the-rise-of-asian-americans/.
4. Jie Zong and Jeanne Batalova, "Asian Immigrants in the United States," *Migration Information Source*, January 6, 2016, www.migrationpolicy.org/article/asian-immigrants-united-states.
5. Pew Research Center, "The Rise of Asian Americans."
6. Zong and Batalova, "Asian Immigrants in the United States."
7. Pew Research Center, "The Rise of Asian Americans."
8. Zong and Batalova, "Asian Immigrants in the United States."
9. Ibid.
10. According to the Pew Research Center, one in five Asian Americans feel they have been unfairly treated because of their race in the last year, and one in ten men-

tion they have been subjected to an offensive label. Pew Research Center, "The Rise of Asian Americans."

11. Pew Research Center, "The Rise of Asian Americans."

12. Kitano, *Race Relations*, 228.

13. Pew Research Center, "The Rise of Asian Americans"; Michael Miller Topp, "Racial and Ethnic Identity in the United States, 1837–1877," in *Race and Ethnicity in America: A Concise History*, ed. Ronald H. Bayor (New York: Columbia University Press, 2003), 73.

14. Kitano, *Race Relations*, 228.

15. Ibid., 229–31.

16. Topp, "Racial and Ethnic Identity in the United States," 74–75.

17. Daniels, "United States Policy towards Asian Immigrants," 313.

18. Ibid., 313–14.

19. Kitano, *Race Relations*, 232.

20. Daniels, "United States Policy towards Asian Immigrants," 316; Pew Research Center, "The Rise of Asian Americans."

21. Daniels, "United States Policy towards Asian Immigrants," 314, 317.

22. Kitano, *Race Relations*, 245–46.

23. Daniels, "United States Policy towards Asian Immigrants," 314.

24. Kitano, *Race Relations*, 252–53.

25. Pew Research Center, "The Rise of Asian Americans."

26. Kitano, *Race Relations*, 254.

27. Ibid.

28. Daniels, "United States Policy towards Asian Immigrants," 319–20.

29. Pew Research Center, "The Rise of Asian Americans."

30. Daniels, "United States Policy towards Asian Immigrants," 325–27.

31. Ibid., 330.

32. Pew Research Center, "The Rise of Asian Americans."

33. Kitano, *Race Relations*, 287, 292–94; Zong and Batalova, "Asian Immigrants in the United States."

34. Topp, "Racial and Ethnic Identity in the United States," 74.

35. Victor Nee and Hilary Holbrow, "Why Asian Americans Are Becoming Mainstream," *Daedalus* 142, no. 3 (2013): 71.

36. Pew Research Center, "The Rise of Asian Americans."

Chapter 4

Latin America and the Caribbean

*Overview of Latin American and Caribbean
Immigration to the United States*

NEWCOMERS FROM LATIN AMERICA AND THE CARIBBEAN represent a heterogeneous group of intersecting cultural and ethnic elements that, in its combined impact, has contributed significantly to the recent altering of the U.S. population's demographic makeup, thus triggering a complex set of responses from the U.S. mainstream. While in 1965, 84 percent of Americans identified as non-Hispanic whites, by 2015 their share had decreased to 62 percent, with the number of Hispanic Americans rising from 4 percent to 18 percent within the same time frame.[1] To put it in another perspective, in 2015 Hispanics constituted 47 percent of all immigrants residing in the United States.[2] Of the four geopolitical sub-areas comprising the region (Mexico, Central America, the Caribbean, and South America), Mexico represents the most common place of origin of these newcomers, having been the nation's largest source country of recently arrived immigrants from the 1980s[3] until 2013, when China and India surpassed it in this regard.[4] Accordingly, data collected in 2014 show that Mexican immigrants account for 28 percent of the 42.4 million foreign-born residents in the U.S. population.[5] In comparison, Central American immigrants represent approximately 8 percent,[6] Caribbean immigrants 9 percent,[7] and South American immigrants 7 percent of all non-native people residing in the United States.[8] In spite of the immigration from these areas slowing down lately, the overall share of foreign-born residents of Hispanic descent is expected to continue to amount to a comparatively large figure in the next decades, specifically 31 percent of all foreign-born immigrants by 2065.[9]

As research shows, such a large influx of migrants from the region has met with relatively low levels of U.S. approval, with the population in question also generally exhibiting a comparatively low degree of economic and educational success in the country. According to the Pew Research Center, many Americans are likely to hold unfavorable opinions of the impact of Latin American immigrants on the United States, with 37 percent of American adults viewing their contribution to the American society as mostly negative, 35 percent perceiving their impact as neither positive nor negative, and a mere 26 percent saying that these newcomers have influenced America in a positive way.[10] By contrast, approximately 47 percent of U.S. adults view the impact of Asians on America as positive overall, and 44 percent hold the same view of immigrants from Europe.[11] Not unrelated to these social attitudes, most immigrants originating from Latin America and the Caribbean also face a higher probability of having lower incomes, living in poverty, not being insured, being less educated, and, in the case of Mexican and Central American immigrants specifically, being less likely to have a good command of English than the overall U.S. foreign-born population.[12] South Americans, arriving in the country predominately from Colombia, Peru, Ecuador, Brazil, and Guyana, represent an exception to these socio-demographic trends, being slightly more educated and having higher incomes than the general immigrant population.[13] Still, they join their larger geopolitical group in its tendency to have a higher likelihood of participating in the U.S. labor force.[14] This shared characteristic points to employment as being a significant driving force behind Latin American and Caribbean migration to the United States.

A careful look at the long-term history of the group's immigration to the country confirms the pivotal role of employment in their arrival patterns, while simultaneously providing additional insight into their challenging position within American society. Mexico, as the region's largest supplier of non-native workers to the United States, serves as a telling example in this context. Repeatedly, Mexicans have been actively invited into the country to address its labor needs. Thus, the large-scale migration from Mexico to the United States that began in the early twentieth century was triggered not only by Mexico's unstable economic conditions and the Mexican Revolution, but also by the shortage of workers in U.S. agriculture and railroad construction,[15] with U.S. recruiters looking for workhands particularly from the west-central Mexican states of Jalisco, Michoacán, and Guanajuato.[16] The purposeful recruitment continued throughout the 1910s and into the late 1920s, when immigration from Southern and Eastern Europe as a key source of inexpensive labor slowed down due to World War I and the quota-based Immigration Act of 1924.[17] Many U.S. employers took advantage of the fact that the entrance of Mexicans was not limited by the new legislation, with Hispanics even granted eligibility for citizenship in spite of being routinely defined as nonwhite by the period.[18] As a result, the annual number of Mexican immigrants entering the country grew from 10,000 in 1913 to 68,000 in 1920 and 106,000 in 1924. According to the same source, approximately 621,000 Mexicans migrated to the United States between 1920 and 1929.[19] A similar situation occurred during World War II, when the federal government initiated the Bracero Program in response to the country's conscription-related shortage of agricultural labor, with Mexicans permitted to be employed in the United States as temporary workers.[20] More specifically, as Durand, Massey, and Zenteno explain, "Mexicans were granted renewable six-month visas to work for approved agricultural growers, located mostly in the southwestern United States."[21] The binational treaty was extended annually until 1964, when pressure from religious and labor organizations caused it to be phased out. During the program's twenty-two years of existence, over 4.6 million Mexican workers were allowed into the country, [22] proving the powerful effect of the legally supported employment-based invitations.

However, the repeated and targeted recruitment of Mexican workers has not necessarily paired up with American society cultivating the migrants' sense of belonging. Fueled by ethnic/racial and class prejudice against them as the immigrant Other, Mexican newcomers have been frequently ostracized, correlating with efforts to tighten the immigration rules controlling their entry or even to expel those already in the country during times of increased economic hardship and/or rising nationalistic fervor. As Kitano observes, Mexican Americans of the early twentieth century "were kept isolated and segregated," with the pre-World War II era also preventing them from participating in the dominant society in a way equal to European immigrants, and the World

War II years continuing to exhibit active signs of Latino economic exploitation as well as "refusal of service in some public and private places; denial of access to real estate and housing; exclusion from jury duty; and terrorism by police officers."[23] Still more disconcerting were the massive repatriations of Mexican immigrants during the Great Depression of the 1930s. While scholarship disagrees about the level of coercion employed and the legality of related orders,[24] there are repeated mentions of some 400,000 to over one million Mexicans and Mexican Americans leaving the United States between 1929 and 1939.[25] The numbers are at best approximate, given the lack of federal records for many of the departures.[26] According to the U.S. Department of Homeland Security, the repatriations were triggered by "some Americans accus[ing] Mexicans, as well as other aliens, of holding jobs needed by U.S. citizens" during a time of severe fiscal crisis and unemployment, with "many agencies f[eeling] pressure to exclude foreign-born applicants from receiving aid."[27] Nevertheless, in Balderrama's opinion, "the procedure . . . praised as a way to ensure that jobs [and welfare benefits] would become available for 'real' Americans . . . turned out to be a foolish policy" since "Mexicans across the country never comprised more than 10 percent of those on welfare."[28] Ryan confirms that, contrary to governmental assumptions, the repatriations did not solve the dire problems of the Great Depression. She also points out that "many of those sent to Mexico were native-born United States citizens and had never been to Mexico."[29] As such scholarly observations show, the deep pain associated with the rather unknown high-impact Depression–era action against Hispanic Americans lives on.

A concentrated official effort, if a much less radical one, to curtail the numbers of Mexican immigrants in the country occurred in another instance in 1986 with the passage of the Immigration Reform and Control Act (IRCA). While the two decades after the phasing out of the Bracero Program witnessed a generally tolerated steady immigration of Mexican workers—about 1.4 million legal and some 1.5 million illegal immigrants arrived from 1964 through 1985[30]— the United States of the late 1980s, plagued by domestic economic problems, attempted to limit the practice while especially targeting unauthorized immigrants. Although IRCA included provisions outlining the path to amnesty for those illegals able to provide evidence of continuous residence in the country for a specific length of time,[31] it also criminalized the hiring of undocumented workers and militarized the Mexico-U.S. border.[32] Nevertheless, as Katz, Stern, and Fader observe, IRCA did not quite succeed in its goals of "crack[ing] down on undocumented migrants"; coinciding with the collapse of the Mexican economy, it merely "shifted the balance even more toward undocumented workers and discouraged immigrants from returning to Mexico."[33] In fact, by 2013, 6.2 million (56 percent) of the approximately 11 million illegal immigrants residing in the United States were from Mexico.[34]

Economic struggles, often occurring alongside political crises, also spurred the immigration from other sub-areas of Latin America and the Caribbean. For instance, Central Americans, arriving in the United States primarily from El Salvador, Guatemala, and Honduras, as well as from Nicaragua, arrived in large numbers in the 1970s and 1980s due to the confluence of civil war, intense political conflicts, and fiscal hardship in the region.[35] Their migration continued in the 1990s and beyond, this time triggered by natural disasters; additional political and socioeconomic volatility, including high homicide rates and gang violence; and the desire for family reunification.[36] Consequently, between 1980 and 2015, the size of the Central American immigrant population increased almost tenfold.[37] Along the same lines, immigrants from the Caribbean started immigrating at accelerated rates in the 1960s, with Jamaica and other former British colonies responding to the U.S. recruitment of English-speaking workers at the time of immigration restrictions in the United Kingdom. Cuba, Haiti, and, to some extent, the Dominican Republic also faced political instability, prompting their citizens to leave.[38] Thus, beginning with fewer than 200,000 immigrants in 1960, the Caribbean population in the United States increased 248 percent in the 1960s, 86 percent in the 1970s, 54 percent in the 1980s, 52 percent in the 1990s, and 35 percent between 2000 and 2014.[39] Of special note in this context are the Cuban Adjustment Act of 1966 and the U.S.-Cuba Migration Accords of the 1994 and 1995, which offered special treatment to Castro-regime Cuban refugees by fast-tracking those who reached U.S. soil for permanent residence and granting them the right to receive public assistance.[40] Finally, as for South America, its immigrants have been primarily highly skilled and educated individuals seeking economic opportunities not available in their countries of origin due to restructuring.[41] They have become the Latin American group to experience the fastest growth since 1960, with the number of 90,000 South American immigrants residing in the country in 1960 having grown to approximately 2.9 million in 2014.[42]

As this brief overview shows, the immigration patterns of Latin American and Caribbean people have been closely dependent on the sociopolitical situation in the immigrants' home countries, as well as on their host culture's economic needs and fluctuating levels of nationalist sentiments. Recently, the levels of U.S. nationalism have been on the rise again, with the newly elected administration of President Donald Trump adopting a correspondingly harsh stance towards Latinos, as reflected, for instance, in its vowing to construct a wall on the approximately 2,000-mile-long U.S.-Mexico border as well as issuing new, stepped-up immigration enforcement policies that have widened the pool of unauthorized immigrants targeted for deportation.[43] Only the future will show how these complex realities impacting the presence of the proportionately large numbers of Latino immigrants in the United States, especially those of undocumented status, play out. The section below offers additional scholarly resources providing insight into this multifaceted issue.

Additional Scholarly Resources

Balderrama, Francisco E., and Raymond Rodríguez. *Decade of Betrayal: Mexican Repatriation in the 1930s.* Albuquerque: University of New Mexico Press, 2006.

De León, Arnoldo, and Richard Griswold del Castillo. *North to Aztlán: A History of Mexican Americans in the United States.* Wheeling, IL: Harlan Davidson, 2006.

Gonzales, Manuel G. *Mexicanos: A History of Mexicans in the United States.* Bloomington: Indiana University Press, 2000.

González, Juan. *Harvest of Empire: A History of Latinos in America.* New York: Penguin Books, 2011.

Gutiérrez, David, ed. *The Columbia History of Latinos in the United States since 1960.* New York: Columbia University Press, 2006.

Gutiérrez, Ramón A., and Tomás Almaguer, eds. *The New Latino Studies Reader: A Twenty-First-Century Perspective.* Oakland: University of California Press, 2016.

Massey, Douglas S., ed. *New Faces in New Places: The Changing Geography of American Immigration.* New York: Russell Sage Foundation, 2008.

Massey, Douglas S., Jorge Durand, and Nolan J. Malone. *Beyond Smoke and Mirrors: Mexican Immigration in an Era of Economic Integration*. New York: Russell Sage Foundation, 2002.

Suárez-Orozco, Marcelo M., and Mariela Páez, eds. *Latinos: Remaking America*. Berkeley: University of California Press, 2009.

Zúñiga, Víctor, and Rubén Hernández-León, eds. *New Destinations: Mexican Immigration in the United States*. New York: Russell Sage Foundation, 2006.

Recommended Children's and Young Adult Books

`ARGENTINA`

Life, After. Sarah Darer Littman. Scholastic, 2010. 978-0-545-15144-3. 281 pp. Historical Fiction. Gr. 7–10.

Selected Awards: Sydney Taylor Book Award (Honor) 2011.

Structured around the contrast between "a Before, which [one] could never return to, and an After, where [one] had to learn to find joy again" (278), this relatively slow-paced, dialogue-driven first-person narrative traces the identity development of the Argentinian Jewish teen Daniela Bensimon as her family immigrates to the United States in 2003 during her home country's prolonged economic crisis. With her father sinking into depression after his pregnant sister's death in a 1994 terrorist attack and his more recent loss of a clothing business, Daniela, while nostalgic, initially shares her mother's optimism about their relocation to a New York suburb—in part because her Buenos Aires sweetheart has moved to Miami. However, faced with the modesty of their new living quarters, persistent linguistic challenges, increasing caregiving responsibility for her younger sister, and bullying at Twin Lakes High, the narrator quickly reevaluates her position. It is only after a series of somewhat contrived plot twists that she gradually overcomes her acute sense of helplessness and Otherness. She finds a close friend in her privileged-background mocker Jess, whose brother with Asperger's syndrome she aids and who also lost a close relative to terrorism. In addition, Daniela successfully confronts Papá about his destructive passivity. Embedded Spanish phrases and references to Jewish holidays add to the authenticity of this emotional narrative on acculturation-related challenges.

Discussion Starters

1. Why is Daniela annoyed that many of her fellow students immediately think of *Evita* when finding out about her Argentinian origin? What have you learned about Argentina from the narrative?
2. What are the pros and cons of the Bensimons immigrating to the United States? Under what circumstances would you be willing to leave/have you left your home country?
3. The book explores several seemingly unlikely friendships. Identify some of them and discuss what helps the characters bond.
4. Why does Daniela's father, an Argentinian, feel confident he can mentor relatives of 9/11 victims?
5. Compare Daniela's and Roberto's adjustment to the United States. In your opinion, is it possible to sustain a long-distance romantic relationship at their age? Why/why not?

Quotes for Interpretation

1. "'Do you think we'll ever belong again, the way we do here?'... 'Or do you think in America, we'll always be *extranjeros?*'" (76).
2. "'These foreigners—if they're going to come to our country, the least they can do is make the effort to learn our language'" (150).

CHILE

I Lived on Butterfly Hill. **Marjorie Agosín. Ill. by Lee White. Trans. by E. M. O'Connor. Atheneum Books for Young Readers, 2014. 978-1-4169-5344-9. 454 pp. Historical Fiction. Gr. 5–9.**

Selected Awards: ALA Notable Children's Books 2015; Pura Belpré Award 2015.

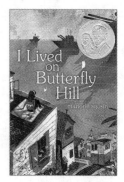

Dedicated to "the countless children who traveled beyond their home-lands in search of freedom and possibility," this lyricism-infused novel by the poet and social rights activist Marjorie Agosín offers a captivating portrayal of the impact of exile and subsequent repatriation on the identity development of a Chilean preteen. The book opens with Celeste Marconi, its perceptive sixth-grade narrator, detailing her idyllic upper-class life in the close-knit coastal community of Valparaíso in Chile. Her circumstances are shown to drastically change following Pinochet's coup d'état, with the narrative drawing explicit parallels between military-controlled Chile and Nazi-occupied Austria that Celeste's Jewish grandmother (Abuela) once fled. As Valparaíso is overtaken by violence and fear, the Marconi family is forced to separate: Celeste's parents, philanthropic doctors perceived as subversive by the new regime, go into hiding within the country, while Celeste travels to her emigrated aunt (Tía) Graciela's Maine residence. The acculturation challenges that Celeste faces as a refugee are explored in the book's second part, with specific attention given to climate differences, linguistic barriers, and initial ostracism by classmates. In an optimistic fashion, Celeste's exile is presented as an ultimately positive experience that results in her significant maturation as well as increased interest in writing and ends with her return to still-troubled Chile after the dictator's death. Given the novel's substantial length, leisurely pace, and relatively complex themes, advanced middle-school readers are likely to be its most appropriate audience.

Discussion Starters

1. Define dictatorship. What freedoms do Chileans lose during Pinochet's regime?
2. What are some of the main differences between Maine's Juliette Cove and Chile's Valparaíso? What helps Celeste gradually adjust to Maine?
3. How does Celeste's Maine experience change her? Think of an event or period in your life that had a transformative effect on you.
4. How does Celeste's habit of writing in her journal help her face hardship? What means do you use to feel better in difficult situations?

Quotes for Interpretation

1. "[Juliette Cove, Maine] isn't Valparaíso, where it seems like everyone has at least one grandparent who came as an exile from somewhere else" (199).
2. "'Yes, I am a refugee. And it is a beautiful word, a beautiful thing. I am an exile. That means I am a traveler of the world, and I belong to nothing but the things I love'" (454).

CUBA

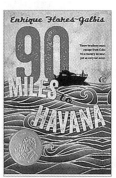

90 Miles to Havana. **Enrique Flores-Galbis. Roaring Brook Press, 2010. 978-1-59643-168-3. 292 pp. Historical Fiction. Gr. 5–8.**

Selected Awards: ALA Notable Children's Books 2011; Notable Social Studies Trade Books for Young People 2011; Pura Belpré Award (Honor) 2011.

Strongly autobiographical, this absorbing first-person historical novel relates the experiences of a preteen forced to flee his home country in the aftermath of the Cuban Revolution. As the pro-Castro armed forces assume control of the island, Julian, a gifted artist, must trade the comforts of his privileged family's house in Havana for the overcrowded child refugee camp in Miami where his desperate parents send him and his two older brothers through the Pedro Pan rescue operation. As Julian soon discovers, the camp's residents are terrorized by a self-proclaimed leader named Caballo. The narrative explores the dynamics of Caballo's bullying at length, prompting readers to identify parallels between his controlling behavior and Cuba's dictatorship. Ways of opposing the bully are analyzed as well, often humorously, with several somewhat didactic passages emphasizing the value of democracy. The story picks up pace when Julian, separated from his brothers and confronted with the prospect of being transferred to a notorious orphanage, runs away, joining his friend Tomás on a rescue mission of fellow Cubans on a makeshift vessel. The heroism the narrator displays during the voyage marks his transformation from a pampered boy to an independent pre-adolescent, foreshadowing his resourcefulness in facing the prejudice of the 1960s Connecticut school system once he is reunited with most of his family. Middle-schoolers of all backgrounds will likely enjoy this rare account of a young refugee's struggle to establish a sense of safety in a new country.

Discussion Starters

1. Research the Cuban Revolution. What were its pros and cons? How are these represented in the book?
2. Why do Julian's parents choose to send him and his brothers alone to the United States? How would you feel if your parents made a similar decision?
3. How does Caballo resemble a dictator? What proves to be the most effective way to oppose him?
4. Discuss Julian's passion for art. How does drawing help him in moments of crisis? What helps you face difficulties?
5. Why do many Americans outside Julian's camp look down on the Cuban child refugees?

Quotes for Interpretation

1. "I never thought my mother could be like the parents waiting in that line, so determined to send their children to a strange country all alone" (48).
2. "'Did you live in a tree house like Tarzan?' . . . 'Did you have a T.V.?' . . . 'Did you eat off plates?' The questions tumble out of the laughing class, each one sillier than the last, and I stare at my two-toned shoes" (285).

Cuba 15. **Nancy Osa. Ember, 2005. 978-0-385-73233-8. 277 pp. Fiction. Gr. 6–10.**

Selected Awards: ALA Best Books for Young Adults 2004; ALA Notable Children's Books 2004; Notable Social Studies Trade Books for Young People 2004; Pura Belpré Award (Honor) 2004.

Osa's witty narrative, inspired by her Cuban American family, traces a multiple-heritage teen's journey toward openly accepting her immigrant cultural background while identifying as simply American. The book's fifteen-year-old narrator, Violet Paz, growing up in Chicagoland, looks more like her Polish American mother and doesn't "even think of [herself] as Cuban" (her father's nationality) (11). Yet, approached by her "customized English"-speaking grandmother (Abuela) (2), she suddenly has to deal with plans for celebrating her assumed transition into womanhood in the traditional Cuban ceremony of *quinceañero*. Most of the novel focuses on Violet's coming to terms with the event by tailoring it to her personality. She enhances its performative character, which allows her to incorporate her high-school speech team-practiced skit on her family's eccentricities. In the process, Violet actively learns more about her cultural roots: she even bypasses her father's resistance to discuss his native culture by participating in a Cuba peace rally, thus causing a major family crisis that teaches her about the older generation's pain over having to leave Cuba due to political circumstances. Violet's best friends, whose families have their own oddities, are masterfully drawn, often adding to the story's humor. A helpful "Readers Guide" and a detailed conversation with the author conclude this action-packed narrative on the possibility of bridging the cultural gap between generations.

Discussion Starters

1. Why did Violet's grandparents leave Cuba? Research the changes that have occurred in U.S.-Cuba sociopolitical relations since the novel's first publication in 2003.

2. Which of Violet's non-American cultural backgrounds dominates in the Paz household and why? Analyze Violet's evolving relationship to that heritage.

3. Why is Violet's father reluctant to answer questions about his native culture? Think of a topic your parents had trouble discussing with you. How did you deal with it?

4. After a major argument, Violet's father insists she is not ready for her *quinceañero* (251, 254). Do you agree with him? Why/why not? Discuss Violet's maturation.

Quotes for Interpretation

1. "'Some of the kids I ran around with thought it was—*afeminado*—to be in a court. To have to . . . learn all those silly dances . . . we just wanted to be Americans, to drive around in cars and be cool'" (68).
2. "'For [Papi] and for Mami, the only Cuba is the Cuba of old. They have no future there anymore, or they think they don't'" (215).

Flight to Freedom. **Ana Veciana-Suarez. Orchard Books, 2002. 978-0-439-38199-4. 215 pp. Historical Fiction. Gr. 6–9.**

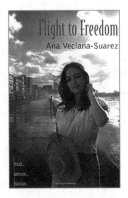

Selected Awards: Notable Social Studies Trade Books for Young People 2003.

Set during the 1960s wave of Cuban exiles flooding into the United States, Ana Veciana-Suarez's first book for middle-schoolers chronicles the bittersweet experiences of thirteen-year-old Yara García as she attempts to find a new home in Miami. Yara's rather formal diary opens in 1967 Havana, detailing the hardships of her close-knit family under the Castro regime: insufficient rations, enforced farm labor, indoctrination, and persecution due to them having applied for emigration are all addressed. The family's escape from Cuba is persuasively linked to immediate benefits but also to significant challenges. The linguistic barrier, differences in cultural practices, and corresponding isolation all take their toll on Yara's sense of self, to the extent that she begins to feel like "nobody" (48). Her parents, who frequently argue based on Mami's progressive emancipation and Papi's involvement with anti-Castro militia, cannot help her navigate the new cultural space very much. Only after Yara makes new friends, succeeds academically, and participates in social activities does she begin to consider herself less uprooted. However, her feeling of being suspended between the two cultures prevails: she concludes that her expatriate family "can never be completely happy" because of what was left behind (178). Historical facts and Cuban cultural trivia are seamlessly embedded in the emotional story, with additional information on Cuban exile offered in the author's afterword on her "Personal Exodus" (207).

Discussion Starters

1. List the advantages and disadvantages of the Garcías moving to the United States. Would you have made the same choice to leave 1960s Cuba? Why/why not?

2. Why are Yara's parents reluctant to let her and her older sister enjoy American social life? Link your answer to the different expectations for young women in the two cultures.

3. Discuss the impact of the exile on Yara's sense of self. If you were her classmate, how could you help her to adjust?

4. How does the family's belief that their stay in Miami is only temporary make their immigration experience potentially more difficult?

5. How would the diary be different if written by another family member, such as Papi?

Quotes for Interpretation

1. "...Mami told us that we are exiles, not immigrants. Big difference, she insisted" (42).

2. "My heart, the one now beating in my chest, feels like it belongs to someone else. It has been transplanted here, and everybody seems to want to force it to feel something it cannot feel" (94–95).

Heat. **Mike Lupica. Philomel Books, 2006. 0-399-24301-1. 220 pp. Fiction. Gr. 5–8.**

Selected Awards: ALA Notable Children's Books 2007.

Likely to appeal to all middle-school baseball fans, this dialogue-driven narrative by the accomplished sports writer Mike Lupica is centered on a Cuban American refugee preteen's aspirations to play in the Little League World Series. Though having recently arrived from Havana, which he still considers his home, twelve-year-old Michael Arroyo is fully bilingual and appears relatively well integrated into his South Bronx multicultural neighborhood. The gift of having "the arm" makes him a lauded pitcher of the Clippers (6), surrounding him with friends and providing him with a sense of direction.

However, upon his father's sudden death, his optimism is seriously challenged, with him and his older brother Carlos attempting to keep the tragedy secret from social services so that they can stay together. After an opposing team's xenophobic player named Justin and Justin's father-coach bestow another blow in the form of questioning his age and having him barred from playing until he produces a birth certificate, Michael resolves to not "expect good things to happen to [him]" (149). To contest such an outlook on life, the narrative presents a series of surprising twists, including Michael receiving help from an admired Cuban-born Yankees player, who is the father of his romantic interest. The ambitious story closes with the well-drawn refugee orphan pitching at his dreamed-about Little League Yankee Stadium game.

Discussion Starters

1. Do you agree with Michael and Carlos's decision to keep their father's death a secret? What are the pros and cons of such a decision? What would you have done in their place?

2. What role does Michael's Cuban origin play in Justin's perception of him?

3. Analyze the episode in which Justin hits Michael in the head with a fastball (67–69). Why is Justin kept in the game? Would Michael as a Cuban refugee be likely to get away with the same action? Why/why not?

4. Discuss the importance of baseball for Michael. Link your answer to him being a refugee orphan.

Quotes for Interpretation

1. "'What'd you do, drop a couple of years on the boat over, like you guys do'" (72)?

2. "Papi never allowed yeah. Speak American, he always said. You're American now" (112).

3. "It was [Michael] against Justin and maybe him against all the other people who didn't want him to be here, or across the street ever, or even in Williamsport" (210).

EL SALVADOR

Journey of the Sparrows. **Fran Leeper Buss and Daisy Cubias. Puffin Books, 2002. 0-14-230209-0. 155 pp. Fiction. Gr. 5–8.**

Selected Awards: ALA Best Books for Young Adults 1992; Jane Addams Children's Book Award 1992.

Fran Leeper Buss's eye-opening first novel, written with the assistance of the Salvadoran American poet and activist Daisy Cubias, provides middle-school readers with the opportunity to learn about the day-to-day struggles of illegal refugees. The fictional account, which is based on interviews Buss conducted with undocumented workers, is centered on the fifteen-year-old artistic narrator María, her older pregnant sister Julia, and their six-year-old sickly brother Oscar, who flee their peasant village in El Salvador following the brutal killings of their father and Julia's husband by government soldiers. After a brief stay in Mexico, they endure a horrendous journey to midwinter Chicago nailed in crates at the back of a smuggler's truck. In documentary-style fashion, the book details the relative absence of safety for them on U.S. soil as well, with the siblings living in constant danger of deportation and enduring life-threating poverty while supporting themselves by the odd jobs of sewing, cleaning, and dish-washing. In spite of the constant setbacks they experience, a thin thread of hope and faith runs through the narrative, as represented by the immigrant/low-income community's solidarity, help by church organizations, the birth of Julia's daughter, and the real possibility of María successfully bringing their youngest sister Teresa to the United States. Much of the natural and religious symbolism that the authors use supports the impression of overall optimism in this beautifully told story on the timely topic of war-triggered migration.

Discussion Starters

1. Research the Salvadoran Civil War. Share your findings with your classmates.

2. Discuss the reasons behind María and her siblings' traumatic journey to the United States. Why do they choose to cross the border illegally?

3. How do the siblings support themselves once in Chicago? What would you do in their position to make a living without the appropriate work permits?

4. How does María's illegal status make her more vulnerable to the poor behavior of others, including her employer?

5. Has the book changed your views on illegal immigration and refugees in any way? Why/why not?

Quotes for Interpretation

1. "'[Beatriz] told us how we would have to live, way up north like this. She said we'd have to be invisible, never complain, never get anybody to notice us'" (14).

2. "'Oh, how we suffer to get up [north], where we're not even wanted, except to do work that others wouldn't do'" (15).

GUATEMALA

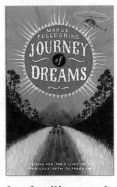

Journey of Dreams. **Marge Pellegrino. Francis Lincoln Children's Books, 2009. 978-1-84780-061-9. 250 pp. Historical Fiction. Gr. 5–8.**

Selected Awards: Outstanding International Books 2010.

Pellegrino's powerful story, based on the author's work with Central American refugees, has the articulated aim to foster "a better understanding of unfamiliar people and situations" (5). For this purpose, the fictional character of Tomasa, a thirteen-year-old Guatemalan of Mayan ancestry, details the systematic military destruction of the Guatemalan highlands and the family's consequent perilous escape through Mexico to Arizona during the 1980s. While closely codependent on each other, the family is forced to separate right from the start, with Tomasa's mother and older brother leaving first due to targeted threats. The narrator, her two younger siblings, and their folk tale-telling father follow. Pellegrino has Tomasa skillfully weave the story of their difficult immigration journey like the fabric Tomasa used to make on the family's loom, with her dreams filling the reader in on the emotions she tries to suppress. Helped by the underground Sanctuary Movement, the family ultimately reunites in Phoenix. While the ending may seem a little too optimistic, given the explicit dangers of multiple illegal border crossings and constant military presence, the characters are well drawn, with the narrative casting a refreshing light on frequently shunned refugees. It shows that their struggle for survival often does not allow for immediate compliance with existing immigration laws. A background note, glossary, and a map of Tomasa's journey conclude this suspenseful narrative.

Discussion Starters

1. Why do Tomasa and her family leave Guatemala? What do you think would have happened if they had stayed?
2. What is the book's position on illegal crossings of borders? Do you agree with that position? Why/why not?
3. Research the Sanctuary Movement. Who was involved and what were the possible sanctions?
4. When Tomasa reads a newspaper story about the soldiers protecting the Guatemalan highlanders, she doubts its accuracy (134). Discuss why. Think of a piece of news you read or heard through the media recently that seemed questionable.

Quotes for Interpretation

1. "As we set up a shelter, I wonder: how can you run from a place you love?" (98).
2. "Away from our home, I must keep my deepest self hidden. This seems impossible. I am always waiting for something to happen" (118).
3. "Each day, I think of when our family will be sewn together again" (205).

HAITI

Fresh Girl. **Jaïra Placide. Wendy Lamb Books, 2002. 0-385-32753-6. 216 pp. Fiction. Gr. 8–12.**

Selected Awards: ALA Best Books for Young Adults 2003; Golden Kite Award 2003.

Distressed by reports of sexual violence in Haiti following its 1991 coup d'état, Jaïra Placide authored a complex debut novel featuring a nar-

rator attempting to overcome her rape-induced trauma while renegotiating her cultural identity. Fourteen-year-old Mardi Desravines, the
only U.S.-born member of her Haitian immigrant family, first experiences a stressful translocation at the age of four when her overworked
parents send her to live with her grandmother in Haiti. After the Aris-
tide government's overthrow by the military, Mardi is forced to revise
her idea of home yet again, moving back in with her estranged parents.
Their life in Brooklyn is far from ideal, with the Creole terms-sprin-
kled narrative offering a unique insight into the relationships between
same-background immigrants: at Taliaferro Junior High, Mardi is bullied not only by her American schoolmates but also by other Haitian
immigrants, who, considering themselves more assimilated, painstakingly dissociate themselves from her. Mardi struggles with her dual
identity as well, "trying to get rid of Haiti in [her] mind" (35) and seeming
too "fresh" to her traditional parents in the process (127). Mardi's identity negotiations are linked closely to her sexual violation by a soldier
when she was fleeing the island, an incident that is hinted at throughout the novel and described fully toward its end. The healing power of
the family's love is explored, with Mardi beginning to move away from
self-mutilating practices after confiding in those who are closest to her.
A brief author's note concludes this ambitious coming-of-age novel on
an abused second-generation immigrant teen's re-creating a sense of
self-worth and belonging.

Discussion Starters

1. What are Mardi's parents' views on young female sexuality? How do
   these differ from mainstream U.S. opinions? How do Mardi and her
   sister deal with this discrepancy?
2. Why does Mardi keep the brutal rape a secret from her family?
   Would you have done the same in her situation? Why/why not?
3. What stereotypes are applied to Mardi at Taliaferro Junior High? Why
   do some other students of immigrant backgrounds look down on her?
4. Does Mardi seem to be more at home in Haiti or in the United States?
   How is her experience of a second-generation immigrant unique
   when compared to those of other immigrants?

Quotes for Interpretation

1. "... when I first started school, [other Haitian kids] were the first ones to accuse me of having Haitian Body Odor. Somehow they knew how to get rid of theirs" (33).
2. "'You're the American. You're born with choices'" (107).

Stormwitch. **Susan Vaught. Bloomsbury Children's Books, 2005. 978-1-58234-952-7. 208 pp. Historical Fiction. Gr. 6–10.**

Selected Awards: ALA Best Books for Young Adults 2006.

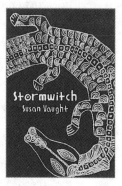

Skillfully combining fantasy and historical fiction, this suspenseful narrative by a neuropsychologist analyzes the identity struggles of a sixteen-year-old Haitian immigrant as she attempts to satisfy the demands of racist Pass Christian, Mississippi, in 1969 while staying true to her upbringing as a Dahomey Amazon war woman. After her maternal Haitian grandmother Ba's death, Ruba is taken in by her American Grandmother Jones, a devout Christian who considers Ruba "dirty" because of her belief "in magic and spirits and many gods" (16). The reflective passages, which include Ruba's heartfelt letters to Ba, show Ruba's distress as she is ordered to sever her connections to her Haitian foremothers' past as represented by her colorful African print garments, French speech, and, most importantly, conjuring. The two females' disagreement about adequate ways to respond to the area's blatant discrimination against African Americans is also addressed, with Ruba siding with radical modes of Black resistance based on her warrior background and Grandmother Jones advocating a Martin Luther King Jr.-inspired nonviolent activism. The book's final chapters ambitiously intertwine a scene on Ruba and her relatives' abuse by a local Ku Klux Klan juvenile affiliate and her fight against Hurricane Camille, whom she believes to be the vengeful stormwitch Zashar. Ruba's victory is presented as made possible by her successful negotiation of the two seemingly incompatible cultures of Haiti and Mississippi. Historical notes and a brief bibliography conclude this magic-infused narrative.

Discussion Starters

1. What are some of the main differences between the Haiti of Ruba's upbringing and 1969 Mississippi? Link your discussion to issues of race, gender, and religion.

2. How does Grandmother Jones try to make Ruba adapt to the new culture? Would you use the same strategies with a new immigrant? Why/why not?

3. Analyze the passage on Ruba using her journal to fight Zashar (190–92). What does it suggest about Ruba's changing relationship to Grandmother Jones?

4. The narrative portrays various ways of responding to racial injustice. Which of them do you consider the most effective and why?

Quotes for Interpretation

1. "I want to go back to Haiti. To a place with ten thousand black faces. Ten million. A place that might make some sense" (46).

2. "Perhaps I will do as my foremothers did . . . slay as many of the enemy as I can find. Show the white man Africa's woman heart. . . . Ba would be proud, but Grandmother Jones would be crushed" (123).

Touching Snow. **M. Sindy Felin. Atheneum Books for Young Readers, 2007. 978-1-4169-1795-3. 234 pp. Fiction. Gr. 8–12.**

Selected Awards: ALA Best Books for Young Adults 2008; National Book Award for Young People's Literature (Honor) 2007.

Inspired by the debuting author's experience of having to navigate different cultures, this coming-of-age novel focuses on Karina Lamond, a bicultural teen growing up in a large dysfunctional Haitian immigrant family in suburban Chestnut Valley, New York, during the 1980s. Even though born in the United States as her mother's pathway to citizenship, Karina, together with her siblings, continues to be subjected to rules predicated on Haitian cultural norms, as enforced especially by her stepfather (the Daddy). As Karina's matter-of-fact narrative voice relays, any deviation from the heavily gendered rules results in brutal beatings, culminating in the "black-as-dirt-and-too-fat-for-his-pants" Daddy's life-threating punishment of her older sister Enid for the children's failure to finish their dinner (3). The book persuasively shows that there is no easy way out of the domestic violence, with the family fearing that the Daddy's imprisonment would result in them having to go on welfare and their illegal alien cousins being deported. However, Karina does gradually manage to transcend the role of a passive victim that she has previously internalized: empowered by her not-quite platonic relationship with the affluent teen Rachael, she becomes instrumental in the Daddy's death, choosing to free herself and her sisters from the stifling Haitian gender paradigms. The narrative's well-nuanced characters and admirable honesty in depicting the immigrant family's struggles make it a valuable addition to any collection or curriculum on hybrid identities.

Discussion Starters

1. How does Karina's having Haitian parents influence her daily life in the United States? Link your answer to her gender. Which culture does she seem to side with and why?
2. Why did Karina's mother have her? What is your opinion on such a decision?
3. Why does Karina decide not to testify against her stepfather? Would you have acted differently in her position? Why/why not?
4. Discuss the relationship between Karina and Rachael. What explains their mutual attraction in spite of the differences in their backgrounds?

Quotes for Interpretation

1. "Ma always said if a family got welfare, then the government wouldn't let their kids go to college. Everyone in Haiti knew that, she said" (83).
2. "'... I think she likes [volunteer work] more now since she's rich and she knows she's never gonna be like the people she helps'" (181).

HONDURAS

Gaby, Lost and Found. Angela Cervantes. Scholastic, 2013. 978-0-545-48945-4. 220 pp. Fiction. Gr. 5–8.

Selected Awards: Notable Children's Books in the English Language Arts 2014.

In this politically charged coming-of-age story, Angela Cervantes portrays the plight of second-generation immigrant children whose parents entered the United States illegally. Ever since Gaby Ramirez Howard's mother's deportation to Honduras three months earlier, the eleven-year-old St. Ann's student has felt abandoned like the animals at the Furry Friends shelter where her class volunteers. Although her estranged white father promises to take care of her, Gaby is mostly on her own, and desperately lacks the financial and emotional support she needs. The narrative implicitly questions the immigration laws behind such an unfavorable mother-daughter separation. It emphasizes that while Ms. Ramirez strove to belong and contribute to her new country for fourteen years, "work[ing] on her English every day" and juggling multiple employments (138), she was still forced out. The dangers associated with illegal border crossings are also addressed, with the preteen gradually realizing that her mother may be unable to reunite with her in Kansas any time soon. Gaby's ability to write persuasive profiles of the shelter's cats and dogs helps her navigate the stressful situation more successfully, boosting her sense of agency as people adopt the animals she advertises. Adding to the pattern of parallels between her and the strays, the book has Gaby also find a new home: her father finally approves of her living with her close friend's family. Occasional Spanish phrases and detailed characterization add genuineness to this emotional narrative.

Discussion Starters

1. Why does Gaby describe herself as "St. Ann's stray" in her own profile (190)?
2. Discuss Gaby's mother's deportation in spite of Gaby being a U.S. citizen. Do you approve of such a practice? Why/why not? What are the chances of Gaby and her mother reuniting?

3. What does Gaby think about her mother's native country? Should she move to Honduras to be with Mom? Why/why not?

4. In your opinion, how can books like *Gaby, Lost and Found* possibly influence people's attitudes toward illegal immigrants?

Quotes for Interpretation

1. "There wasn't any money to buy Gaby a ticket to Honduras. Plus, Gaby had been born in the United Sates. She didn't know Honduras" (16).

2. "'... you tried to save me from being deported. I remember how you'd come with your rosary when I was detained. You told everyone that would listen how you were my daughter and that you wanted me home'" (194).

JAMAICA

Every Time a Rainbow Dies. **Rita Williams-Garcia. HarperCollins, 2001. 0-688-16245-2. 166 pp. Fiction. Gr. 8–12.**

Selected Awards: ALA Best Books for Young Adults 2002; ALA Top Ten Best Books for Young Adults 2002.

This tender coming-of-age story by an acclaimed young-adult novelist examines the healing power of love. Thulani, the book's well-drawn sixteen-year-old Jamaican-born protagonist who has "no plans, [and] no friends" (49), has intentionally isolated himself ever since his mother returned to their Jamaican homeland to die of cancer. The narrative's third-person lyrical voice portrays him as spending much of his time atop the Brooklyn brownstone he shares with his older brother and sister-in-law, tending to his pet pigeons. His emotional pain darkens even his perceptions of Jamaica, whose patois he no longer speaks, making him immune to their tenant's pastoral descriptions of the country—the notion of his mother's grave near his estranged father's house is simply unbearable to him. However, after witnessing and stopping the openly described brutal rape of Ysa, an ambitious Haitian teen, Thulani gradually reevaluates his attitude toward life and his home country, guided by the supportive love bond that forms between him and Ysa based on his persistence. Ysa's rainbow-colored silk skirt, which he finds at the rape scene and pins to his bedroom wall, is symbolic of his transformation, with the world no longer seeming "drab" and "dead" to him (89). This engaging story of a troubled adolescent's transition into adulthood closes with Thulani returning to Jamaica temporarily, attempting to access his future by exploring his origins.

Discussion Starters

1. Why is Thulani so strongly attracted to Ysa? Why does she initially reject him?
2. Discuss Thulani's unwillingness to listen to Mr. Dunleavy's descriptions of Jamaica. Why does he later decide to visit the country?
3. How does schooling influence Thulani's attitude towards his heritage? In your opinion, what can U.S. schools do to support immigrant students' maintaining a positive view of their native cultures?
4. Analyze the symbolism of the colorful skirt Thulani nails to his bedroom wall.
5. The novel ends on an anticipatory note. What do you envision will happen because of Thulani's decision to travel to Jamaica?

Quotes for Interpretation

1. "Thulani himself no longer spoke patois, thanks to a prekindergarten teacher, a strict Jamaican woman, who advised his mother to speak only proper English, if he was to succeed in school. This start-and-stop talking of trying to speak proper English confused him . . . It was easier to be quiet" (46).
2. "'. . . you will see the place you were born. Your father. How rich the land. You'll be home'" (165).

MEXICO

Any Small Goodness: A Novel of the Barrio. Tony Johnston. Ill. by Raúl Colón. Blue Sky Press, 2001. 0-439-18936-5. 128 pp. Fiction. Gr. 4–7.

Selected Awards: John and Patricia Beatty Award 2002; Notable Children's Books in the English Language Arts 2002; Notable Social Studies Trade Books for Young People 2002.

Dedicated to "everyone who gives up a part of himself," Johnston's authentic book focuses on the possibility to programmatically create goodness in the economically challenged, gang-ridden immigrant barrios of Los Angeles. In a series of vignettes, Arturo Rodriguez, an eleven-year-old newcomer from Mexico, relays the encounters of his loving family with individuals who serve as a source of inspiration to him as he tries to find his place in the new country. The chapters feature a talented pianist sacrificing her musical career to teach her neighborhood's children, an NBA player training the underfunded school's basketball team, a librarian with a secret identity donating titles to the library, and others who produce change through their generosity and love. After Arturo's family becomes the target of a local gang's drive-by shooting, the narrator makes a conscious decision to contribute to the creation of good, forming his own gang that fights violence through anonymous acts of charity. The hope-filled narrative pays special attention to immigrants' options for resisting the dominant culture's efforts to erase signs of their ethnic affiliations. When Arturo's teacher Americanizes his name to Arthur, the boy successfully opposes this pro-mainstream attempt to change his identity as he grows to understand his name's connection to his heritage. Adding to the spirit of honoring minority cultural identities, the narrative is interspersed with numerous Spanish words and phrases, with a glossary at the book's end.

Discussion Starters

1. Why does the teacher Americanize Arturo's name and those of other Hispanic students? What is Arturo's initial response? How and why does it change later on?

2. In your opinion, how is a name linked to one's sense of self?
3. Based on the book, what are some of the challenges that children face when immigrating into poor U.S. neighborhoods?
4. The book shows many examples of people trying to foster goodness in tough parts of the city. List some. Then talk about a time when you helped someone in need.

Quotes for Interpretation

1. "In solemn ceremony we retrieve our names. Our selves" (20).
2. "'If you do not find enough of the good, you must yourself create it'" (103).

Becoming Naomi León. **Pam Muñoz Ryan. Scholastic, 2005. 978-0-439-26997-1. 246 pp. Fiction. Gr. 4–7.**

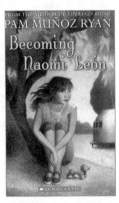

Selected Awards: ALA Notable Children's Books 2005; Notable Children's Books in the English Language Arts 2005; Pura Belpré Award (Honor) 2006; Tomás Rivera Mexican American Children's Book Award 2005.

This suspenseful chapter book explores the transformative power of a bicultural child's newly established connection with the country of her father's origin on her identity. Fifth-grader Naomi Soledad León Outlaw is aware that she is half Mexican, but does not consider herself affiliated with that culture in any way. Growing up in a California trailer park with her physically disabled but gifted brother (Owen) and great-grandmother (Gram), she faces social challenges related to their modest living conditions and her selective mutism, but she is relatively content. However, when her alcoholic mother, a somewhat two-dimensional character, shows up on the trailer's doorstep, demanding that Naomi come to live with her and her insensitive tattoo artist boyfriend, the family has to flee to Mexico in an attempt to gain support from the children's father regarding custody. The trip becomes symbolic of Naomi's journey toward a balanced hyphenated identity. Through her participation in the Oaxacan radish-carving festival, her gradual acquisition of Spanish, a sense of belonging based on the culture's concept of the extended family, and the realization that her father has always loved her and Owen, Naomi begins to identify with Mexico to the extent that she is reluctant to leave it. Having to return to California for a court interview, Naomi displays the strengthening effect of her cultural transformation: she breaks through the metaphorical wall of her condition by choosing to speak to the judge, thus beginning to live up to the león (lion) attribute of her name.

Discussion Starters

1. What is a family? How is Naomi and Owen's family different from others? How is it similar?
2. What are some of the worries Naomi has about Mexico at the beginning of the trip? How do her views change?
3. What challenges do Naomi and Owen face when dealing with their peers in California? Why do they seem more accepted in Mexico?
4. How does Naomi's relationship with her Mexican father help her break through her selective mutism?

Quotes for Interpretation

1. "'I can already tell you are a different girl since you went to Mexico. Before you were a mouse, but now you have the countenance of a lioness'" (243).

The Circuit: Stories from the Life of a Migrant Child. **Francisco Jiménez. Houghton Mifflin Company, 1999. 0-395-97902-1. 116 pp. Short Stories/ Fiction. Gr. 6–9.**

Selected Awards: ALA Best Books for Young Adults 1999; Américas Award for Children's and Young Adult Literature 1997; Boston Globe-Horn Book Award 1998; Jane Addams Children's Book Award (Honor) 1998; John and Patricia Beatty Award 1998.

Blending the author's childhood memories with background research, this masterful collection of chronologically arranged short stories provides significant insight into the daily lives of migrant workers and their children. The narrative opens in the late 1940s with little Francisco, nicknamed Panchito, describing the attempt of his ever-growing family to escape the dire poverty of rural Mexico by crawling under the barbed wire fence that separates them from the United States, thus relating the desperation that often triggers illegal immigration. Once in California, Panchito's family does not quite make the "good living" (1) Papá had counted on; they continue instead to reside in substandard housing and are paid meagre wages for back-breaking menial labor as they follow the exhausting cycle of migration associated with crop picking. The related problem of migrant child education is addressed as well. The narrator and his siblings frequently change schools and miss instruction due to them helping in the fields, which makes their English-language acquisition particularly difficult. In spite of the intensity of the family's struggles, the semiautobiographical collection maintains an optimistic tone, highlighting the close-knit family's perseverance as they pursue the American Dream. A closing "Note from the Author," mentioning his graduation from Columbia University, alludes to their eventual success. This moving narrative is likely to inspire lively classroom discussions on current immigration themes.

Discussion Starters

1. What does Panchito's family hope for as they plan to cross the border? To what extent do their wishes come true?
2. How does the family's taking on crop-picking jobs make it difficult for them to improve their lives? What would you do in their situation to break the cycle of poverty?
3. How do schools deal with Panchito and his siblings' lack of English proficiency? In your opinion what else could be done to help them succeed?
4. Why is Panchito so excited about returning to Bonetti Ranch in spite of its dilapidated condition (97–100)?

Quotes for Interpretation

1. "'I remember being hit on the wrists with a twelve-inch ruler because I did not follow directions in class,' Roberto answered in a

mildly angry tone when I asked him about his first year of school. 'But how could I?' he continued. 'The teacher gave them in English'" (12).

2. "'You have to be careful,' [Papá] warned us . . . 'You can't tell a soul you were born in Mexico. You can't trust anyone, not even your best friends'" (96).

CrashBoomLove: A Novel in Verse. Juan Felipe Herrera. University of New Mexico Press, 1999. 978-0-8263-2114-5. 155 pp. Poetry/Fiction. Gr. 8–12.

Selected Awards: Américas Award for Children's and Young Adult Literature 1999.

In this eye-opening free-verse narrative, the 21st Poet Laureate of the United States draws on the experiences of Chicano teens to present a pained, yet ultimately hopeful account of the challenges associated with growing up as a child of working-class Mexican immigrants in contemporary America. The novel's protagonist and voice, the tenth-grader César García, is constantly pulled toward self-destructive behavior as he struggles with his migrant-worker father's abandonment and a desire to establish a sense of belonging within the ethnically cliquish Rambling West High in Fowlerville, California, that automatically profiles him as a disposable teen. To escape the mainstream culture-sanctioned shame he feels for his Chicano heritage, César seeks approval with equally disadvantaged classmates by experimenting with drugs and alcohol, participating in violent fights, and committing an act of petty crime. The poetic sequence, interspersed with annotated Spanish slang terms, shows that César's only hope of breaking free from this devastating downward spiral comes in the form of positive pedagogical intervention and his mother's love reflected in her direct in-school advocacy for him after his serious injury in a car accident. His second chance at life is metaphorically represented by his finding a creative outlet through music and writing, as well as his recognition of the heroism involved in his demographic group's day-today struggles. The book's raw, fast-paced narrative is sure to resonate with marginalized immigrant youths across the United States.

Discussion Starters

1. What are the most significant challenges César faces after enrolling at Rambling West High? What are his options? What would you do in his position if faced with the same challenges?
2. How does César's attitude towards his Mexican immigrant migrant-worker heritage evolve throughout the narrative?
3. What role does the educational system play in the choices César makes? In your opinion, how can U.S. schools support minority youths of immigrant background?
4. Discuss the importance of having a voice. How does César's ability to finally "speak" relate to his metaphorical rebirth?

Quotes for Interpretation

1. "high-fives and long stretched voices, cries, circle me
   and my mother's face who knows crooked English and
   my father's face who leaves me in a knot
   and my empty living room back home and Mrs. Tinko
   and Mr. Santos who don't speak Spanish
   and Xeng who stomps on my new shoes
   and my naked body that everyone sees—" (30–31).

Esperanza Rising. **Pam Muñoz Ryan. Scholastic, 2000. 978-0-439-12041-8. 262 pp. Historical Fiction. Gr. 6–9.**

Selected Awards: ALA Best Books for Young Adults 2001; ALA Notable Children's Books 2002; ALA Top Ten Best Books for Young Adults 2001; Jane Addams Children's Book Award 2001; Notable Children's Books in the English Language Arts 2001; Notable Social Studies Trade Books for Young People 2001.

Based on the author's Mexican grandmother's story, this compelling narrative details a teenage girl's struggles with her new geographic and socioeconomic placement in the 1930s American Southwest. Having lived as the privileged daughter of a rich landowner in Mexico for thirteen years, Esperanza has to drastically adjust her life expectations after her father is murdered by bandits and their house is burned to the ground by an evil uncle plotting to force Esperanza's mother into remarriage. Out of desperation, Esperanza and her mother join their servants' family and secretly escape to a California Mexican farm workers' camp. Here the young immigrant must learn to tend to babies, do domestic chores, pick and pack produce, and rise again as the family's new *patrona* when her mother falls gravely ill. The chapter titles are based on the harvesting times of fruits and vegetables to mimic the time frame of a field worker. Ryan, who is sympathetic to the plight of hired field hands, documents the dire conditions in the farm camps, including the hard decisions they face with regard to the opportunity to strike. The segregation of laborers on the basis of race/ethnicity and the aftermath of the 1929 Deportation Act that legalized the "repatriation" of thousands of Mexicans and Mexican Americans regardless of their immigration and citizenship status are also addressed in this honest narrative and are likely to result in thought-provoking discussions.

Discussion Starters
1. Why is the book titled *Esperanza Rising?*
2. Describe Esperanza's changing relationship with Miguel.
3. How does the main character's social consciousness evolve throughout the narrative?
4. Initially, Esperanza cannot hear the earth's "heartbeat" once in California (91), but she regains this ability later on (249). Explain why.
5. What types of discrimination and stereotypes did Mexicans and Mexican Americans face in America in the 1930s? Has this changed compared to current views of Mexican immigrants? Why/why not?

Quotes for Interpretation
1. "'Esperanza, people here think that all Mexicans are alike. They think that we are all uneducated, dirty, poor, and unskilled'" (187).
2. "'They call it a voluntary deportation. But it is not much of a choice'" (207).

3. "'Miguel, do you not understand? You are still a second-class citizen because you act like one, letting them take advantage of you like that'" (222).

Home at Last. Susan Middleton Elya. Ill. by Felipe Davalos. Lee & Low Books, 2002. 1-58430-020-5. 1 volume (unpaged). Picture Book/Fiction. Gr. 1–3.

Selected Awards: Notable Social Studies Trade Books for Young People 2003.

Dedicated to English as a Second Language students, their teachers, and "all immigrant mothers," Elya's picture book focuses on immigrant empowerment through English-language acquisition, while highlighting the important role children often play in this regard in relation to their parents. Having recently arrived from Mexico, members of the featured Patiño family are shown to experience varying degrees of difficulty in adjusting to the different culture. Eight-year-old Ana soon feels comfortable in her encouraging school environment, and her English is improving daily. Similarly, her father, employed at a canning factory, is provided with the opportunity to learn and acculturate quickly. However, Ana's mother, spending most of her days inside the apartment of an unnamed U.S. farming community while caring for the family's twins, is rather isolated, and suffers from intense homesickness. The narrative skillfully illustrates the inversion of roles that frequently occurs between the immigrant child and her parents in these situations, with Ana acting as Mamá's guide to the new culture. Initially, Mamá resists Ana's urgings that she also learn English, but after being unable to ask for help when one of the twins becomes ill, Mamá agrees to enroll in an evening class. The book ends on a triumphant note, showcasing the positive impact of Mamá's newfound English skills on her self-confidence and sense of belonging. Davalos's vibrant illustrations enhance this engaging story about an immigrant family's enabling support of each other.

Discussion Starters

1. What is immigration? Why is immigration harder on Mamá than on Ana or Ana's father?
2. Why does Ana insist her mother learn English? How does knowing the country's language make one's life easier?
3. How do some people treat Mamá when they cannot understand her? Would you do the same in their situation? Why/why not? How could one still help Mamá?
4. How does living in the United States sometimes make Ana act as Mamá's parent rather than her child, especially outside of their home? Find examples from the book.

Quotes for Interpretation

1. "The night of the test Mamá sat silently during the drive to class. Ana knew she was worried. How she wished she could take the test for Mamá!"

Illegal. **Bettina Restrepo. Katherine Tegen Books, 2011. 978-0-06-195342-2. 251 pp. Fiction. Gr. 7–11.**

Selected Awards: Notable Social Studies Trade Books for Young People 2012.

Raw and empathy-provoking, Bettina Restrepo's coming-of-age novel offers a first-person portrayal of the extreme hardships that illegal immigrants face in the contemporary United States while fully committed to succeeding in the country. The book opens by depicting the desperate conditions that often trigger illegal border crossings. With the school in impoverished Cedula, Mexico, closed, church services stopped, and the family in danger of losing their drought-stricken orchard, fourteen-year-old Nora does not seem to have another option but to leave her native community in search of Papa, who went to Texas a few years ago but recently stopped sending back money. Accompanied by her mother, Nora undergoes a life-threatening immigration journey at the back of a fruit truck. As with many other illegal immigrants, their arrival in Houston lacks the redemptive effect Nora hoped for. While able to secure jobs through fake paperwork, she and Mama continue to be plagued by dire poverty, gang violence, and racial clashes. The theme of them as sexual prey is also explored. After finding out about Papa's construction job-related death, with him being thrown "away like trash" (212), the always-persevering Nora loses faith—in God and her new country. However, through a series of optimistic twists predicated on the generous acts of others, including the credulity-stretching smuggling-in of her grandmother, the hope-filled narrative has Nora's belief in the possibility of a better future restored. A detailed glossary of embedded Spanish terms completes this eye-opening novel.

Discussion Starters

1. Why do Nora and her mother leave for Texas? In your opinion, how would the story develop if they had stayed in Cedula?
2. Research basic options for immigrating into the United States legally. Use this information to explain Nora and Mama's decision to be smuggled across the border instead.
3. Discuss Nora's desire for education. Given her situation, do you consider her views on its importance exaggerated? Why/why not?
4. How do Nora's illegal status and gender make her particularly vulnerable to violence? What are her options for seeking justice when something goes wrong?
5. What makes gangs appealing to youth in areas such as Nora's immigrant neighborhood?

Quotes for Interpretation

1. "'I know I'm here in America, where everything is supposed to be better. But it isn't. I want to live in a place that doesn't smell like garbage. I want my quinceañera. I want to be fifteen again'" (201).
2. "'We can start over. We may not matter to America, but we are important to each other'" (229).

La Línea. **Ann Jaramillo. Roaring Brook Press, 2006. 978-1-59643-154-6. 131 pp. Fiction. Gr. 8–12.**

Selected Awards: ALA Best Books for Young Adults 2007; Notable Social Studies Trade Books for Young People 2007.

Inspired by real-life stories of the author's newly immigrated English as a Second Language students, this gripping narrative focuses on the dangers and hopes associated with unauthorized border crossings. The book's narrator, fifteen-year-old Miguel, has longed to reunite with his parents ever since they left their struggling rural Mexican community for better opportunities in California almost seven years ago. When his father finally pays a local human smuggler for his passage, Miguel's dream seems to come within reach. However, as the action-packed, tightly woven chapters show, getting over *la línea* (the borderline) without appropriate paperwork is never easy. Unexpected complications accumulate quickly, from Miguel's younger sister Elena secretly joining him on the journey, to the siblings being confronted by a corrupt police officer and robbed by a street gang. Lacking other options, the teens mount a northbound train fittingly nicknamed "mata gente, the 'people killer'" (62), facing a new set of rather graphically described dangers. The close, trusting bond they form as a result helps them succeed in the final trial of their journey—a multi-day crossing of the border-area desert. The narrative ends rather abruptly, leaving readers to speculate on the details of the family's reunion but offering a very brief overview of Miguel's and Elena's accomplishments within the ten-year period following their entering the United States. Frequently embedded Spanish phrases enhance the authentic feel of this sympathy-provoking narrative.

Discussion Starters

1. Compare the immigration journey of Miguel and Elena's family to that of European immigrant working-class families in the late nineteenth and early twentieth centuries. What has changed? What has remained the same?

2. Why does Miguel feel betrayed by Papá's leaving for the United States?

3. What is Miguel's first response to having crossed *la línea* in the desert? Think of an experience that had a similar emotional effect on you.

4. In your opinion, can this book change people's views of illegal immigrants? Why/why not? Name a literary text that ignited social change.

Quotes for Interpretation

1. " ... I'd been only partly alive anyway, for a long time. Papá took a big part of me with him to California when he left" (71).

2. "I thought I'd find the real Miguel, the one I thought I couldn't be in Mexico, once I crossed *La línea*. I didn't understand that there are thousands of *líneas* to cross in a life" (124).

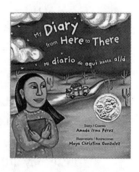

My Diary from Here to There/Mi Diario de Aquí Hasta Allá. **Amada Irma Pérez. Ill. by Maya Christina Gonzalez. Children's Book Press, 2015. 978-0-89239-230-8. 31 pp. Picture Book/Fiction. Gr. 2–4.**

Selected Awards: Pura Belpré Award (Honor) 2004.

Inspired by Pérez's personal experience of immigration, this book is written in the belief that newcomers to the United States "strengthen each other by telling these stories." Within that compositional frame, the book's narrator Amada uses her diary to detail her emotions, consisting mainly of fears but also hopes, as her Mexican family moves from Juárez to Mexicali and later to Los Angeles in search of better economic conditions. Set during Cesar Chávez's attempts to unionize farm workers, the family's immigration is made possible by their American-born father's citizenship, which enables Amada, her five brothers, and her mother to obtain green cards with the sole inconvenience of a wait time. As the family settles down in Los Angeles, Amada concludes that her initial worries of losing her cultural identity do not necessarily materialize as she continues to carry her heritage with her through her memories, language, and emotional connections. Gonzalez's eye-catching full-page illustrations in vibrant tones of turquoises, golden browns, and deep reds serve as a beautiful backdrop to the optimism-filled story. The narrative is bilingual, with English and Spanish passages alternating in the position of primacy to resist hierarchical interpretations of the two languages and cultures.

Discussion Starters

1. How does Amada, compared to her brothers, respond when she learns the family will be moving to the United States? Why do they react so differently?
2. What are green cards? Why doesn't Amada's father need one if the rest of the family has to apply for them?
3. How and why do Amada's feelings about immigration change by the end of the story?
4. Have you ever had to move away from a familiar neighborhood, or even a country? If so, how did it make you feel? What made your move seem easy, or difficult?

Quotes for Interpretation

1. "You know, just because I'm far away from Juárez and Michi and my family in Mexicali, it doesn't mean they're not here with me. They're inside my little rock; they're here in your pages and in the language that I speak; and they're in my memories and my heart" (30).

My Name Is Jorge: On Both Sides of the River. **Jane Medina. Ill. by Fabricio Vanden Broeck. Word-song/Boyds Mills Press, 1999. 1-56397-811-3. 48 pp. Poetry/Fiction. Gr. 3–7.**

Selected Awards: Notable Children's Books in the English Language Arts 2000.

This touching collection of bilingual poems accompanied by simple black-and-white illustrations focuses on the identity crisis an immigrant child experiences based on the painful discrepancy between the sense of self he developed in his home country and the self produced by his interactions with the Anglocentric culture in the United States. In Mexico, eleven-year-old Jorge "used to be the smartest one" in his grade (32), impressing many by masterfully reciting poetry. Now he appears "dumb" (9), discriminated against and ridiculed for his limited English proficiency and acculturation. The book uses the relatively common U.S. cultural practice of Americanizing immigrant children's names as a focal point to highlight the stressful pressure on the narrator to conform. Addressed as George in the classroom, the boy deeply resents his beginning to respond to his altered name, and he later pleads with his teacher to call him Jorge. Gradually, he establishes some sense of connectedness, as evidenced by his forming a friendship with a non-Hispanic classmate, only to have his identity put to the test yet again: as the book closes, the family plans to return to Mexico after Jorge's grandmother's death. Written in easily accessible verse but structured around a relatively complex theme, the book is best suited for upper-level elementary or middle-school readers. A short glossary of selected Spanish-English terms is included in the volume.

Discussion Starters

1. Why does Jorge oppose his name being changed to George? Discuss the relationship between a person's name and his sense of self.
2. Which U.S. experiences make Jorge feel that his heritage is not respected?
3. How can a new immigrant's inability to speak good English make him or her seem "dumb" (9)?
4 What helps Jorge gradually feel a little more at home in the United States? List ways to make a recently immigrated classmate feel welcome.

Quotes for Interpretation

1. "(Free books
   Standing still . . .
   Anybody
   Can open them
   And wander inside.
   Their halls of dreams.

Anybody,
but *Mamá*
and me)" (17).

2   "This hard, white country
stung at first, too" (46).

***Prizefighter en Mi Casa.* e. E. Charlton-Trujillo. Delacorte Press, 2006. 978-0-385-73325-0. 210 pp. Fiction. Gr. 6–8.**

Selected Awards: Notable Social Studies Trade Books for Young People 2007.

Set in contemporary south Texas, this authentic first-person narrative sprinkled with slang and Spanish phrases explores a Mexican American preteen's journey to self-acceptance in an environment that stigmatizes her based on her second-generation immigrant origin and challenging health condition. Growing up in the Circle, a low-income ethnic neighborhood differing strikingly from the privileged Squaretown, seventh-grader Chula Sanchez has always been marginalized. However, when her father's drunken driving results in an accident that paralyzes him and leaves her with epileptic seizures that are negatively interpreted by her own community, Chula's sense of non-belonging intensifies. The painful isolation causes her to bond with El Jefe, a large-bodied prizefighter her father brought over from Mexico City in hopes of winning money through illegal boxing matches. Discovering compassion under El Jefe's fear-inducing physique, Chula feels accepted in previously unexperienced ways, gaining new courage and confidence in the process. She also embraces her Mexican immigrant heritage more explicitly, improving her Spanish and nurturing visions of Mexico as a semi-mythical space. Her journey towards empowerment is shown to be quite superior to the choices made by her older brother Richie, who views his ethnic origin as a permanent stigma and copes through prosecutable gang involvement. The absorbing narrative thus encourages young readers to perceive their uniqueness as a source of strength rather than an incapacitating burden.

Discussion Starters

1. Why do Chula and El Jefe bond in spite of their visible differences?
2. In Chula's middle school, how do students of different backgrounds interact with each other? How does it compare to the vision of America as a melting pot? Relate this discussion to the situation in your school.
3. Analyze Chula's and Richie's relationships to their Mexican immigrant heritage. How do they evolve throughout the narrative?
4. What challenges do Mexican American children growing up in the Circle face? In your opinion, what are their options for successfully overcoming those challenges?

Quotes for Interpretation

1. "... gringos who smiled back at us when they were really thinking, 'Filthy Mexican. Go back to your country.'
   'Like we're already in our freakin' country, pendejos,' Richie would say when it came up" (14).
2. "'You're a Mexican and you'll always be Mexican. It ain't nothing to drop your head about but that year-round tan of yours means you'll always have to fight for what you want'" (163).

The Quiet Place. **Sarah Stewart. Ill. by David Small. Farrar, Straus and Giroux, 2012. 978-0-374-32565-7. 1 volume (unpaged). Picture Book/Fiction. K–Gr. 3.**

Selected Awards: Notable Social Studies Trade Books for Young People 2013.

In this charming picture book by critically acclaimed husband-and-wife collaborators, the newly arrived Mexican immigrant Isabel writes a series of letters to her aunt Lupita to share her impressions about adjusting to the life in the United States in the 1950s. The narrative focus is on the child's need to establish a familiar refuge in the midst of the demanding chaos that the acculturation experience represents. Often feeling insecure about her less-than-perfect English and anxious about not quite belonging, Isabel transforms the empty refrigerator box her father gave her into a space where she can escape to feel safe. As she gradually establishes successful connections with members of the new culture, the function of the box as the book's central metaphor changes. After a rainstorm ruins her cardboard retreat, Isabel rushes to find an adequate replacement, only to realize that she no longer needs a hiding place—having befriended a group of neighborhood children through the parties her mother caters, she is ready to open her sanctuary to everyone. Small's detail-oriented illustrations, culminating in a vivid double-page foldout portrayal of the collectively enjoyed festivities of Isabel's birthday, perfectly capture the evolving emotions of the young immigrant. All readers who have had to leave a beloved place for a less familiar one are likely to relate to this narrative.

Discussion Starters

1. Think of a time when you had to move or leave your home for quite a long time. How did it make you feel?
2. What is immigration? What are some of the difficulties Isabel faces after coming to the United States? How is immigrating to another country different from moving within the country?
3. Why is Isabel so excited when her father gives her an empty refrigerator box? What does she use it for?
4. How and why does Isabel's use of her box and its replacement change by the end of the story?

Quotes for Interpretation

1. "I am still too shy to make friends. But I have started something—a quiet place for me and my books."
2. "When I get your letter every week, the Span-
ish words are like friends."

Return to Sender. Julia Alvarez. Yearling, 2010. 978-0-375-85123-0. 325 pp. Fiction. Gr. 4–7.

Selected Awards: ALA Notable Children's Books 2010; Américas Award for Children's and Young

Adult Literature 2010; Notable Social Studies Trade Books for Young People 2010; Pura Belpré Award 2010.

Claiming fictionality while also establishing a direct connection to current sociopolitical reality, Julia Alvarez's novel offers a thought-provoking view of illegal immigrants. The story is told from the alternating perspectives of two sixth-graders—Mari Cruz, a Mexican-born daughter of undocumented laborers, and Tyler Paquette, a son of Vermont dairy-farm owners—and it shows that the preconceived notions some hold about the presence of illegal aliens in the United States are subject to renegotiation once the groups establish an interpersonal relationship. Correspondingly, Tyler's third-person sections illustrate his initial ambivalence about the employment opportunity his family provides to the Cruzes following his father's farming-related accident. However, his friendship with Mari allows him to develop an understanding of the lack of choices the undocumented workers face, to the extent that he later assists in retrieving Mari's mother from abusive people smugglers. Mari's first-person sections in epistolary and diary form further encourage compassionate views of illegal immigrants by demonstrating the constant fear of deportation they live in. The complex identity issue of undocumented migrants' children, both U.S.- and Mexican-born, is also addressed. While the Cruzes are ultimately forced to return to Las Margaritas in Mexico, the book's overall tone is optimistic in view of the mutually supportive connection the two families form. A reader's guide and conversation with the author conclude this powerful narrative.

Discussion Starters

1. Why does Mari's family choose to enter the United States illegally? How does their undocumented status impact their everyday life?
2. How do Mari's and Tyler's families help each other survive?
3. Where is Mari's true home? Why does she feel more lonely and confused about her identity than her sisters or her dad and uncles? What makes a place a home to you?
4. Discuss the view of hiring illegal immigrants as unpatriotic. Where does the novel stand on this issue? Do you agree with that position? Why/why not?

Quotes for Interpretation

1. "'It's not wrong in God's eyes,' his dad explains. Sometimes, a country has these laws that have nothing to do with what's right or what's best for most of the people involved" (56).
2. "I used to feel so alone, neither Mexican nor American. But now that I have a special friend, I feel like I don't have to be one thing or another" (202).
3. "... the function of freedom is to free someone else" (221).

Separate Is Never Equal: Sylvia Mendez & Her Family's Fight for Desegregation. Duncan Tonatiuh. Ill. by the author. Abrams Books for Young Readers, 2014. 978-1-4197-1054-4. 40 pp. Picture Book/Nonfiction. Gr. 2–5.

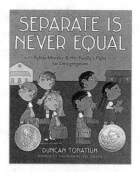

Selected Awards: ALA Notable Children's Books 2015; Jane Addams Children's Book Award 2015; NCTE Orbis Pictus Award (Honor) 2015; Notable Social Studies Trade Books for Young People 2015; Pura Belpré Award (Honor) 2015; Robert F. Sibert Informational Book Award (Honor) 2015; Tomás Rivera Mexican American Children's Book Award 2015.

Inspired by the lawsuit the Mendez family filed against California's segregated school system in the 1940s, this highly informative yet concise picture book shows that children of immigrants perceived as nonwhite often face discrimination even when born in the United States. As a second-generation Mexican immigrant, third-grader Sylvia Mendez considers herself an American and speaks "perfect English" (9); yet, due to her skin color, hair texture, and last name, she is interpreted as an undesirable social Other by the cultural mainstream. The 17th Street Westminster school refuses to enroll her and her two brothers, sending them to an inferior Mexican school instead. The narrative details the relentless struggle of Sylvia's parents to redress this unfair practice, from their formation of the Parents' Association of Mexican-American Children to a successful legal action which paved the way for the landmark 1954 *Brown v. Board of Education* court case. Readers are likely to be delighted at the family's court victory but appalled by the stereotypes of Mexican Americans that freely circulated in mid-century America. Tonatiuh's multimedia illustrations, influenced by the ancient art of the Mixtecs, add visual interest to the empowering narrative that provides children of all backgrounds with the knowledge that "their voices are valuable" (36). A well-researched bibliography, glossary of terms, and an index are included.

Discussion Starters

1. Define segregation. Why does the 17th Street Westminster school reject Sylvia and her brothers but accept her cousins?
2. What are some of the differences between the 17th Street Westminster school and the Hoover Elementary Mexican school? How can these differences influence the children's future?
3. What is a stereotype? What stereotypes of Mexican Americans are used in the Mendez court case in defense of segregated schooling? In your opinion, has today's society moved away from such prejudice? Why/why not?
4. Sylvia claims to be an American in spite of her Mexican immigrant heritage. Do you agree with her? Why/why not? What makes one an American?

Quotes for Interpretation

1. "Why do I have to go to the Mexican school? Sylvia wondered. She was not Mexican—she was American. She spoke perfect English. Her father was from Mexico, but he had become a U.S. citizen. Her mother was from Puerto Rico, which was a U.S. territory" (9).

¡Sí, Se Puede! / Yes, We Can!: Janitor Strike in L.A. **Diana Cohn. Ill. by Francisco Delgado. Trans. by Sharon Franco. Cinco Puntos Press, 2002. 0-938317-66-0. 31 pp. Picture Book/Fiction. Gr. 1–5.**

Selected Awards: Jane Addams Children's Book Award (Honor) 2003.

Inspired by the successful Los Angeles Justice for Janitors Campaign in April 2000, Cohn's bilingual narrative draws the reader's attention to the plight of many urban Latino immigrants who are forced by circumstances to take on low-skilled jobs at meagre pay. Hope in the form of the workers uniting to fight for the improvement of their conditions is also offered. Through its narrator Carlitos, a first-generation Mexican immigrant, the book relates the story of his widowed mother, who works long hours at night scrubbing the floors and windows of a "tall glass office building" in downtown Los Angeles (5) and supplements her income by cleaning other people's houses and doing their laundry on weekends, yet is unable to adequately support her family. Frustrated at being overworked, underpaid, and underappreciated, Mamá joins other janitors in a powerful strike that attracts many supporters. At first unsure about how he could help, Carlitos gets an excellent idea when watching Mamá make a speech on the TV news: he creates a sign expressing pride in her work and, assisted by his teacher, showcases it with his classmates during the strikers' march. The brightly illustrated narrative closes with writer Luis J. Rodríguez's strongly pro-union afterword featuring Dolores Sánchez, an immigrant social activist who in many ways seems to resemble Carlitos's mother.

Discussion Starters

1. What are some possible reasons behind Carlitos and Mamá immigrating to the United States from Mexico?
2. Why do you think Mamá as a recent immigrant takes on the janitor job? What else does she do to make money? Think of someone you know who works more than one job.
3. In your own words, explain what a strike means. Why do the janitors strike?
4. How do Carlitos and his classmates help the strikers?
5. What changes for Carlitos's family once the strike is over?

Quotes for Interpretation

1. "'You bet they won! When many people join together, they can make a strong force'" (14).

2. "When my mamá took the bus to scrub, mop and polish in the tall glass office buildings that shoot up from the streets, I dreamt that angels came down to Los Angeles and sang songs to her while she worked" (24).

Sofi Mendoza's Guide to Getting Lost in Mexico. Malín Alegría. Simon Pulse, 2008. 978-0-689-87811-4. 289 pp. Fiction. Gr. 9–12.

Selected Awards: Society of School Librarians International Book Award (Honor) 2007.

Inspired by a real-life story, Alegría's emotional coming-of-age novel draws attention to the plight of Mexican American adolescents who, unaware of their illegal immigrant status, voluntarily deport themselves by visiting their native country. The book's central character, seventeen-year-old Sofi Mendoza, has always considered herself "as American as her friends" (6); having immigrated at the young age of three, she is preoccupied mostly with boys, clothes, and her milieu's party scene, and she carefully distances herself from her "old-school typical Mexican" protective immigrant parents (4). However, when she secretly joins her girlfriends on their weekend trip to a graduation bash near Tijuana, Mexico, her comfortable life takes a drastic turn. Denied reentry into the United States because her green card is deemed counterfeit, the shocked, not-quite Spanish-proficient Sofi has to move in with Mexican relatives she has never met before. Her new living quarters lack a phone, Internet, and occasionally electricity, with her strict aunt expecting help with babysitting and household chores. A good portion of the narrative focuses on Sofi's romantic adventures in the struggling community, but her inner transformation, including her revised attitude toward her Mexican heritage, is portrayed in detail as well. Allowed to return to California upon the confirmation of her estranged grandmother's (Abuela's) U.S. citizenship, the teen is shown to have become a true "bridge between cultures" (276), fully accepting her hybridity. An extensive glossary of embedded Spanish terms closes the action-packed narrative.

Discussion Starters

1. Why does Sofi know so little about Mexico at the book's beginning? Discuss the possible pros and cons of immigrant children fully embracing American culture regardless of their heritage.
2. How does Sofi's forced stay in Rosarito impact her sense of self?
3. Where does the narrative stand on the issue of illegal immigration? Do you agree with such a position? Why/why not?
4. Draft an alternative ending to the story that would be structured around Sofi not being allowed to legally reenter the United States. What would her options be?

Quotes for Interpretation

1. "[Sofi] couldn't believe that Officer Cohn had called her an illegal. How could she be? She was infinitely more American than she was Mexican" (92).
2. "'What those fools don't understand is that it is we Mexicans who make it possible for them to have big cars, big houses, and even bigger guns . . . You can't have a superpower nation without stepping on someone's back to get there'" (125).

***Under the Mesquite.* Guadalupe Garcia McCall. Lee & Low Books, 2011. 978-1-60060-429-4. 224 pp. Poetry/Fiction. Gr. 8–12.**

Selected Awards: ALA Best Fiction for Young Adults 2012; ALA Notable Children's Books 2012; ALA Top Ten Best Fiction for Young Adults 2012; Pura Belpré Award 2012; Tomás Rivera Mexican American Children's Book Award 2013.

In this lyricism-infused free-verse debut for young adults, Guadalupe Garcia McCall traces the maturation of a Mexican American high-schooler as she attempts to anchor her identity while struggling with the reality of her mother's terminal illness. Lupita, having immigrated on a green card with her large, close-knit family at the age of six, has always considered herself "transplanted" (10). While her Texan bilingual border town does not marginalize her, she continues to consider rural Mexico her home. Yet, as the heartfelt vignettes show, Lupita is also willing to continue to adapt to the new culture's mainstream in order to succeed. Upon her teacher's prompting, she intentionally suppresses her accent so that she can advance her acting aspirations. Accused by her peers of trying to "be white" as a result (80), Lupita takes solace by concluding that it is her feeling of solidarity with same-background individuals, not the audible or visible signs of being Mexican, that matter. Upon her mother's diagnosis with cancer that leaves her temporarily in charge of her seven younger siblings and impoverishes her family, Lupita experiences her sense of self further destabilized. The narrative highlights the healing power of creative self-expression in such situations, with Lupita managing to overcome her depression by writing under the mesquite tree (a powerful metaphor for resilience), an act that empowers her enough to pursue college. A detailed list of Spanish terms and cultural references closes the evocative narrative.

Discussion Starters

1. Discuss the symbolism of the mesquite tree in the narrative.
2. How does Lupita attempt to balance the demands of her Mexican heritage with the pull of American culture? Do you agree with her schoolmates' claim that she is "acting white" (83)? Why/why not?
3. Compare the uprooting that Lupita experiences as a result of her family's immigration with her dislocation due to leaving for college. Which transition is she more accepting of and why?
4. How does writing help Lupita overcome despair? What do you do to feel better at moments of crisis?

Quotes for Interpretation

1. "... I nibbled on school lunches
of fish sticks and macaroni
while my soul craved
the chocolaty gravy of mole
on a bed of Spanish rice.
But Mami said we were
the luckiest children because
we had two homes" (39).

2. "'Changing how I talk

   doesn't change who I am.

   I know where I came from'" (95).

PERU

***Marisol McDonald Doesn't Match/ Marisol McDonald No Combina.* Monica Brown. Ill. by Sara Palacios. Trans. by Adriana Domínguez. Children's Book Press, 2011. 978-0-89239-235-3. 31 pp. Picture Book/Fiction. PreK–Gr. 3.**

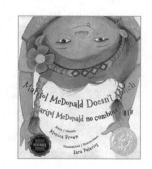

Selected Awards: ALA Notable Children's Books 2012; Pura Belpré Award (Honor) 2012.

Based on the renowned author's personal experience of not fitting neatly into one identity category because of her multiethnic origin, this bilingual narrative tells the story of a delightfully unique, artistic girl named Marisol McDonald who is of mixed Peruvian- Scottish-American heritage. With Marisol as the narrative's implied second-generation immigrant, nothing seems to quite match: her fiery hair clashes with her cinnamon brown skin, she likes to eat peanut butter and jelly burritos, creates outfits out of polka-dot and striped pieces, mixes English and Spanish, writes her Latino-Scottish name in print and cursive, and prefers to play soccer when dressed as a pirate. While Marisol initially freely and creatively intertwines the multiple strands of her heritage, her confidence comes to a test when others express discomfort at her distinctiveness. In an attempt to act in accordance with accepted norms, she briefly adjusts her ways, only to find the result extremely boring. Encouraged by her teacher, she re-embraces her multilayered identity, proudly announcing that her nonconformity is of her own choosing and proceeding to buy a mismatched puppy, whom she names Kitty. Palacio's vibrant double-page illustrations combine a variety of media, including newsprint collage, childlike drawings, and more formal cartoon art, further underscoring the book's message that it is often the unlikely blending of things that produces significant delight. All children of complex origin who have experienced others trying to tell them what they should and should not be will find this narrative quite empowering.

Discussion Starters

1. What is unique about Marisol McDonald? Why do her cousin, brother, and friends see her as mismatched?

2. How does Marisol feel about being different at the book's beginning? How and why do her feelings change throughout the story?

3. Why does the book use both Spanish and English, sometimes even mixing them together?

4. What is special about you? Did the book change your feelings about being unique in any way? Why/why not?

Quotes for Interpretation

1. "At breakfast I say, 'My name is Marisol McDonald and I don't match because . . . I don't want to!'" (26).

Notes

1. Pew Research Center, "Modern Immigration Wave Brings 59 Million to U.S., Driving Population Growth and Change through 2065," last modified September 28, 2015, www.pewhispanic.org/2015/09/28/modern-immigration-wave-brings -59-million-to-u-s-driving-population-growth-and-change-through-2065.

2. Ibid.

3. Ibid.

4. Jie Zong and Jeanne Batalova, "Mexican Immigrants in the United States," *Migration Information Source*, March 17, 2016, www.migrationpolicy.org/article/ mexican-immigrants-united-states.

5. Ibid.

6. Gabriel Lesser and Jeanne Batalova, "Central American Immigrants in the United States," *Migration Information Source*, April 5, 2017, www.migrationpolicy.org/ article/central-american-immigrants-united-states.

7. Jie Zong and Jeanne Batalova, "Caribbean Immigrants in the United States," *Migration Information Source*, September 14, 2016, www.migrationpolicy.org/article/ caribbean-immigrants-united-states.

8. Jie Zong and Jeanne Batalova, "South American Immigrants in the United States," *Migration Information Source*, March 1, 2016, www.migrationpolicy.org/article/ south-american-immigrants-united-states.

9. Pew Research Center, "Modern Immigration Wave Brings 59 Million to U.S."

10. Ibid.

11. Ibid.

12. Lesser and Batalova, "Central American Immigrants in the United States"; Zong and Batalova, "Caribbean Immigrants in the United States"; Zong and Batalova, "Mexican Immigrants in the United States."

13. Zong and Batalova, "South American Immigrants in the United States."

14. Lesser and Batalova, "Central American Immigrants in the United States"; Zong and Batalova, "Caribbean Immigrants in the United States"; Zong and Batalova, "Mexican Immigrants in the United States"; Zong and Batalova, "South American Immigrants in the United States."

15. Harry H. L. Kitano, *Race Relations* (Upper Saddle River, NJ: Prentice Hall, 1997), 153.

16. Jorge Durand, Douglas S. Massey, and Rene M. Zenteno, "Mexican Immigration to the United States: Continuities and Changes," *Latin American Research Review* 36, no. 1 (2001): 109.

17. Ibid.

18. Andrew R. Heinze, "The Critical Period: Ethnic Emergence and Reaction, 1901–1929," in *Race and Ethnicity in America: A Concise History,* ed. Ronald H. Bayor (New York: Columbia University Press, 2003), 138, 140; Michael B. Katz, Mark J. Stern, and Jamie J. Fader, "The Mexican Immigration Debate: The View from History," *Social Science History* 31, no. 2 (2007): 166.

19. Durand, Massey, and Zenteno, "Mexican Immigration to the United States," 109.

20. Katz, Stern, and Fader, "The Mexican Immigration Debate," 166.

21. Durand, Massey, and Zenteno, "Mexican Immigration to the United States," 110.

22. Ibid., 110–11.

23. Kitano, *Race Relations,* 153.

24. See, for example, Francisco E. Balderrama, "The Emergence of Unconstitutional Deportation and Repatriation of Mexicans and Mexican Americans as a Public Issue," *Radical History Review* 93 (2005): 107–8; and U.S. Department of Homeland Security, "INS Records for 1930s Mexican Repatriations," last modified February 11, 2016, https://www.uscis.gov/history-and-genealogy/our-history/historians-mailbox/ins-records-1930s-mexican-repatriations, for dissenting views.

25. Balderrama, "The Emergence of Unconstitutional Deportation and Repatriation," 107; Pam Muñoz Ryan, "From the Author: Learn about Pam Muñoz Ryan," https://www.scholastic.com/esperanza/popups/authornote.htm; U.S. Department of Homeland Security, "INS Records for 1930s Mexican Repatriations."

26. U.S. Department of Homeland Security, "INS Records for 1930s Mexican Repatriations."

27. Ibid.

28. Balderrama, "The Emergence of Unconstitutional Deportation and Repatriation," 108.

29. Ryan, "From the Author."

30. Durand, Massey, and Zenteno, "Mexican Immigration to the United States," 111.

31. Kitano, *Race Relations*, 160.

32. Durand, Massey, and Zenteno, "Mexican Immigration to the United States," 112; Katz, Stern, and Fader, "The Mexican Immigration Debate," 167.

33. Katz, Stern, and Fader, "The Mexican Immigration Debate," 166–67.

34. Zong and Batalova, "Mexican Immigrants in the United States."

35. David G. Gutiérrez, "A Historic Overview of Latino Immigration and the Demographic Transformation of the United States," in *The New Latino Studies Reader: A Twenty-First-Century Perspective*, ed. Ramón A. Gutiérrez and Tomás Almaguer (Oakland: University of California Press, 2016), 114.

36. Lesser and Batalova, "Central American Immigrants in the United States."

37. Ibid.

38. Zong and Batalova, "Caribbean Immigrants in the United States."

39. Ibid.

40. Ibid.

41. Gutiérrez, "A Historic Overview of Latino Immigration," 116.

42. Zong and Batalova, "South American Immigrants in the United States."

43. Pew Research Center, "Latinos and the New Trump Administration," last modified February 23, 2017, www.pewhispanic.org/2017/02/23/latinos -and-the-new-trump-administration.

Chapter 5

Europe

Overview of European Immigration to the United States

EUROPEAN IMMIGRATION TO THE UNITED STATES, ONCE remarkably robust, has been on a steady proportionate decline since the mid-1960s, with that immigrant population presently enjoying a generally favorable reputation and substantial success but historically not immune to having several of its subgroups constructed as an undesirable, often racialized minority. As for the group's changing numerical representation, Zong and Batalova posit that while in 1960, 75 percent of the total U.S. immigrant population was European, by 2014 this number had plunged to 11 percent, or 4.8 million European immigrants of the 42.4 million total non-native U.S. population.[1] The decrease is often attributed to the Immigration Act of 1965, which removed the national-origin quota system that had strongly favored Western and Northern European immigration. As a result, Asian immigrants were able to join Latin American newcomers in dominating the U.S. immigration scene.[2] The long-term expansion of the post-World War II economies of Western Europe initially triggered by the Marshall Plan played its role in this ethnic shift as well, with the region's residents no longer necessarily perceiving the United States as a place of clear financial and/or social advantage.[3] Correspondingly, most of the Europeans wishing to emigrate in the post-1960s climate were from Eastern Europe,[4] with the period between 1990 and 2010 in particular witnessing "a sizeable inflow" of migrants from such areas as the dissolved Soviet Union, Czechoslovakia, and Yugoslavia.[5] In fact, in

2014 immigrants from Eastern Europe constituted 44 percent (2.1 million) of all European-born residents in the United States, as compared to Western Europe (960,000) and Northern Europe (931,000) contributing roughly 20 percent each and Southern Europe (775,000) accounting for 16 percent.[6] The overall number of new immigrants from all of the European areas has remained small since 1970, approximately 88,000 individuals per year.[7]

The current public perception of the European immigrant population tends to be relatively positive, paired with the population's considerable educational and economic success. More specifically, as the Pew Research Center documents, approximately 44 percent of Americans view the impact of European immigrants on U.S. society in "mostly positive" terms.[8] Even though older and "less likely to participate in the labor force," European immigrants are also more educated and have higher household incomes than the total foreign- and native-born populations.[9] Thus, in 2014, the median income of a household with a European immigrant at its head was $60,000, as compared to the $49,000 median income of the overall immigrant household and the $55,000 median income of native-born households.[10] In addition, newcomers from Europe exhibit higher levels of English proficiency, are more likely to speak English at home, and become naturalized citizens at higher rates than the overall U.S. foreign-born population.[11]

In sharp contrast to the European newcomers' current reputation and achievement trends, the history of their immigration has been marked at certain points by prejudice and discrimination, manifested especially in the resettling experience of the non-Protestant and non-Anglo-Saxon European immigrant subgroups. The Irish were the first subgroup to be subjected to markedly hostile attitudes[12] upon arriving after the failure of the potato crop and the resulting famine that struck their homeland between 1845 and 1849.[13] Unlike the sixteenth- to eighteenth-century wave of European settlers, who were a "mix of well-to-do individuals and indentured servants" of mostly Protestant faith from the British Isles,[14] the Irish immigrants were overwhelmingly Catholic, impoverished, poorly educated, and employed in low-paying, menial jobs often requiring manual labor.[15] As outlined in chapter 1, these characteristics, combined with the large numbers of this immigrant Other, produced a severely negative reaction in the nativist mainstream, culminating in a concentrated effort to challenge the "whiteness" of the Irish and to present them as inherently and unchangeably inferior, thus justifying their exploitation and oppression. Specifically, the Irish immigrants were associated typologically with stereotyped African Americans,[16] as reflected in their being assigned such features as apelike appearance, "low intelligence, wickedness, a fighting stance, [favoring] a jug of whiskey, ignorance, and [being] a threat to orderly politics."[17] While some historians point out that the nonwhite identity construct was applied to the Irish quite inconsistently, since they were eligible for naturalization under the 1790 Naturalization Act that only permitted whites access,[18] it did take until the early twentieth century for the Irish to gradually free themselves from the discriminatory stereotypes and join the American mainstream.[19]

The outlined pro-nativist practice of constructing incoming groups of European immigrants differing from the earlier settlers as biologically inferior took on an even more pronounced shape in relation to the influx of Southern and Eastern Europeans during the early twentieth-century wave of U.S. immigration. Between 1900 and 1930, roughly 10 million Slavs, Eastern European Jews, and Italians immigrated, with more than half of them remaining in the United States.[20] Their large number was predicated on such developments as the unification of Italy and the resulting political and economic repression of the Italian south;[21] the persecution of multiple ethnic groups in tsarist Russia, especially the Jews; and new problems produced by the Bolshevik Revolution of 1917.[22] The corresponding proportionate decrease of the "old" immigration from Northern and Western Europe in American society was a source of the mainstream's great alarm, with pro-nativist thinkers of the era rushing to warn against the vulgarization and criminalization of American life by the new immigrant masses.[23] To support such bleak predictions, they claimed that there was "something inherently different and wrong" about the new migrants "that prevented them from ever becoming 'real' Americans no matter how hard they might try."[24] Heinze adds detail to the implied biological devaluation of the incoming Southern and Eastern European immigrants by explaining that, "relying on spurious theories of racial genetics, [the early twentieth-century pro-nativist] natural scientists, psychologists, and sociologists" tried to offer a persuasive breakdown of humankind into several essentialized, racially predetermined groups of varying hierarchical quality with the Nordic/Anglo-Saxon race at its top, Africans on the bottom, and "everyone else . . . somewhere in between."[25] In line with these theories, the eugenicists Madison Grant, Lothrop Stoddard, and Kenneth Roberts are known to have spoken of the "'worthless,' 'weak, broken, and mentally crippled' races from the Mediterranean, the Balkans, and Poland."[26] Also within this framework, Italians, who were particularly detested for their physical difference from the WASP ideal and their Catholicism,[27] were often singled out and widely portrayed as "habitual criminals . . . quick with a stiletto knife, who brought organized crime" into America.[28] An additional frequent target of stereotyping were the Eastern European Jews, with Madison Grant using their example to caution that these (supposedly racially inferior) newcomers "adopt the language of the native American; . . . wear his clothes; . . . steal his name, and . . . are beginning to take his women, but . . . seldom adopt his religion or understand his ideals" while pushing "the white Anglo-Saxon American out of his home."[29] Statements like these point to the pro-nativist mainstream's fear that the new immigration of the early twentieth century would result in the "older" immigration losing its position of dominance, with the genetic theories of the intrinsic lowliness of the new migrants used to prevent such a prospect from materializing.

The immigration laws of the early 1920s represented an even more powerful means employed by pro-nativists in attempts to curtail the potential influence of Southern European, Eastern European, and other non-Protestant and non-Anglo-Saxon immigrant groups on American society. Dovetailing with the then current eugenics theories, the laws were drafted in such a way that the individual country entrance quotas set up within them strongly favored Western and Northern European immigrants, a goal accomplished by using U.S. ethnic composition data prevailing before immigration from the unwanted regions had really begun.[30] Thus, in 1921 the Congress passed a one-year First Quota Act that was ultimately extended until the passing of the 1924 Act to Limit the Immigration of Aliens into the United States,[31] with the legislation allocating each country the quota of "2 percent of the foreign-born population of that nationality as enumerated in the 1890 census."[32] The highly discriminatory national-origins quota system remained in effect until the mid-1960s, when it was replaced with a seven-category preference and hemispheric-limits system.[33]

World Wars I and II again fueled the legally sanctioned animosity towards certain newer groups of European immigrants, especially Germans and Italians. The Germans, representing with the Irish the largest group of Europeans immigrating to the United States between 1837 and 1877, were initially not subjected to pronounced vilification.[34] While facing occasional challenges, Germans' reputation as highly educated and highly skilled workers of mostly Protestant background had enabled them "to take advantage of American expansionism and industrialization" since their early arrival.[35] However, the situation changed drastically with the onset of World War I, which produced a strong anti-German hysteria. Even prior to the United States entering the war, German Americans were often accused of being "un-American" whenever they lobbied the government for the adoption of pro-German policies.[36] During the United States' involvement in World War I in 1917–18, these sentiments escalated into frequent physical attacks on the ethnic group as rumors of German espionage and subversion abounded.[37] In addition, according to Jaret, "schools stopped teaching the German language, newspapers written in German were banned, and German music was boycotted."[38] In response to such violent antipathy, individuals and businesses with German-sounding names "Americanized" them,[39] while also distancing themselves from many of the cultural practices associated with being German.[40]

The Italians are known to have similarly attempted to repress the visible signs of their ethnic identity in relation to the intensified discrimination against them during the years of an international armed conflict, this time "War II.[41]" Already stereotyped as part of the anti-immigrant movement in early twentieth-century nativist America, Italian Americans became targeted even more intensely after the attack on Pearl Harbor solidified the country's fear that "the greatest threat to national security [could] come from within": together with newcomers from Japan and, again, Germany, they became classified as "enemy aliens."[42] By January 1942, the stigmatizing designation was applied to anyone of Italian descent (approximately 600,000 individuals), with the population subjected to curfews and harassment, including the closing of its Italian-language schools.[43] Perhaps most alarmingly, 250 Italian Americans were confined in internment camps for a period of up to two years until the government decided to release them in attempts to "generate political support for the war" from Italians as the nation's most numerous ethnic group.[44] Due to these complex developments, many Italian immigrants became eager to move more definitively toward full acculturation and Americanization—a decision ultimately contributing to their upward mobility but also threatening to erase their ethnic particularity.[45]

As this discussion has shown, many European immigrants have not been spared the discrimination that has often been associated primarily with immigrants from different continents. Anti-immigrant sentiments predicated on what Jaret describes as "common fears that generate conflict"[46] negatively influenced the resettlement experience of such subgroups as the Irish, Slavs, Jews, Italians, and even the Germans. Due to societal fears that their presence in the United States would threaten the position of cultural and economic primacy of the earlier European settlers, these populations were subjected to constructs signaling their inherent inferiority, treacherousness, and non-belonging. As they became more assimilated and better known, the country gradually redefined them, allowing them to join the ranks of the "quality white" mainstream. Not insignificantly, their absorption into the "real" America has been frequently enabled by the arrival of newer, lesser known, and thus more feared and ostracized subgroups of the immigrant Other. This circumstance signals that the pro-nationalistic mainstream's antipathy towards the immigrant Other does not tend to completely dissipate—it simply tends to reshift its focus on another target. The section below offers a brief list of additional scholarly resources on the topic of the evolving reception of European immigrants in the United States, focusing especially on the periods roughly spanning the turn-of-the-century large waves of immigration and current immigration in line with the historic scope of the included preK–12 books.

Additional Scholarly Resources

Daniels, Roger. *Coming to America: A History of Immigration and Ethnicity in American Life.* New York: Perennial, 2002.

Dolan, Jay P. *The Irish Americans: A History.* New York: Bloomsbury, 2008.

Epstein, Lawrence J. *At the Edge of a Dream: The Story of Jewish Immigrants on New York's Lower East Side 1880–1920.* San Francisco: Jossey-Bass, 2007.

Guglielmo, Jennifer, and Salvatore Salerno, eds. *Are Italians White?: How Race Is Made in America.* New York: Routledge, 2003.

Ignatiev, Noel. *How the Irish Became White.* New York: Routledge, 2009.

Jacobson, Matthew Frye. *Whiteness of a Different Color: European Immigrants and the Alchemy of Race.* Cambridge, MA: Harvard University Press, 1999.

Kirschbaum, Erik, and Herbert W. Stupp. *Burning Beethoven: The Eradication of German Culture in the United States during World War I.* New York: Berlinica, 2015.

Michalikova, Nina. *New Eastern European Immigrants in the United States.* New York: Palgrave Macmillan, 2017.

Roediger, David R. *Working Toward Whiteness: How America's Immigrants Became White: The Strange Journey from Ellis Island to the Suburbs.* New York: Basic Books, 2006.

Zahra, Tara. *The Great Departure: Mass Migration from Eastern Europe and the Making of the Free World.* New York: W.W. Norton, 2016.

Recommended Children's and Young Adult Books

ARMENIA

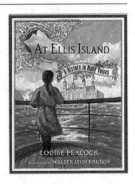

***At Ellis Island: A History in Many Voices.* Louise Peacock. Ill. by Walter Lyon Krudop. Atheneum Books for Young Readers, 2007. 978-0-689-83026-6. 44 pp. Picture Book/Historical Fiction. Gr. 3–6.**

Selected Awards: Society of School Librarians International Book Award (Honor) 2007.

Louise Peacock's picture book represents an interesting—if not completely successful—structural experiment: it intertwines a large multiplicity of voices in the effort to portray young immigrants' experiences of entering America through Ellis Island during the first decades of the twentieth century. The central voice belongs to Sera Assidian, a ten-year-old Armenian whose journey to join her father in the United States to escape the Ottoman Empire's systematic genocide of her people is recorded in her letters to her late mother. Sera's rather dramatic narrative is paralleled by that of an unnamed modern child, who visits the island wishing to learn more about her grandmother's grandmother, a pre-World War I immigrant at the age of sixteen. The two fictional voices are accompanied by quotations from actual child and teen immigrants of European descent as well as by other individuals (an interpreter, surgeon, immigration inspector, and other officials) who closely witnessed the great immigration wave. While the author provides a brief introductory note explaining her intentions, and varies the color and type of font used in the passages to visually distinguish between the individual voices, young readers may feel somewhat confused. However, if provided with additional guidance and paying close attention to the included archival photographs as well as Krudop's evocative gouache paintings, they are likely to get a good general sense of the specific challenges their turn-of-the-century peers faced on their quest for freedom and safety.

Discussion Starters

1. The book shows that children and teens came to the United States for various reasons in the early twentieth century. List at least some of these reasons. How does this list compare to the motives of people immigrating here today?
2. What are some of the difficulties that many of the book's immigrants faced during their immigration journey?
3. What was the purpose of the examinations and questioning at Ellis Island? Who was often denied entry, and why?
4. What do you know about your family's origin? Interview other family members if necessary.

Quotes for Interpretation

1. "And to this day I think I'm a better American than a lot of them born here, because when I sing 'God Bless America,' I'm in tears" (17).
2. "'You're in America now. You have nothing to be afraid of. Nothing at all'" (42).

CZECH REPUBLIC

Madlenka. **Peter Sís. Ill. by the author. Frances Foster Books/Farrar, Straus and Giroux, 2000. 978-0-374-39969-6. 1 volume (unpaged). Picture Book/Fiction. PreK–Gr. 3.**

Selected Awards: Horn Book Fanfare 2000.

In this visually stunning book, Madlenka, a character based on the immigrant author's daughter, is excited to find out that her tooth wiggles. She wants to inform the entire world, represented by her culturally diverse New York City block, about this life-changing event. Mr. Gaston, the French baker; Mr. Singh, the Indian news vendor; Ciao, the Italian ice-cream man; Ms. Grimm from Germany; Mr. Eduardo, the Latin American greengrocer; Cleopatra, her school friend with African roots, and Mrs. Kham, the Asian shopkeeper, are all notified that she is "a big girl now." Using the method of die-cut windows, multiple frames, and complex, almost mythical illustrations as well as simpler, childlike pictures with verbal descriptions, Sís creates a portrayal of each immigrant's culture through the landscapes, animals, artifacts, historic landmarks, well-known narratives, and fictional characters associated with it. The resulting imagery provides the book's young readers with an intriguing tapestry, inspiring them to create their individualized understanding of the cultures described. The narrative also shows readers that the difference in backgrounds within a community does not prevent interconnectedness and empathy: Madlenka relates her experience easily and successfully to a widely diversified group of people as if they were one large, close-knit multicultural family.

Discussion Starters

1. Have you ever lost a tooth? Whom did you tell? Who are the people that Madlenka tells about her wiggling tooth? Where are they from?
2. Choose one of the countries or geographic areas that the characters or their ancestors came to the United States from and find it on a map. What did you learn about this country or area from the book?

3. How do different adults and children on the city block respond to Madlenka's news? How well do they know Madlenka?

4. What does "multicultural" mean? In your opinion, what are some of the good things about living in multicultural neighborhoods?

Quotes for Interpretation

1. "Madlenka! Where have you been?
   Well . . . I went around the world."

GERMANY

How I Became an American. **Karin Gündisch. Trans. by James Skofield. Cricket Books, 2001. 0-8126-4875-7. 120 pp. Historical Fiction. Gr. 4–7.**

Selected Awards: ALA Notable Children's Books 2002; Mildred L. Batchelder Award 2002; Notable Social Studies Trade Books for Young People 2002.

Translated from German, this turn-of-the-century immigration story of a German-speaking family from Siebenbürgen in Austria-Hungary is told through the eyes of young Johann Bonfert. This likeable fictional boy chronicles the hardships that he, his mother, and three of his siblings (Regina, Emil, and Eliss) endure on their journey to join his immigrant father and older brother Peter in Youngstown, Ohio, to secure a more affluent future. In the Promised Land, the family faces new difficulties, including Eliss's death, Peter and his father's long working hours at the steel mills, and the whole family's need to assimilate culturally and linguistically. They continue to work hard and manage to thrive, largely thanks to their resourcefulness as reflected in the mother's chicken farm and egg business, Johann's selling newspapers, Regina's becoming a housemaid, and Emil's helping out in a bakery. The book's language, especially its dialogue, seems stiff at times, but is livened up by the inclusion of propaganda songs, folk tales, and humorous passages structured around the differences in speed with which the younger and older generations acculturate. Based on actual immigrants' letters from 1902 to 1986, the narrative seems quite realistic and shows that the struggles of immigrants have not really changed that much over the course of a century.

Discussion Starters

1. Trace the immigration journey of Johann's family on a map. What difficulties and dangers do they encounter while traveling?
2. Describe the immigrant screening process at Ellis Island—who is accepted and who is turned away? What role does a person's socio-economic status play in these decisions?
3. How does the family's life in Youngstown compare to their life in Siebenbürgen in terms of its advantages and disadvantages? In your opinion, was it wise of them to have left Austria-Hungary?
4. What does the episode about Regina's refashioning an old boot (112) suggest about the differences in the older and younger generations' ability to adapt to the new country?

Quotes for Interpretation

1. "In Siebenbürgen, we were Americans before we'd even left the country; here in Youngstown, we're only European immigrants" (22).
2. "We're going to keep our name. You see, I think you can be named Bonfert *and* be an American" (70).
3. "'Johnny, promise me that you'll succeed in finishing school, and that you'll learn something, because that's your best chance!'" (72).

GREECE

Marianthe's Story: Painted Words and *Spoken Memories*. Aliki. Ill. by the author. Greenwillow Books, 1998. 978-0-688-15662-6. 1 volume (unpaged). Picture Book/Fiction. K–Gr. 3.

Selected Awards: Jane Addams Children's Book Award 1999.

In two closely intertwined narratives, Aliki explores the ways a newly immigrated child can use varying means of communication to share her story with others, thus establishing a sense of belonging. While the main character's country of origin is not named, the author has linked it to Greece, from which her mother immigrated at the age of six. In part one, *Painted Words,* readers meet Marianthe (Mari) shortly after she became immersed in the new culture without being able to access it linguistically: not only does she not speak its language, but its alphabet is inaccessible to her as well, with letters looking "like sticks and chicken feet, humps and moons." The narrative demonstrates how isolating such an experience can be, with some classmates taking advantage of Mari's silence to bully her. The solution presents itself in the immigrant child's use of art: encouraged by her teacher, Mari is able to tell her story in a sequence of drawings. In part two, *Spoken Memories,* readers learn more about Mari's background while witnessing the progress she has made towards becoming a full member of her new society: she is now able to describe her pictures in freshly acquired words. Aliki's empowering narrative is accompanied by beautiful examples of the very medium it proposes as an alternative to words—soft-toned art rendered in colored pencil and crayon—making it a perfect read-aloud piece.

Discussion Starters

1. Think of a situation when you could not understand what others were saying. How did it make you feel? How can one communicate without words?
2. How does drawing help the main character feel more at home in the new country?
3. Why do some villagers in Mari's home country think she doesn't need to go to school? Why does her mother feel differently about it? What is your opinion on only boys getting an education?
4. Why does Mari draw a picture of a bleeding girl? If this happened in your class, what could you do to make her feel better?

Quotes for Interpretation

1. "'... there is more than one way to tell a story. Someday Mari will be able to tell us with words.'"
2. "'Girls don't need books to clean the house.'
   'Girls need books to find other worlds, just like boys,' said Mama."

HUNGARY

Man of the Family. **Kathleen Karr. Farrar, Straus and Giroux, 1999. 0-374-34764-6. 179 pp. Historical Fiction. Gr. 4–8.**

Selected Awards: ALA Notable Children's Books 2000.

Karr's absorbing novel, based on her Hungarian immigrant family's history after World War I, explores the year of 1924 that precedes the ten-year-old narrator István (Stephen) Csere's premature transformation into the "man of the family" due to his father's unexpected appendicitis-related death (12–13). Much of the book focuses on the deep father-son bond, detailing the boy's admiration for his cheerful, music-loving Apa who, having fled Europe's war with his wife, continues to embrace the latest technological innovations in efforts to adequately support his rather large family. The immigration-related sacrifices of the Cseres are examined as well, with the narrator mentioning his mother's suffering from intense bouts of homesickness and his educated but moderately English-proficient father's having to exchange his Hungarian teaching career for his South Jersey chicken farm enterprise. István, as the Cseres's first U.S.-born son, often assumes the related role of the parents' acculturation/English language coach, with the narrative making clear that he as a second-generation immigrant is not spared identity struggles either: the different names assigned to him at home and at school, with their sociolinguistic implications, make him ask, "Which one was [he]" (22). The lively yet touching narrative closes with the boy facing the reality of the family's uncertain economic future under his new leadership.

Discussion Starters

1. List the advantages and disadvantages of the Cseres's immigration. What would you/did you miss the most when leaving your native country?

2. How does István/Stephen help his parents, especially his mother, feel more at home in America? Think of a situation when you acted as your parents' or caregivers' teacher or guide.

3. What impact does the family's immigrant status have on István's/
   Stephen's sense of who he is?
4. The book ends with Apa's sudden death. Outline how the story could
   continue given what we know about the individual characters. What
   is likely to happen now that István/Stephen is in charge?

Quotes for Interpretation

1. "'In Hungary my hands were never like this. They were smooth as
   a woman's, with clean nails. In Hungary an educated man is not
   expected to do physical labor'" (11).
2. "'In Europe [being educated] wasn't enough. In America it is everything'" (108).

IRELAND

Ashes of Roses. **Mary Jane Auch. Henry Holt and
Company, 2002. 0-8050-6686-1. 250 pp. Historical Fiction. Gr. 7–10.**

*Selected Awards: ALA Best Books for Young Adults
2003; Notable Social Studies Trade Books for Young
People 2003.*

Inspired by the infamous 1911 Triangle Shirtwaist Factory fire, this variation on the classic
turn-of-the-century immigration tale relays the experiences of sixteen-
year-old Rose Nolan as she, dissatisfied with Ireland's limiting prospects
for women, attempts to create a better life for herself in New York City.
As the narrative shows through a series of surprising twists, the teen
narrator has to repeatedly reevaluate her optimistic view of America.
First, her sick baby brother is denied entry to the United States, and her
father has to take him back to Limerick in Ireland. Then her mother and
youngest sister, disappointed by the less-than-warm welcome by their
prosperous American relatives, return as well. Refusing to give up,
rebellious Rose is left alone with her twelve-year-old sister in the city
that holds many dangers to "greenhorn[s]" (78). Denied fair pay and sex-
ually assaulted by a sweatshop owner, she finds new hope when Gussie,

her Jewish landlord's daughter and a passionate union organizer, helps her secure employment at the women's blouses-producing factory. The novel provides insight into the immigrant working girl lifestyle, illustrating Rose's ability to enjoy life in spite of the plant's exploitative working conditions. However, any happiness she finds is short-lived—after the fire breaks out, she and her sister barely escape, with Gussie and other friends perishing. Radicalized by the somewhat graphically described events, Rose vows to join the union. The "Author's Note" commenting on the genesis of the story closes this informative and emotional narrative.

Discussion Starters

1. How do Rose's views of America evolve throughout the narrative?
2. Why does Uncle Patrick's family look down on the newly arrived relatives?
3. Discuss Rose and her sister's decision to make it on their own in New York City. What would you have done in their place?
4. Why are the book's new immigrants, especially women, vulnerable to employers' abuse? Has the situation changed since the early twentieth century? Why/why not?
5. What does the narrative suggest about ethnic hierarchies between immigrant groups? Have these prevailed?

Quotes for Interpretation

1. "'... Italians are not respected here. But it will change. They say there was a time when everyone looked down on the Irish. Now they run the whole city'" (80).
2. "I was goin' to reach out and grab this new life in America with all my strength, because I was brought here for a purpose" (245–46).

ITALY

Penny from Heaven. Jennifer L. Holm. Random House, 2006. 0-375-83687-X. 274 pp. Historical Fiction. Gr. 5–8.

Selected Awards: ALA Notable Children's Books 2007; Newbery Medal (Honor) 2007.

Set in New Jersey in the summer of 1953, this witty yet touching first-person narrative explores the affiliation struggles of Penny, an eleven-year-old Brooklyn Dodgers fan, whose parental families differ significantly in their cultural backgrounds and habits. Her late Italian-immigrant father's family is Catholic, favors large and loud gatherings, and serves delicious meals. In sharp contrast, the "plain old American, and Methodist" grandparents that Penny and her widowed mother live with rarely have any visitors, are generally rather quiet, and eat unappetizing food (13). After an unfortunate wringer-washer accident that almost costs her her right arm, Penny discovers that the lack of contact between the two sets of relatives can be attributed largely to the politically charged circumstances surrounding her father's death. In the context of Italy's siding with Germany and Japan during World War II, her non-naturalized father was wrongfully accused of being a spy and died in an internment camp. Penny's helping the families address their collective grief and find forgiveness results in them socializing again, allowing her to navigate the differences between them more successfully. The vignette-style coming-of-age narrative closes with an informative "Author's Note" that further discusses the war-triggered historical discrimination against Italian immigrants.

Discussion Starters

1. Describe the differences between Penny's father's and mother's families. Which set of relatives does she seem to be more comfortable with? Why?
2. How did Penny's father die? Link your answer to his Italian immigrant origin. Why did her family keep the true cause of his death secret from her for years?

3. What is your opinion on the U.S. persecution of Italian Americans because of Italy's World War II affiliations? Which other immigrant groups were historically subjected to a similar treatment?

4. Apart from losing her father, how is Penny affected by the prejudice against Italian immigrants? Do you think this prejudice still lives on? Why/why not?

Quotes for Interpretation

1. "It's times like these that I wish I understood Italian. But they won't teach it to any of us kids because they say it's our job to speak English and be good Americans" (59).

2. "'Doll,' she says sadly, 'his only crime was being Italian'" (226).

3. "'You have to understand, none of them were very happy about our marriage, except Dominic. They had an Italian girl all picked out for your father'" (250).

Peppe the Lamplighter. **Elisa Bartone. Ill. by Ted Lewin. Lothrop, Lee & Shepard Books, 1993. 0-688-10269-7. 1 volume (unpaged). Picture Book/Historical Fiction. Gr. 1–5.**

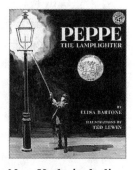

Selected Awards: ALA Notable Children's Books 1994; Caldecott Medal (Honor) 1994.

Reflecting on the challenges many European immigrant families faced in turn-of-the century New York, including the reliance on child labor, Bartone's thoughtful narrative details the mixed emotions of the Italian American school-age boy Peppe about his job of lighting the neighborhood's gas street lamps. While initially feeling proud of helping to support his eight sisters and ill father and infusing his job with almost metaphysical importance—he envisions each small flame as representing a "promise for the future"—Peppe's enthusiasm is dampened when the family's patriarch perceives the task as falling short of the promise America should hold for his only son. Peppe gradually begins to internalize his father's perception of the job to the extent that he refuses to light the lamps one night. However, when his decision results in his younger sister not returning home because of her fear of the dark, Papa recognizes the value of his son's social contribution, which prompts Peppe to return to the streets and fulfill the task with a recovered sense of contentment. Lewin's stunning watercolors are structured around the interplay between the dark tones of the immigrant community's streets and tenement buildings and the soft yellows of the street lamps, thus underscoring the narrative's message of giving credit where it is due. Many young readers are likely to enjoy this emotion-filled slice of historical reality with its special focus on the children of immigrants.

Discussion Starters

1. Where did Peppe and his family immigrate from? What do you know about your family's origin?
2. Why does Peppe need to look for a job even though he is still just a boy?
3. Why does Papa at first disapprove of Peppe being a lamplighter? How and why does his view change?
4. Can you think of any jobs in your community that may not be appreciated by others until they are not done?

Quotes for Interpretation

1. "'Did I come to America for my son to light the streetlamps?' [Papa] said. Then he walked out, slamming the door behind him."
2. "So Peppe lit the streetlamps once again, pretending with all his might that each one was a small flame of promise for tomorrow."

A Place for Joey. **Carol Flynn Harris. Boyds Mills Press, 2001. 1-56397-108-9. 90 pp. Historical Fiction. Gr. 3–6.**

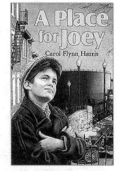

Selected Awards: Society of School Librarians International Book Award 2002.

Harris's novel, dedicated to "all immigrants who found their dream and ... those who are still seeking" (90), takes readers back to the immigrant world of the North End of Boston in the early twentieth century. Twelve-year-old Joey Calabro loves his neighborhood with its specific smells and sounds and does not mind its economic hardships much. Therefore, he strongly resents his immigrant family's dream of staying there only until they save enough money to buy a farm in Watertown. "You only get respect when you're the boss," his older brother explains (25). Joey begins to skip school in hopes of finding employment that would allow him to gain his own kind of independence outside of his family, which he views as too Italian. During his quest, he is frequently subjected to stereotypes demonstrative of the city's ethnic rivalries, especially those between the Irish and the Italians. Only after Joey witnesses the tragic aftermath of a molasses-tank explosion at the waterfront and he saves a policeman's life does he begin to comprehend his family's plans, embrace his Italian roots, and vow to dedicate his life to protecting others. Readers are likely to enjoy this believable portrait of the identity conflict resolution of a young immigrant who can barely remember his home country and attempts to dissociate himself from it, yet continues to be pulled back to his cultural, linguistic, and religious heritage.

Discussion Starters

1. How does Joey feel about speaking in Italian, his mother tongue? How does his attitude change throughout the narrative?
2. Discuss the portrayed tensions between the Irish and Italian immigrants. Why do the groups dislike each other?
3. Why does Joey's family want to buy a farm?
4. What is Joey's dream as the book closes? Why is it, in his Mama's words, "a big, big dream" (85)? Would he face the same challenges if he was trying to achieve that dream today?

Quotes for Interpretation

1. "'Don't call me Giuseppe, Mama. Call me Joey. That's my American name'" (9).
2. "'Maybe you ain't heard it, you little Eye-talian, but there's veterans of the Great War looking for jobs. Any jobs there is here go to Americans'" (37).
3. "Joey listened to the voices in his heart. He heard voices in Italian, and he heard voices in English. And he understood them both" (84).

KOSOVO

***Drita, My Homegirl.* Jenny Lombard. Puffin Books, 2008. 978-0-14-240905-3. 135 pp. Fiction. Gr. 3–5.**

Selected Awards: William Allen White Children's Book Award (Master List) 2008–2009.

Inspired by the author's experience teaching in the New York City public schools, this chapter book uses a dual-narrator strategy to portray the vulnerable social position of a newly arrived refugee and the empowering character of her friendship with a well-established local. Drita, whose Muslim family fled war-torn Kosovo, is relieved to reach the comparative safety of Brooklyn, only to find herself disillusioned by its cramped living conditions and her classmates' pronounced prejudice toward her as a barely English-speaking, unacculturated immigrant. Maxie, a troubled but popular African American classmate, is given the task of learning about Drita as part of her social studies project, and an initially unlikely friendship is born between the two girls. In alternating first-person chapters, the two ten-year-olds provide insight into their gradual overcoming of linguistic and cultural barriers to realize how much they have in common. The narrative culminates with Maxie's report on Drita's immigration story to an assembly of classmates and parents, with the prediction that Drita will make "a lot of new friends" as a result (135). Readers learn as much about the plight of refugees as about the possibility of finding common ground with someone of a different cultural background from this easy-to-read book with its credible character development.

Discussion Starters

1. How does Drita's family's life in the United States compare to their life in Kosovo?
2. Why is Drita being bullied? Are newly arrived immigrant children more likely to be picked on? Why/why not?
3. Why doesn't Drita report that her classmates shun and bully her? If you witnessed someone in her situation, how could you help?
4. How does Maxie overcome her initial dislike of Drita and befriend her?

5. Why does the book have two narrators? Discuss the importance of the closing chapter for the book's narrative strategy.

Quotes for Interpretation

1. "Now I have a new home and a new country . . . But as I look around, I begin to feel sad" (4).
2. "I look over at the new girl who's sitting at my desk. I got to say, I don't like her. I don't like her hair, I don't like her clothes, I don't like her face and I don't like her eyes" (19).
3. " . . . when I got to know Drita, I started finding out that even though on the outside we were different, on the inside we were just the same" (134–35).

POLAND

Rivka's First Thanksgiving. **Elsa Okon Rael. Ill. by Maryann Kovalski. Margaret K. McElderry Books, 2001. 0-689-83901-4. 1 volume (unpaged). Picture Book/Historical Fiction. Gr. 1–3.**

Selected Awards: Sydney Taylor Book Award 2001.

Described by Rael as "the story of one child's first Thanksgiving in a new homeland" inspired by the author's family memory, this witty narrative focuses on the desire of a young second-generation Jewish immigrant from Poland to belong culturally by participating in the celebration of an iconic American national holiday. Having learned about the history and meaning of Thanksgiving at school, nine-year-old Rivka tries to persuade her mother and grandmother that the holiday is for them as well, in spite of the family's distinctive religious affiliation. Doubtful, the women decide to consult with the Rabbi, who sides with them, deeming Thanksgiving unsuitable for Jews. But Rivka is persistent and she appeals the decision, outlining convincingly the connection between Jewish newcomers to "the Golden Haven" and immigrant groups of other religious backgrounds. The books closes with the immigrant family's successful incorporation of their culturally specific foods and ceremonies into the American holiday. Kovalski's whimsical illustrations help bring the story to life, while anchoring it firmly in the early twentieth century through its lively street and tenement building scenes in New York's Lower East Side. While some readers may find the narrative's premise of the learned Rabbi's limited knowledge of the holiday ("'So tell me about this ... celebration, this Thanksgiving'") problematic, the book serves as a powerful reminder that it is possible to bridge cultural and religious differences while maintaining particularity.

Discussion Starters

1. Why did Rivka's family emigrate from Poland? According to Rivka, what are the benefits of them living in America?
2. Why are Rivka's mother and grandmother unsure if the family should celebrate Thanksgiving?
3. Why does Rivka want to celebrate the holiday? How does she persuade the Rabbi that Thanksgiving is for immigrant Jews as well?
4. How does Rivka's family's Jewish immigrant background influence the way they celebrate Thanksgiving? What do they eat? Who visits? How does it compare to your family's Thanksgiving traditions?

Quotes for Interpretation

1. "'It sounds to me as though this is a party for Gentiles,' Mama added. 'It's not for us.'"
2. "'Thanksgiving is for all Americans, Bubbeh. Aren't we Americans, too?'"

`RUSSIA`

The Always Prayer Shawl. **Sheldon Oberman. Ill. by Ted Lewin. Boyds Mills Press, 1994. 1-878093-22-3. 1 volume (unpaged). Picture Book/Historical Fiction. K–Gr. 3.**

Selected Awards: Sydney Taylor Book Award 1994.

Oberman's tender narrative focuses on the anchoring power of cultural and religious traditions on an immigrant child's identity development. Adam, a Jewish boy growing up in tsarist Russia, is forced to abandon his familiar village when a military conflict, contextually likely related to the Russian Revolution, spreads into the area. While Adam's parents are leaving with him, his beloved grandfather stays behind because he is "too old to change anymore." For the sake of spiritual continuity, the grandfather hands his grandson a prayer shawl that, just like Adam's name, was previously passed down through generations. The ceremonial object helps to foster a sense of belonging and stability in Adam during the years of his substantial adjustment to life in urban America and his maturation, with the boy wearing the shawl every Sabbath as a reminder that in spite of his psychosomatic changes, he is "always Adam." The tradition is further strengthened when Adam, now aged, promises to pass the heirloom onto his American grandson, while explaining the story behind it. Oberman's sparse, straightforward prose is accompanied by Lewin's beautiful soft watercolor illustrations, which alternate between black-and-white tones and brighter colors to help readers distinguish between past and present events. While non-Jewish children may need additional assistance understanding the details of the prayer shawl's use, this is an important narrative that demonstrates to young readers of all backgrounds the significance of ritualistic traditions for one's sense of self.

Discussion Starters

1. What is immigration? Why does Adam's family decide to leave Russia?
2. Compare Adam's life in Russia to his life in America. What changes? What stays the same?
3. Why is the Always Prayer Shawl so special for Adam after his immigration to America?
4. Think of something that has been passed down through generations in your family. Why is it important? What do you have that you would like to hand down to your children or grandchildren one day and why?

Quotes for Interpretation

1. "Every Saturday Adam put on the prayer shawl and he said, 'I am always Adam and this is my Always Prayer Shawl. That won't change.'"

Anya's Ghost. **Vera Brosgol. Ill. by the author. First Second, 2011. 978-1-59643-713-5. 221 pp. Graphic Novel/Fiction. Gr. 9–12.**

Selected Awards: ALA Notable Children's Books 2012; Horn Book Fanfare 2011.

Brosgol's debut graphic novel tells the story of the troubled teenager Anya, who, having immigrated to the United States from Russia at the age of five, struggles significantly with her ethnic identity. Desperate to fit in based on her childhood experience of being bullied for her accent and secondhand clothing, Anya strives to erase any signs of her cultural heritage—including painstakingly dissociating herself from her only Russian classmate, Dima, whom she describes as acting too "fobby," that is, fresh off the boat (57). Anya's lack of self-esteem and corresponding cultural attitudes undergo a significant transformation after she befriends a ghost named Emily, whom she found in an abandoned well. After Emily, helpful at first, becomes threatening and almost takes over Anya's life, the discontented teenager realizes that appearances may not always correspond to reality and that she and Emily are alike in the sense that they both desire to assume the identity of others. This realization provides Anya with the courage to be different and to assert herself culturally as an individual of a hybrid background. She rejects the sexual advances of the heartthrob Sean, bonds with Dima, and begins using her Russian last name with confidence. This coming-of-age story of a teen immigrant is often haunting and comical at the same time, with the purplish tones of the sequential black-and-white images enhancing its supernatural elements.

Discussion Starters

1. How does Anya feel about her Russian heritage? What are some of the formative experiences behind her outlook, and how does the latter evolve in the narrative?
2. Discuss Anya's attitude towards Dima. Why does she try so hard to distance herself from him?
3. What does the ghost symbolically represent? Why does Emily want Anya to be with Sean?
4. What is the book's position on the issue of immigrant assimilation? How does that compare with your view on the matter?

Quotes for Interpretation

1. "Oh boy, again with the back in Russia. I don't think American boys really go for girls that look like rich men" (4).
2. "The only thing that's different about me now versus then is that I got some better clothes and got rid of my accent" (151).
3. "Impressing a bunch of snooty teenagers is a pretty lame life goal to have" (151).

Brooklyn Bridge. **Karen Hesse. Feiwel and Friends, 2008. 978-0-312-37886-8. 229 pp. Historical Fiction. Gr. 6–12.**

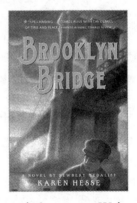

Selected Awards: Sydney Taylor Book Award 2009.

In this compelling variation on the rags-to-riches story, critically acclaimed author Karen Hesse chronicles the immigrant Michtom family's successful attempt to make a fortune by selling America's first teddy bears in the early twentieth century. Written from the perspective of fourteen-year-old Joseph, the book explores the intergenerational and intercultural clashes within the family that accompany this effort. The narrator's parents, having escaped anti-Semitic Russia and the poverty they experienced there, want all family members to devote every possible minute of their time to their booming business in order to secure lasting prosperity. In contrast, Joseph, the family's first U.S.-born member, nurtures a vision with more immediate rewards: to visit the glittering new amusement park on Coney Island. Ultimately, the family makes it to Luna Park just before the summer is over, unified by the joyful event of Joseph's uncle's marriage. The travails of the extended family, including its three eccentric aunts, are addressed as well. This historical novel is intricately woven, with the main story accompanied by vintage newspaper excerpts reporting on the fair's grandeur as well as by mystery-infused, italicized vignettes focusing on the daily struggles of homeless children living under the Brooklyn Bridge. Teenage readers are likely to have a hard time putting down this spellbinding work on the complex socioeconomic reality of immigrant New York in the early twentieth century.

Discussion Starters

1. Discuss the conflict between the narrator and his parents about how he should spend his summer. Think of a time when you had similar issues with your parents or caregivers. How does the Michtoms' immigrant status help fuel this quite common conflict?
2. Why does Joseph list Pauline's being "no immigrant" (20) as one of the things that attract him to her?
3. What types of people did Aunt Golda help immigrate? In your opinion, why did she keep the information secret from the family?
4. What is the function of the mini-stories on children living under the Brooklyn Bridge? Why did the author decide to use them as a parallel to the main story?

Quotes for Interpretation

1. "'I'm dying . . . and . . . I . . . never became . . . a citizen . . . . Joseph . . . I want to . . . die an American'" (59).

Journey to the Golden Land. **Richard Rosenblum. Ill. by the author. Jewish Publication Society, 1992. 0-8276-0405-X. 1 volume (unpaged). Picture Book/Historical Fiction. PreK–Gr. 4.**

Selected Awards: Sydney Taylor Book Award (Honor) 1992.

Rosenblum's picture book provides a solid introduction to the challenges of immigrating from Eastern Europe at the turn of the century. Told in short, simple sentences, the story focuses on Benjamin and his family, who leave behind their familiar village life in poor and oppressive tsarist Russia for the prosperity and freedom of the Golden Land. Having received funds from an uncle already settled in America, the family undertakes a perilous and exhausting passage that involves multiple means of transportation and ends with them successfully getting through the rigorous examination at Ellis Island—with the sacrifice of having to change their last name because they cannot spell it. The narrative creates a sense of universality by leaving out geographic names (other than Russia and New York) and suppressing the featured family's religion, which is likely Judaism, judging from the references to their persecution. Similarly, the class-based treatment of immigrants is alluded to rather than explored in detail. The author's elaborate black-and-white illustrations contribute to the feeling of generality through scenes documenting the magnitude of the turn-of-the-century immigration wave. While more sophisticated readers are likely to view this attempt at universality as resulting in a lack of depth, the narrative's subtle allusions to discrimination still make it an effective springboard for immigration-focused discussions.

Discussion Starters

1. Why does Benjamin's family decide to leave Russia?
2. Think of a time when you had to leave your home for a place you did not know. How did it make you feel? How does Benjamin feel about setting off for America?
3. Look closely at the picture of the ship. How is traveling on it different for different passengers?
4. What is Ellis Island? How are people in the book treated there? Who gets turned away by the officials? Why? With the help of your teacher or parents/caregivers, find out how it compares to who is being turned away these days.

Quotes for Interpretation

1. "Along with most of the other passengers, Papa, Mama, Benjamin, and Ruth watched as they passed the Statue of Liberty. The statue had a very special meaning for them."
2. "Officials watched them as they climbed. They were searching for the lame and the weak."

Letters from Rifka. **Karen Hesse. Square Fish, Henry Holt and Company, 2009. 978-0-312-53561-2. 148 pp. Historical Fiction. Gr. 4–8.**

Selected Awards: ALA Best Books for Young Adults 1993; ALA Notable Children's Books 1993; Horn Book Fanfare 1992; Phoenix Award 2012; Sydney Taylor Book Award 1992.

In this page-turner based on her great-aunt's memories, Karen Hesse has created an unforgettable portrayal of the trials of a young adolescent's immigration journey from Russia in the early twentieth century. The book's unique contribution lies in viewing the passage through the prism of one's religious and gender markings. In a series of unmailed letters written in the blank spaces of a poetry book by Pushkin, twelve-year-old Rifka Nebrot records how her being a Jew and "just a girl" (54) affects her efforts to find safety and opportunity across the ocean. Having fled anti-Semitic Russia in 1919 with two of her brothers and parents, Rifka survives typhus and a humiliating medical inspection only to be separated from her family after contracting ringworm: she is sent to Belgium to get better while they sail to the United States. When her hair refuses to grow back after her recovery, the society's gender prejudice, hinted at throughout the narrative, comes to full light: finally at Ellis Island, Rifka is quarantined out of fear that her baldness makes her unmarriageable, and will thus make her the U.S. government's "social responsibility" (95). Fortunately, the outspoken Rifka is able to persuade the immigration authorities that her intelligence and compassion will result in her not being a burden, and she is released. The emancipatory, well-written narrative closes with a contextualizing historical note and an interview with the author.

Discussion Starters

1. What makes Rifka's family flee Russia?
2. There are occasions when Rifka thinks about giving up on her journey to America. Think of an example. What keeps her going?
3. How does Rifka's being a Jew and a girl influence her immigration journey?
4. Define anti-Semitism. Discuss the relationship between Russia's anti-Semitism and Rifka's family's dislike of all Russians. How does Rifka overcome both forms of prejudice?
5. Think of a time when you did not like someone because of the social group he or she belonged to, and then you changed your opinion after getting to know the person.

Quotes for Interpretation

1. "In Russia, all America meant to me was excitement, adventure. Now, coming to America means so much more. . . . In America, I think, life is as good as a clever girl can make it" (90–91).
2. "To turn my back on the part of me that is Russian is impossible. I am Jewish, yes, but I am Russian too . . . And I am also more" (117).

Shy Mama's Halloween. **Anne Broyles. Ill. by Leane Morin. Tilbury House, 2000. 0-88448-218-9. 1 volume (unpaged). Picture Book/ Fiction. PreK–Gr. 4.**

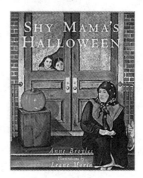

Selected Awards: Notable Social Studies Trade Books for Young People 2001.

Broyles's book, "written in the hope that there will always be welcome in the United States for immigrants and their unique perspective," offers a fresh look at the Halloween tradition by emphasizing its potential for generating a sense of inclusion for non-mainstream groups. Details in Morin's bright and realistic illustrations set the story of a family that has recently emigrated from Russia in the early twentieth century. The narrator Anya and her three younger siblings prepare excitedly for their first chance of joining the festivities of the holiday, only to experience a deep sense of disappointment when their father falls ill. They assume that their mother, frightened by Halloween and shy even in the old country, will not be taking them trick-or-treating. To their surprise, Mama, prompted by the children's desire to feel connected culturally in America, overcomes her bashfulness and ventures out into the unfamiliar jack-o'-lantern-lit world. By the time the night is over, Mama is dressed in pieces of the children's costumes and has accepted the holiday as her own. The text thus highlights the positive impact that immigrant children, who are generally likely to acculturate faster than their parents, may have on the older generation's ability to fit in with the new culture. The book concludes with a spread providing background information on immigration and offering related discussion questions.

Discussion Starters

1. At the book's beginning, what do the children think about Halloween? How about Mama?
2. What helps Mama change her mind about the holiday?
3. Think of a time when you had a chance to celebrate a holiday or an occasion that was new to you. How did it make you feel?
4. How does Halloween help the family feel part of America?
5. How can we help someone be more at home in a new culture?

Quotes for Interpretation

1. "Outside, on the busy street, Halloween happened without us. I felt a sudden sense of longing for the familiarity of my old home."
2. "Here, in the darkness, surrounded by what seemed like hundreds of other children, we, too, were American."
3. " . . . [Mama] replied, sounding serious and joyful at the same time, 'Now I know this Halloween,' and sighed with pleasure."

SCOTLAND (UNITED KINGDOM)

HALF and HALF

Half and Half. **Lensey Namioka. Dell Yearling, 2004. 0-440-41890-9. 136 pp. Fiction. Gr. 4–6.**

Selected Awards: Notable Social Studies Trade Books for Young People 2004.

Namioka's short chapter book centers on Fiona Cheng's multiculturally and biracially fueled identity dilemmas. As the daughter of a Scottish-immigrant mother and a Chinese American father, the eleven-year-old narrator has had to engage in much introspection lately. When filling out an enrollment form for a class at the recreation center, Fiona is unsure if she should check the box for "White" or "Asian" since she is "half of each" (3). She also refuses the category of "Other" because she senses its implications of marginality. Her concerns become more pronounced when her self-identification could potentially hurt the feelings of close family members. As the annual Seattle Folk Fest approaches, Fiona has to decide if she will perform with her Scottish grandfather's dance troupe or participate in her author/illustrator father's book talk, wearing a silk garment made by her Chinese grandmother especially for that occasion. To everyone's relief, she finds a clever way to resolve the scheduling conflict between the two events, ultimately showcasing both her Scottish and Chinese cultural affiliations and realizing that her identity does not have to be predicated on her physical appearance. While the plot seems a little schematic at times, with the narrator explicitly describing the cultural and racial stereotypes rather than letting them unfold through action, the book successfully addresses the struggles of complex heritage children facing the societal demand to fit into neat categories.

Discussion Starters

1. Why is Fiona confused about who she is? How and why would you identify your culture or race if you were her?
2. Why does the narrator dye her hair? Think of a time when you altered your appearance for similar reasons.

3. Fiona's identity conflict is mainly about her Scottish and Chinese heritage. Why doesn't she seem to doubt being an American?
4. How and why do Fiona's grandparents' and parents' expectations differ when it comes to her identity?

Quotes for Interpretation

1. "Suddenly I became angry. 'Why do grown-ups always have to sort people into boxes anyway'?" (4).
2. "Normally I don't mind looking Chinese. But now I was very conscious that I didn't belong. I felt like a prune in a bowl of strawberries" (47).
3. "I wasn't 100% anything—except myself" (136).

`UKRAINE`

Brave Girl: Clara and the Shirtwaist Makers' Strike of 1909. **Michelle Markel. Ill. by Melissa Sweet. Balzer + Bray, 2013. 978-0-06-180442-7. 1 volume (unpaged). Picture Book/Biography/Nonfiction. K–Gr. 3.**

Selected Awards: Flora Stieglitz Straus Award 2014; Jane Addams Children's Book Award 2014; NCTE Orbis Pictus Award (Honor) 2014; Notable Social Studies Trade Books for Young People 2014.

Markel's critically acclaimed picture-book biography, anchored in the premise that it is especially on American soil that one can successfully stand up for what is right, features Clara Lemlich, a Jewish Ukrainian immigrant who led the strike of thousands of New York garment factory workers in 1909. Having come to the United States at a young age with very limited English, Clara, like many other preteen and teen female Eastern European immigrants, found employment in the textile industry. Soon she became dissatisfied with its inhumane working conditions, which included meagre wages, long working hours, and unsanitary facilities. Inspired by her late-night efforts to educate herself, Clara began encouraging fellow workers to strike, thus going against the general perception that lower-class women of immigrant background could not organize. While male union leaders advised caution, Clara demanded a radical action in the form of a general walkout. Her efforts were effective, culminating in the largest strike of female workers at that point in U.S. history. Sweet's illustrations combining watercolor, gouache, and mixed media provide an outstanding backdrop to the story, making it even more accessible to emergent readers, who will appreciate the book's short sentences and clear language. The empowering narrative closes with a background note on the history of working conditions in the garment industry and a bibliography of selected sources.

Discussion Starters

1. Why do Clara and other immigrant girls have to work at such a young age?
2. Describe the conditions at the clothing factory where Clara works. Would you enjoy working there? Why/why not?
3. Why do the men at the factory think that the women there are not "tough enough"? How do Clara and her coworkers prove them wrong?
4. Has your family (including grandparents, great-grandparents, etc.) always lived in America? If not, where did they/you come to the United States from and why?

Quotes for Interpretation

1. "Clara smolders with anger, not just for herself, but for all the factory girls, working like slaves. This was not the America she'd imagined."
2. "... she has helped thousands of people. Proving that in America, wrongs can be righted, warriors can wear skirts and blouses, and the bravest hearts may beat in girls only five feet tall."

UNIDENTIFIED EUROPEAN COUNTRY

When Jessie Came Across the Sea. **Amy Hest. Ill. by Patrick James Lynch. Candlewick Press, 1997. 0-7636-0094-6. 1 volume (unpaged). Picture Book/Historical Fiction. Gr. 1–4.**

Selected Awards: Christopher Award 1998; Kate Greenaway Medal 1997; Sydney Taylor Book Award (Honor) 1997.

In this quintessential turn-of-the-century immigration story, thirteen-year-old Jewish orphan Jessie leaves her underprivileged native village in an unnamed European country in hopes of securing a better future in America. Her journey is enabled by the local rabbi's generous gesture of gifting his transoceanic ticket to her and finding a job for her at his widowed sister-in-law's dress shop on Manhattan's Lower East Side. The narrative discusses many of the typical challenges that such a dramatic change of geographic locations and cultures represents, including the necessity of leaving behind an aging relative, experiencing intense homesickness, and having to learn English. However, emphasis is placed on the benefits of immigrating into the "land of plenty," such as Jessie's prospering financially by lacemaking and thriving educationally. Jessie also finds love in the new country and, by the book's end, manages to reunite with her beloved grandmother by relentlessly saving for a ticket to the United States for her. Lynch's strikingly detailed double-page watercolor and gouache illustrations masterfully capture the emotional roller-coaster of Jessie's immigration story, including the awe she and other passengers experience when seeing the Statue of Liberty for the first time. Given its visual appeal, the book represents an excellent option for introducing younger readers to the hopes and hardships of the large wave of European immigrants in the late nineteenth and early twentieth centuries.

Discussion Starters

1. Why does Jessie leave for America? How does she feel about it? How would you/did you feel when leaving your home country for good? What would you/did you bring with you when only able to pack what you could carry?

2. What visions of America do Jessie and the other passengers talk about while on board the ship? Do any of the visions prove true for Jessie?

3. What are some of the difficulties Jessie faces because of immigration? How does she cope?

4. In your opinion, how would Jessie's life have been different if she had stayed in her native village? What would be the possible advantages/disadvantages of that?

Quotes for Interpretation

1. "On a fine fall day they sailed past the Statue of Liberty. America! No one swapped stories or argued. Babies hushed. Even the oldest passengers, and the most seasick, stood against the rail. America!"

Notes

1. Jie Zong and Jeanne Batalova, "European Immigrants in the United States," *Migration Information Source,* December 1, 2015, www.migrationpolicy.org/article/european-immigrants-united-states.

2. Faye Hipsman and Doris Meissner, "Immigration in the United States: New Economic, Social, Political Landscapes with Legislative Reform on the Horizon," *Migration Information Source,* April 16, 2013, www.migrationpolicy.org/article/immigration-united-states-new-economic-social-political-landscapes-legislative-reform; Zong and Batalova, "European Immigrants in the United States."

3. Roger Daniels, "United States Policy towards Asian Immigrants: Contemporary Developments in Historical Perspective," *International Journal* 48, no. 2 (1993): 330; Douglas S. Massey, "The New Immigration and Ethnicity in the United States," *Population and Development Review* 21, no. 3 (1995): 637.

4. Daniels, "United States Policy towards Asian Immigrants," 330.

5. Zong and Batalova, "European Immigrants in the United States."

6. Ibid.

7. Massey, "The New Immigration and Ethnicity in the United States," 642.

8. Pew Research Center, "Modern Immigration Wave Brings 59 Million to U.S., Driving Population Growth and Change through 2065," last modified September 28, 2015, www.pewhispanic.org/2015/09/28/modern-immigration-wave-brings-59-million-to-u-s-driving-population-growth-and-change-through-2065.

9. Zong and Batalova, "European Immigrants in the United States."

10. Ibid.

11. Ibid.

12. Michael Miller Topp, "Racial and Ethnic Identity in the United States, 1837–1877," in *Race and Ethnicity in America: A Concise History*, ed. Ronald H. Bayor (New York: Columbia University Press, 2003), 65.

13. Harry H. L. Kitano, *Race Relations* (Upper Saddle River, NJ: Prentice Hall, 1997), 216.

14. Zong and Batalova, "European Immigrants in the United States."

15. Topp, "Racial and Ethnic Identity in the United States," 65–66; Zong and Batalova, "European Immigrants in the United States."

16. Topp, "Racial and Ethnic Identity in the United States," 66.

17. Kitano, *Race Relations*, 217.

18. Topp, "Racial and Ethnic Identity in the United States," 67.

19. Kitano, *Race Relations*, 217.

20. Andrew R. Heinze, "The Critical Period: Ethnic Emergence and Reaction, 1901–1929," in *Race and Ethnicity in America: A Concise History*, ed. Ronald H. Bayor (New York: Columbia University Press, 2003), 131.

21. Kitano, *Race Relations*, 220.

22. Heinze, "The Critical Period," 135.

23. Charles Jaret, "Troubled by Newcomers: Anti-Immigrant Attitudes and Action during Two Eras of Mass Immigration to the United States," *Journal of American Ethnic History* 18, no. 3 (1999): 11.

24. Ibid., 29.

25. Heinze, "The Critical Period," 146.

26. Jaret, "Troubled by Newcomers," 11.

27. Kitano, *Race Relations*, 220.

28. Jaret, "Troubled by Newcomers," 30.

29. Ibid., 29.

30. Daniels, "United States Policy towards Asian Immigrants," 316.

31. Ibid., 315.

32. Muzaffar Chishti, Faye Hipsman, and Isabel Ball, "Fifty Years On, the 1965 Immigration and Nationality Act Continues to Reshape the United States," *Migration Information Source*, October 15, 2015, www.migrationpolicy.org/article/fifty-years-1965-immigration-and-nationality-act-continues-reshape-united-states.

33. Hipsman and Meissner, "Immigration in the United States."

34. Topp, "Racial and Ethnic Identity in the United States," 69.

35. Ibid.

36. Jaret, "Troubled by Newcomers," 20.

37. Heinze, "The Critical Period," 145; Jaret, "Troubled by Newcomers," 20.

38. Jaret, "Troubled by Newcomers," 20.

39. Ibid.

40. Heinze, "The Critical Period," 145.

41. Kitano, *Race Relations,* 222.

42. Paula Branca-Santos, "Injustice Ignored: The Internment of Italian-Americans during World War II," *Pace International Law Review* 13, no. 1 (2001): 160–61.

43. Ibid., 164–65, 167.

44. Ibid., 165, 169.

45. Kitano, *Race Relations,* 222–23.

46. Jaret, "Troubled by Newcomers," 20.

Chapter 6

Africa and the Middle East

Overview of African and Middle Eastern Immigration to the United States

NEWCOMERS FROM THE GEOGRAPHICALLY INTERCONNECTED Africa and the Middle East, while ethnically and culturally diverse, share quite a few similar characteristics. Along these lines, the history of their immigration also significantly intersects at points when their arrivals were severely curtailed or were made more possible through revisions to U.S. immigration legislation. The following sections explore these connections.

Characteristics of African Immigrants

As for African immigrants, their share within the overall U.S. immigrant population has been increasing at an accelerated rate in recent decades, a development accompanied by dramatic changes to the group's demographic composition. According to Anderson, while migrants from Africa currently account for only 4.8 percent of the total U.S. immigrant population, they have experienced an extremely fast growth rate.[1] Thus, if there were approximately 80,000 African migrants residing in the United States in 1970, in 2000 their number increased to 881,000, to further grow to 2.1 million in 2015.[2] Correspondingly, newcomers from Africa are markedly more likely than the total of immigrants from other world regions to be recent arrivals.[3] In comparison to other immigrant groups, they also exhibit a much higher likelihood of admittance through the refugee and diversity visa programs: in 2010, 46 percent of African immigrants entered through one of these two admission classes, as compared to 18 percent of U.S. immigrants overall.[4] That said, the majority of Africans still immigrate through family-based visas, with 48 percent of them legally admitted through family provisions, either as immediate relatives of U.S. citizens or through other family-sponsored preferences, in 2010.[5]

The substantial increase in the African immigrant population's size has been accompanied by a noteworthy shift in its racial configuration, dominant subregions of origin, and prevailing cultural backgrounds. As research shows, in the mid-twentieth century, the majority of African-born newcomers were white, arriving predominantly from Morocco and South Africa.[6] By contrast, in 2009, 74 percent of African immigrants self-identified as black,[7] with the immigration from Northern and Southern Africa steadily declining.[8] Currently, almost two-thirds of the population arrive from Eastern and Western African countries,[9] with Nigeria, Ethiopia, Ghana, and Kenya representing the top source countries of African migrants.[10] As for the refugee subgroup specifically, their leading countries of origin have been Somalia, Liberia, Sudan, Ethiopia, Burundi, the Democratic Republic of Congo, Eritrea, and Sierra Leone.[11] According to Thomas, contrary to theoretical predictions, "larger emigration increases were [simultaneously] found in Africa's non-English than English-speaking countries," with the contemporary African immigrant group being more culturally and linguistically diverse than its migrant predecessors.[12] This change is driven by the nations from African French-, Portuguese-, and Arabic-speaking countries, whose inhabitants exhibit a greater willingness to move to areas outside of their traditional emigration destinations, such as Europe.[13]

Given their rising diversity, the subgroups of African immigrants to the United States display varying levels of preparedness to succeed in the new country. Overall, newcomers from the African continent tend to "fare well on integration indicators,"[14] which can be partially linked to the comparatively high levels of their educational attainment and employment rates as well as to their slightly younger age.[15] Their general likelihood to be more English-proficient than other U.S. immigrants and to speak English at home also represents a positive factor in this regard.[16] In opposition to these overall trends, however, the population's refugee subgroups tend to exhibit relatively low levels of formal education while also facing more difficulties integrating than their non-refugee counterparts.[17] Women from Muslim countries, such as Morocco, Somalia, and Sudan, constitute another variant subgroup within the population—they are less likely to be employed than other African newcomers.[18] In spite of such differences, the experience of the subgroups often overlaps in their higher-than-average probability of living under the poverty line.[19] The situation can be attributed in part to the documented underemployment of many high-skill African migrants, which is in turn likely caused by the recent character of their arrival, the frequent non-transferability of the credentials they earned in their home countries, and discrimination against them on the labor market.[20]

Characteristics of Middle Eastern Immigrants

Immigrants from the Middle East exhibit some of the same overall characteristics as the African newcomers. As for their size, Zong and Batalova's recent report discussing the Middle East and North Africa (MENA) as a collective entity mentions that the immigrant group is also quite small, at approximately 1.02 million, or 2.5 percent of the total U.S. immigrant population.[21] Iraq, Egypt, Lebanon, and Saudi Arabia are cited as the top countries of their origin.[22] With the intensification of the Syrian civil war that began in 2011, the numbers of Syrians granted asylum have increased as well,[23] with the Obama administration surpassing its goal of admitting 10,000 Syrian refugees in 2016, up from a mere 36 in 2013.[24] Like the African immigrant group in general, the incoming Middle Eastern migrants tend to be more educated than the overall foreign- and native-born populations, with 43 percent of MENA immigrants reported to have a bachelor's degree or higher in 2013.[25] Simultaneously, those who arrived earlier generally display higher educational attainment than those immigrating more recently.[26] MENA migrants are also comparatively more likely to be English-proficient, but, unlike African newcomers in general, are less inclined to speak only English at home and are less likely to be employed.[27] While research presents conflicting information about their average household incomes,[28] data confirm that quite a few are employed in high-skill fields such as computer science, engineering, and health care, thus enjoying higher incomes than the total U.S. population.[29]

In relation to the prominence of Islam in the Middle East and the war- and terrorism-exacerbated levels of Islamophobia in the United States, the perception of Middle Eastern immigrants to the United States has been increasingly negative.[30] As Jaret eloquently puts it, "suspicion and fear that [they] engage in terrorism on behalf of Arab nationalism or Islamic fundamentalism was strong during the Iranian-United States hostage crisis of the late 1970s, the Persian Gulf War, . . . after the bombing of the World Trade Center,"[31] and, one could add, the later events of 9/11 and the Boston Marathon bombing. Accordingly, Middle Eastern immigrants, especially those of Arab-Muslim background, have been subjected to discrimination in multiple areas of their socioeconomic life, with the media tending to fuel their mistreatment by further demonizing them.[32] Al Wekhian argues that, contrary to the popular concept of the United States as a diverse country tolerant of all, it thus "should be noted that the hostility against Arab immigrants [has been] more tolerated than toward almost any other minorities."[33] As a result, the Middle Eastern immigrant population constructed as a dangerous Other has experienced a higher likelihood of feeling depressed, inferior, or traumatized, with its members often preferring to stay within their own ethno-religious community and, accordingly, struggling with acculturation.[34]

The Impact of Immigration Laws on Middle Eastern and African Migrants

The evolving position of Middle Eastern and African immigrants in American society, including the mentioned ostracism of them, is historically closely linked to immigration legislation, most prominently the laws of the 1910s–1920s and the 1960s. Middle Easterners first started arriving in significant numbers in the late nineteenth century, when modestly educated male Arab Christians from the Ottoman province of Syria (currently, Lebanon, Palestine, and Syria) were coming into the United States to escape the region's stagnant economy as well as the armed conflicts between the Druze and Christians.[35] However, the immigration wave was stopped by acts passed during the second and third decades of the twentieth century. Specifically, in 1917 Congress approved the Asiatic Barred Zone Act,[36] which applied to the Middle East very directly since

Syrians—as almost all of the migrants from the region were called at that time—were classified as Asians by the U.S. government.[37] In response to this unfavorable development, Middle Eastern immigrants lobbied to have their racial classification changed to white, with many also intentionally suppressing their ethnic distinctiveness by Americanizing their names and choosing not to teach their native language to their children.[38] Nevertheless, the 1921 one-year First Quota Act, which was eventually extended until the passing of the 1924 Act to Limit the Immigration of Aliens into the United States,[39] only reinforced the attempts to severely curtail arrivals from the Middle East. It endorsed a national-origin quota system strongly favoring Western and Northern European immigration by allocating each world country the share of "2 percent of the foreign-born population of that nationality" as listed in the 1890 census,[40] that is, at a time when Middle Easterners represented just a tiny fraction of the U.S. population.

Given they strongly pro-Anglo-Saxon character, the early twentieth-century acts' negatively affected the African immigrant population as well. The history of African migration to the United States is comparatively long, with the first Africans arriving in what constitutes the current U.S. territory in 1519.[41] However, having resulted from the trans-Atlantic slave trade, these early arrivals were not voluntary[42] and do not represent immigration in the traditional sense of the word despite the high numbers involved: scholars estimate that by 1867, when the slave trade officially ended, some 10 million Africans had been forcefully transported to the Western Hemisphere, with approximately 360,000 of them landing in the United States.[43] Not surprisingly, with the abolition of slavery, the annual numbers of African newcomers to the United States, now voluntary, dramatically declined: for instance, only 350 African immigrants arrived in the United States between 1891 and 1900.[44] The 1920s immigration laws further significantly curtailed the already very limited flow of migrants from Africa.[45] Driven mostly by nonblack South Africans, post-1920s immigration from the continent produced very few new admissions, with Africans correspondingly accounting for only 1 percent of all U.S. immigrants by the mid-1960s.[46]

The situation began slowly changing again in 1965, when the Immigration and Nationality Act replaced the national-origins quota rules with a seven-category preference system.[47] Assigning greater importance to immigrants' family relationships with U.S. citizens and/or legal permanent residents as well as their skills, and less to their ethnic background,[48] the 1965 act attracted additional migrants from both Africa and the Middle East. As for Africans, while in the 1970s, the volume of their arrivals remained relatively small, it became gradually much more robust in the ensuing decades,[49] especially following the passing of two additional pieces of legislation making the United States even more accessible to African migrants. More specifically, the Refugee Act of 1980, making immigration from conflict-stricken areas easier, and the Diversity Visa Program of 1990, encouraging migration from underrepresented countries, contributed substantially to the growing presence of African migrants in the United States.[50] As Thomas asserts, by the 1980s "African emigration to the U.S. was occurring at a faster rate compared to any other time in the twentieth century."[51]

The overwriting of the 1920s immigration legislation with less restrictive laws increased the flow of Middle Eastern migrants to the United States as well. They began immigrating in larger numbers again in conjunction with the 1948 Arab-Israeli War, with Palestinian refugees representing the leading subgroup of this wave.[52] The Palestinians were soon joined by members of elites from countries such as Egypt, Iraq, and Syria, who fled the popular revolutions and new regimes in their home countries.[53] However, it was not until the passing of the 1965 Immigration and Nationality Act that their numbers began rising particularly rapidly, with a comparatively larger percentage of the newcomers adhering to the Muslim faith.[54] According to the Migration Policy Institute, between 1980 and 2010, the number of MENA newcomers in the United States grew fourfold, from 223,000 to 861,000; and between 2010 and 2013 it rose by an additional 18 percent, to 1,017,000.[55] Foad mentions that, in addition to the cited legislative changes, such events as "a general increase in religious, ethnic, and sectarian tensions in their homelands," the Lebanese Civil War, and the two Gulf Wars contributed heavily to the influx of Middle Easterners to the country in the decades after the mid-1960s.[56]

In terms of what the future holds for the influx of Middle Eastern and African migrants, any developments will closely depend on the changing situation in their regions of origin as well as on the immigration-related regulatory decisions made by the current administration. The years since 9/11 have resulted in a much "more robust" U.S. immigration system,[57] with the Trump cabinet recently adding a new twist to the situation by making the immigration laws affecting the Middle Eastern and African populations, especially their Muslim and/or refugee subgroups, quite exclusionary again. As outlined in chapter 1, during his first weeks in the office the 45th president signed an executive order barring citizens from seven Muslim-majority countries (Iran, Iraq, Libya, Somalia, Sudan, Syria, and Yemen) from entry for 90 days, suspending the U.S. refugee program for 120 days, and shutting down the Syrian refugee program indefinitely.[58] The judicial branch's opposition to such an executive decision, coupled with a conflicting public response, resulted in the decision's subsequent revisions, but the existing policies are still likely to substantially reduce the stream of Middle Easterners and Africans into the country—at least for the nearest foreseeable future. The brief section below offers additional scholarly resources that provide insight into the complexities surrounding the two groups' immigration trends in the United States.

Additional Scholarly Resources

Bakalian, Anny P., and Mehdi Bozorgmehr. *Backlash 9/11: Middle Eastern and Muslim Americans Respond.* Berkeley: University of California Press, 2009.

Bayoumi, Moustafa. *How Does It Feel to Be a Problem?: Being Young and Arab in America.* New York: Penguin Books, 2009.

DeSipio, Louis, and Rodolfo O. de la Garza. *US Immigration in the Twenty-First Century: Making Americans, Remaking America.* Boulder, CO: Westview, 2015.

Greer, Christina M. *Black Ethnics: Race, Immigration, and the Pursuit of the American Dream.* New York: Oxford University Press, 2013.

Gualtieri, Sarah M. A. *Between Arab and White: Race and Ethnicity in the Early Syrian American Diaspora.* Berkeley: University of California Press, 2009.

Haines, David W. *Safe Haven?: A History of Refugees in America.* Sterling: Kumarian, 2010.

Halter, Marilyn, and Violet Showers Johnson. *African & American: West Africans in Post-Civil Rights America*. New York: New York University Press, 2014.

Jacobs, Linda K. *Strangers in the West: The Syrian Colony of New York City, 1880–1900*. New York: Kalimah, 2015.

Naff, Alixa. *Becoming American: The Early Arab Immigrant Experience*. Carbondale: Southern Illinois University Press, 1993.

Shaw-Taylor, Yoku, and Steven A. Tuch, eds. *The Other African Americans: Contemporary African and Caribbean Immigrants in the United States*. Lanham, MD: Rowman & Littlefield, 2007.

Recommended Children's and Young Adult Books

AFGHANISTAN

Come Back to Afghanistan: A California Teenager's Story. **Said Hyder Akbar and Susan Burton. Bloomsbury, 2005. 978-1-58234-520-8. 339 pp. Autobiography/Nonfiction. Gr. 9–12.**

Selected Awards: ALA Best Books for Young Adults 2006; ALA Top Ten Best Books for Young Adults 2006.

In this gripping eyewitness account that grew out of the young author's radio documentaries for *This American Life*, Said Hyder Akbar, aided by editor Susan Burton, reports on his unique encounters in post-Taliban Afghanistan during the three summers of 2002 to 2004. While born in Pakistan and raised in California, Akbar continues to experience a strong pull toward his refugee parents' homeland, feeling "more Afghan" than American (8). Accordingly, after his father sells his hip-hop clothing store in Oakland, California, in the aftermath of 9/11 to serve as the Afghanistan president Hamid Karzai's spokesman and, later, the governor of Afghanistan's volatile Kunar border province, the high-school senior decides to take his final exams early and accompany him. His journalistic-style narrative intriguingly describes not only the country's pained attempts at democratic reconstruction while facing unsettled conflicts and scarcity of resources, but also his personal struggle with establishing a definitive sense of belonging in one cultural space over another. Although his identity conflict is never quite resolved, the summer visits do substantially deepen his attachment to Afghanistan—to the extent that the book's epilogue finds him asserting that being "an active observer . . . isn't enough" and vowing to become "an active participant in moving the country forward" instead (333). The author's descriptions of war-related violence, including mass massacres, tend to be quite graphic, assuming a certain level of maturity from the book's audience.

Discussion Starters

1. Discuss the reasons behind the narrator's father returning to Afghanistan. How does his role there differ from his position in the United States?
2. How do the repeated visits to Afghanistan change the narrator?
3. Based on the book's representation of the status of women in Afghanistan, how would the narrator's experience there likely differ if he were an Afghan-American female?
4. Why is the narrator detained at the San Francisco Airport upon his return in the summer of 2004? Is it correct to assume that his stay in Afghanistan radicalized him? Why/why not?

Quotes for Interpretation

1. "If you went by paper, I was American, but if you went by instinct, I was Afghan. I could spend years deciding which was the real me, but nothing would ever change that fact" (110).
2. "'A lot of people in America do not have real goals in life. I wasn't sure if you had any goals you wanted to achieve. But now I see your major goal is to bring change to Afghanistan. I see you working hard . . . reading books, educating yourself'" (240).

Shooting Kabul. **N. H. Senzai. Simon & Schuster**
Books for Young Readers, 2010. 978-1-4424-
0194-5. 262 pp. Fiction. Gr. 5–8.

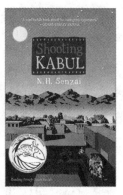

Selected Awards: Asian/Pacific American Award
for Literature 2010–2011; Middle East Book Award
2010; Notable Social Studies Trade Books for
Young People 2011.

Basing her semi-documentary novel on her husband's Soviet-era experience of fleeing Afghan-
istan but setting it in 2001 instead, N. H. Senzai presents a touching
portrayal of the efforts of the preteen Fadi Nurzai and his family to find
refuge in the United States as the Taliban increasingly abuses its power
in their homeland. Much of the novel's plot revolves around the Nurzais
leaving their youngest daughter Mariam behind in the chaos surrounding their escape from Kabul. Like his parents and older sister, the eleven-year-old narrator blames himself for the tragedy, vowing to restore
his honor by finding and rescuing Mariam—a determination that substantially clouds his early experiences in the San Francisco area. The
book explores additional factors influencing Fadi's acculturation, most
significantly the events of 9/11 and the resulting wave of Islamophobia that makes him a prime target of bullying. To fight potential cases
of similar prejudice in the readership, care is taken to explain the difference between the terrorists and other Muslims. Gradually, Fadi is
shown to overcome the sense of isolation he suffers from in spite of his
family having lived in the United States briefly before (his father stud-
ied in Wisconsin): he makes friends by joining a photo club, and he even
helps a group of schoolmates teach the bullies a lesson. The optimistic
feel of the novel is further enhanced by Mariam's safe reunion with the
family. A detailed glossary, author's note, and a helpful list of additional
readings accompany this complex refugee story.

Discussion Starters

1. What are Fadi's initial experiences at Brookhaven Middle School
   like? How can others help refugees feel more at home in America?

2. What did you learn about Islam from the book? Pay special attention to the differences between the Taliban and the 9/11 terrorists on one hand and Fadi's family on the other.
3. What does the attack on Mr. Singh, the ice-cream vendor, suggest about the hatred toward Muslims in the United States after 9/11 (164–66)?
4. What is the reason behind Fadi not revealing the names of his attackers to his parents or the school personnel? In your opinion, is this the right decision? Why/why not?

Quotes for Interpretation

1. "For all the problems in Afghanistan, this was still home" (15).
2. "... Fadi sat alone, watching students flurry around him like snowflakes in a blizzard. He felt as though he were hidden behind a camera lens, watching another world whirl past in shattered fragments" (84).

EGYPT

Coming to America: A Muslim Family's Story.
Bernard Wolf. Ill. by the author. Lee & Low Books, 2003. 1-58430-177-5. 1 volume (unpaged). Photo-Essay/Nonfiction. Gr. 2–5.

Selected Awards: Notable Social Studies Trade Books for Young People 2004.

This informative photo-essay promotes an understanding of Muslim culture by providing a glimpse of the everyday life of a close-knit family who recently immigrated to New York from Alexandria, Egypt. The narrative highlights the advantages of the transition, such as a more supportive school system and better wages, while also showing that the move comes with its challenges: the father's work schedule is quite demanding, and the family occasionally feels homesick. Out of the two portrayed generations, it is the younger one that bridges the cultures more successfully: all of the Mahmouds' three children (Rowan, 8; Dina, 12; and Amr, 13) thrive academically and socially in the United States yet maintain a close connection to their Islamic origin. The book's treatment of Muslim culture is relatively broad. While aiming to offer a basic explanation of the religion itself, it addresses related cultural issues as well, from food preferences to gender roles. Unfortunately, more problematic sociopolitical topics concerning the featured immigrant group, such as the increasingly negative attitudes towards them after 9/11, are not discussed. That said, the narrative does implicitly counter those attitudes: it serves as a powerful reminder that all human beings, in spite of the visible markers of their religious and cultural differences, share the same desire to secure a better future for their loved ones.

Discussion Starters
1. Why do the Mahmouds leave Egypt? Why does the father come to the United States alone at first?
2. Why is education so important to the Mahmouds? How might this be a common value for many immigrant families?
3. How can getting used to a new country be more difficult for stay-at-home mothers? Use Soad as an example.
4. What do the Mahmoud family members hope for? How are these hopes similar to what you and your family wish for?
5. What are some of the additional challenges Muslim immigrants may face compared to immigrants of non-Muslim backgrounds?

Quotes for Interpretation
1. "Sometimes memories of her life in Alexandria come rushing back to Rowan. She misses her neighborhood, where everyone knew everyone else. She misses the excitement of festive holidays. . . . Most of all she misses the many friends she left behind and her large, loving, extended family."

ETHIOPIA

Faraway Home. **Jane Kurtz. Ill. by E. B. Lewis. Harcourt, 2000. 978-0-15-200036-3. 1 volume (unpaged). Picture Book/Fiction. K–Gr. 3.**

Selected Awards: Notable Social Studies Trade Books for Young People 2001.

FARAWAY HOME

WRITTEN BY *Jane Kurtz* • ILLUSTRATED BY *E. B. Lewis*

In this heartwarming tale about an intergenerational gap widened by the difference in cultural backgrounds, an African American girl named Desta experiences anxiety after receiving the news that her father will travel to his native Ethiopia to spend time with his ill mother. Since Desta has never visited the country and does not speak its language, Ethiopia represents a large unknown to her. She fears that her father's home is "too wild" and that he may never come back to her. To help his daughter visualize and emotionally connect to the geographic area he loves, the father begins to share vivid imagery-filled stories of pink clouds of flamingos, cold winds whooshing through silver blue eucalyptus trees, and barefoot walks to school. His strategy proves successful. Gradually, Desta leaves behind her mistrust of her father's native country to the extent that she attempts to test some of his childhood experiences on U.S. soil—she decides to take off her shoes on her way back from school. As a result of this bonding, Desta is able to acknowledge her father's right to miss and visit his homeland, while not doubting that he will return to her. Lewis's luminous watercolors relay the tender lyricism of the story. While this book is an insightful and enjoyable read for all children, second-generation immigrant children who experience a similar lack of connection to their immigrant parents' home countries and cultures are especially likely to relate to this narrative of newfound understanding.

Discussion Starters

1. Think of a time when you had to be away from your parents or caregivers. How did it make you feel?
2. Look up Ethiopia on the map. What did you learn about the country from the book?
3. Why doesn't Desta want her father to go back to Ethiopia?
4. How does Desta's father help her understand why he misses his native country?
5. Why does Desta take off her shoes on her way back from school? How does this help change her view of Ethiopia?

Quotes for Interpretation

1. "'Ethiopia is so far away,' Desta says. 'I don't want you to go.'
   'For me, Ethiopia is never far away,' her father says."

2. "He will come back. Until he does, she can hold his stories in her
   heart."

**Of Beetles & Angels: A Boy's Remarkable Jour-
ney from a Refugee Camp to Harvard.** Mawi
Asgedom. Little, Brown and Company, 2002.
978-0-316-82620-4. 142 pp. Autobiography/
Nonfiction. Gr. 9–12.

*Selected Awards: Notable Social Studies Trade
Books for Young People 2003.*

In this memoir of intense suffering, struggle,
and ultimate triumph, Mawi Asgedom documents his family's passage
from civil war-torn Ethiopia through a Sudanese refugee camp to an
affluent but prejudiced Chicago suburb. Following his father's example
of hard work and treating all people, regardless of their appearance and
behavior, with the utmost kindness and respect as if they were heav-
en's angels, Asgedom gradually overcomes socioeconomic obstacles to
succeed by securing a full-tuition scholarship to Harvard. The book's
style appears influenced by Asgedom's background of a motivational
speaker, as reflected in his occasional tendency for self-aggrandize-
ment. Slightly glorified are also Asgedom's father Haileab, an Ethiopian
medical professional turned U.S. janitor, and his older brother Tewolde,
a generous teenager with a great business sense. In contrast, the female
family members, including Asgedom's mother Tsege to whom the story
is dedicated, are rendered rather sketchily, indicating that the author
has not completely left behind his home culture's gender paradigms.
Nevertheless, the narrative's honesty in detailing both the positive and
negative sides of the refugee life in America is admirable. Readers are
also likely to be impressed by the author's ability to maintain an optimistic attitude when facing life's harshest adversity. Asgedom's 1999
Harvard commencement address, Habesha recipes, and discussion
questions conclude this inspiring story.

Discussion Starters

1. Discuss the difference between the myth of Ameri*kha* as told in the African refugee camps and the reality of the Asgedoms' life in the United States.

2. Why is the book titled *Of Beetles & Angels?* Apply the concept to your life. Who are the angels? Who the beetles?

3. What is the author's mother's role in the story? Why does Asgedom dedicate the book to her while writing more about his father?

4. The refugee family receives significant help in Wheaton but is also subjected to prejudice, especially at school. How does this prejudice manifest itself, and what are its causes? What could U.S. schools do to help refugees feel more accepted?

Quotes for Interpretation

1. "One day, upon awakening, Haileab Asgedom found himself, in America, transformed into a monstrous black beetle" (95).

2. "... in the comfort of the United States, my mother gave me another piece of advice, this one less obvious. 'Always remember where you came from,' she told me just before I left for Harvard" (135).

IRAN

Borderline. **Allan Stratton. HarperTeen, 2010. 978-0-06-145111-9. 298 pp. Fiction. Gr. 8–12.**

Selected Awards: ALA Best Fiction for Young Adults 2011; John Spray Mystery Award (Finalist) 2011.

This coming-of-age thriller focuses on the destructive power of the stereotypes that are frequently applied to Muslims. The book's narrator, U.S.-born fifteen-year-old Mohammed Sami Sabiri, has been continuously ostracized in his white neighborhood near Rochester, New York, based on his family's religious affiliation and Iranian roots. After his transfer to an all-male private academy, the shunning increases, with a ring of bullies frequently attacking him and the school administration turning a blind eye to the incidents. The mainstream society's implied tendency to tolerate the harassment of Muslims is explored more openly in relation to Sami's father's arrest due to his alleged involvement in a planned terrorist attack. The FBI is portrayed as violently breaking into the Sabiri household, with the media helping to further strengthen the Muslim-terrorist stereotype and the academy shamelessly expelling Sami out of fear of bad publicity. The narrative significantly picks up pace in these passages, resulting in a credulity-stretching plot resolution: Sami tracks down the escaped leader of the would-be terrorist group in Toronto, using the information he gains in the process to prove his Dad innocent, thus mending the broken father-son bond and coming to terms with his heritage. Nevertheless, the thoughtfulness of the portrayal of the identity conflict experienced by a second-generation Middle Eastern immigrant during the post 9/11 Muslim scare redeems the narrative, making the book a worthy addition to any young-adult diversity collection or reading list.

Discussion Starters

1. What strategies do Sami and his parents employ in an attempt to fit in with mostly white, Christian suburbia? How successful are they in these efforts?

2. How adequate is Sami's response to being bullied because of stereotypes applied to him as a Muslim Iranian American? What could you do differently in his situation?

3. How does Sami's relationship to his father evolve throughout the narrative? How does it correspond to his changing view of his cultural and religious heritage?

4. Discuss the history teacher's attitude towards Sami. Why does he, unlike other teachers and school officials, tend to protect him?

5. Sami's class is asked to explain where they would "draw the line between liberty and security" (188). What is your take on the topic?

Quotes for Interpretation

1. "'Belonging isn't the same as fitting in,' Dad replied" (15).

2. "'... we're lucky to be alive. I say we round'em [the terrorists] up and send'em back where they came from.'

I whirl around. 'I was born here, Eddy, same as you'" (186).

ISRAEL

The Importance of Wings. **Robin Friedman. Charlesbridge, 2009. 978-1-58089-330-5. 170 pp. Fiction. Gr. 5–9.**

Selected Awards: Sydney Taylor Book Award 2010.

This coming-of-age story follows Roxanne (Ravit) Ben-Ari, an Israeli American teenager growing up in New York City in the 1980s, as she learns to accept her hybrid identity. With her mother in Israel to take care of a sick relative and her father working long hours as a cab driver, Roxanne and her younger sister Gayle (Gili) live on a meagre diet of cereal, canned mushrooms, and the occasional hotdogs bought from a neighborhood friend. Roxanne is obsessed with anything "All-American," including the blond heartthrob Eddie (145), and prefers the created, idyllic reality of a never-ending supply of American TV shows. The TV world nurtures a sense of fitting in and justice that seems to be lacking in her real life. When Liat, another Israeli American girl, moves into the "cursed" pink house on the block (48), Roxanne's self-deprecating view of herself as a "fake American" gradually changes (25). Having repeatedly witnessed Liat's pride in her "tough" Israeli heritage (114), as represented by such acts of resistance as her unwillingness to Americanize her name, Roxanne's self-confidence increases—she comes to appreciate her less-than-ideal family with its multicultural lifestyle. The unexplainable fire that destroys Liat's house and Liat's family's subsequent decision to move back to Israel seem a little bit forced; however, the characters are compelling, equipping the story with the potential to serve as a metaphoric window into the identity struggles of immigrant teens.

Discussion Starters

1. One of Roxanne's long-term fantasies is being a Wonder Woman (14). Explain her fascination with this pop culture icon.

2. Why is being Israeli difficult for Roxanne? Think of a time when you felt very different from others. How did you cope?

3. How does Liat's view of her family and Israeli heritage compared to Roxanne's view? Which of the characters seems more mature, and why?

4. How do the narrator's feelings about her dual cultural identity change throughout the book and why?

Quotes for Interpretation

1. "Liat looks into my eyes in the mirror's reflection.
   'I don't know.... Some things are more important than wings.'
   'Nothing's more important than wings,' I shoot back" (99).

2. "Liat leans forward. 'We're Israeli, Roxanne. Israelis are tough. Israelis are *sabras*'" (114).

3. "Nobody wants to be American more than me. But I can't pretend I wasn't born in Israel" (136).

NIGERIA

No Laughter Here. **Rita Williams-Garcia. HarperCollins, 2004. 0-688-16247-9. 133 pp. Fiction. Gr. 5–8.**

Selected Awards: ALA Best Books for Young Adults 2005.

Written in response to the scarcity of materials on "the brutal ritual of female genital mutilation" for young readers (132), this coming-of-age story details the dismal effect of parents' insistence on performing the internationally contested, discriminatory ritual on their preteen daughter even though she emigrated from her African home country almost a decade ago. The book's ten-year-old narrator, Akilah Hunter, cannot help but notice her best friend's negative transformation upon her return to Queens, New York, from her summer trip to her native Nigeria: the previously cheery and chatty Victoria Ojike is suddenly joyless and withdrawn. Halfway into the narrative, Akilah learns that Victoria's family had her circumcised in efforts to preserve her status as "a clean and proper Nigerian girl" (108). In an age-appropriate way, the book alludes to the generally problematic character of the repressive rite of passage, while highlighting that immigrant girls whose hybrid cultural identity prevents them from fully identifying with their native land's practices suffer the most. Women's participation in their own oppression is also addressed: it is the Ojike family's adult females who are particularly insistent that the surgery be done. Closing on a semi-optimistic note, the narrative points to the possibility of the heroines reclaiming their right to agency: they plot to share Victoria's story in order to "warn girls everywhere" (130). Young readers are likely to be quite intrigued about the despotic construct of female purity that follows many female African emigrants across borders.

Discussion Starters
1. Why does Victoria act so differently after returning from Nigeria?
2. Define a ritual. What is the purpose of the Nigerian ritual portrayed in the book? How does Victoria's living in the United States make it more difficult for her to accept the practice?
3. Compare the responses of Victoria's mother, Akilah's mother, and Akilah's teacher to Victoria's circumcision. Whom would you side with? Why?
4. In your opinion, should parents insist that their immigrant children follow the traditions of their native country when these conflict with the beliefs of their new culture? Why/why not?

Quotes for Interpretation
1. "'If Victoria had lived in her family's village all of her life, she might have been prepared for her rite of passage'" (115).
2. "I was mad because everyone was right and Victoria was silent. Well, Victoria had spoken to me, but we still couldn't laugh together. And that wasn't right" (122).

SIERRA LEONE

Diamonds in the Shadow. **Caroline B. Cooney. Water-Brook Press, 2007. 978-1-4000-7423-5. 228 pp. Fiction. Gr. 7–12.**

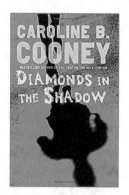

Selected Awards: Christopher Award 2008; Notable Social Studies Trade Books for Young People 2008.

Cooney's page-turner for young adults focuses on the difference between the worldviews of African refugees and their U.S. sponsors and the adjustments they each make as a result of living together. The Finches, a Connecticut upper-middle-class family of four (philanthropic parents, self-absorbed high-schooler Jared, and bubbly middle-schooler Mopsy), feel entitled to their first-world privileges and nurture the corresponding belief that "bad things [aren't] really happening" (183). In a brilliantly drawn contrast, the Amabos (close-knit adults Celestine and Andre and polite teenagers Mattu and Alake), who are taken in by the Finches, suffer from an acute awareness of their vulnerability and mortality—a viewpoint produced by their unimaginable suffering during the African civil war, as represented most poignantly by Andre's chopped-off hands and Alake's muteness. Through a series of nail-biting transitions revolving around the presence of a fifth refugee, the war criminal Victor who made the Amabos smuggle in blood diamonds, the narrative shows that even in America, with its prosperity and relative safety, one is not immune from evil. In the process, the Amabos' fake identity as a family is revealed and their geographic origin is linked to Sierra Leone rather than the initially assumed Liberia, with readers invited to decide for themselves if the measures the refugees adopted to escape Africa are fully justifiable. The plot's final resolution, while somewhat melodramatic, is linked to an empowering sense of mutual understanding and affection that the characters develop for each other.

Discussion Starters

1. How does Jared's attitude towards the refugees evolve throughout the narrative, and why? How would you react if your parents wanted you to share your room with a refugee?

2. Analyze the Amabos' taking on the killed family's identity to get to the United States. Do you find their actions justifiable? Why/why not?

3. What is the difference between the two cultures' views of one's past actions? Link your answer to Alake.

4. The Finches consider themselves to be the refugees' teachers, but ultimately they also learn a lot from them. Discuss the details of this exchange.

5. Research the following issue: How does the first-world countries' hunger for diamonds help fuel African war conflicts?

Quotes for Interpretation

1. "'What did that African family do to deserve all this help? ... How come the church can't help inner-city people right here in America, who probably wouldn't mind a free car and job assistance?'" (109).

2. "That is the difference, thought Alake. In Africa, everything is impossible. But in America, everything is possible" (179).

SUDAN

Home of the Brave. **Katherine Applegate. Feiwel and Friends, 2007. 978-0-312-36765-7. 249 pp. Poetry/Fiction. Gr. 5–8.**

Selected Awards: Golden Kite Award 2008; Josette Frank Award 2008; Notable Social Studies Trade Books for Young People 2008.

Written in sparse free verse, this hope-driven first-person narrative centers on a preteen Sudanese refugee's struggle to accept Minnesota as his new home despite the differences in climate, landscape, and day-to-day practices. As Applegate poetically relates, Kek attempts to establish a sense of connectedness to his new cultural space by viewing it through the prism of what he already knows. Thus, he describes the airplane he arrived on as a "flying boat" (3) and the warm coat given to him as a "fat shirt" (4). The most significant of the bridges Kek forms between the two seemingly incompatible worlds proves to be his caring for a widowed farmer's cow. Having come from a tribe of herders, the boy experiences the comforting feeling of temporarily reacquiring all he has "lost" and "want[s]" through the animal (16)—however illusionary that feeling may be, given his father's and older brother's deaths and his mother's disappearance in the Sudanese genocide. Kek's ability to maintain a generally optimistic outlook on the acculturation process is contrasted with his war-mutilated cousin's skepticism. Ultimately, the narrative seems to side with Kek's sentiments, highlighting acts of philanthropy over racially inspired hatred towards him and offering a redeeming ending. Amusing acculturation mishaps, such as Kek mistakenly washing his aunt's dishes in a laundry machine, lighten the otherwise potentially heavy emotional tone of the inspiring story, increasing its accessibility to middle-school readers of all backgrounds.

Discussion Starters

1. Research the civil war in Sudan that serves as the historical backdrop of the story. What was the conflict based on? How long did the war last?
2. What are some of the portrayed differences between Sudan and Minnesota? Which of them prove most difficult for Kek to deal with?
3. Discuss Kek's observation that staying with his aunt and cousin makes him more homesick (39).
4. Why is Kek drawn to the aging cow? If/when emigrating, what could/did make you feel more at home in the new culture?
5. How do Kek's and his cousin's views of America differ? Who do you side with and why?

Quotes for Interpretation

1. "You come here to make a new life,
   but the old life is still haunting you" (44).
2. " . . . you'll never really feel like an American,
   Ganwar says. You'll see.
   Why? I ask.
   Ganwar shrugs.
   Because they won't let you" (87).

***My Name Is Sangoel.* Karen Lynn Williams and Khadra Mohammed. Ill. by Catherine Stock. Eerdmans Books for Young Readers, 2009. 978-0-8028-5307-3. 1 volume (unpaged). Picture Book/Fiction. Gr. 1–3.**

Selected Awards: Notable Social Studies Trade Books for Young People 2010.

In this noteworthy addition to picture books on non-native children's identity-building, Williams and Mohammed portray an eight-year-old Sudanese refugee boy's struggle to preserve his sense of self while attempting to integrate successfully into American society. The struggle is centered on the act of (re)naming. Having embraced his village elder's advice to always "be Sangoel. Even in America," the Dinka tribe boy accepts the ways of the new country but fights the implicit and explicit external pressures to Americanize his name. This decision severely affects his sense of belonging until he thinks of a clever way to teach his classmates how to pronounce the name that connects him firmly to the heritage of his father and other ancestors: he graphically represents its components while using the linguistic referents the classmates are familiar with (sun and goal). Soon many other students employ the same strategy to introduce themselves to him and a bond is formed. Stock's illustrations, executed mainly in soft watercolors with the occasional presence of photos or fabric collage, add additional detail to the story by portraying closely the emotions that Sangoel and his family experience when facing the challenge of trying to adapt to the new culture. The sensitive narrative communicates to readers the hope that the challenge can be met without the refugee child having to leave behind his home country affiliations.

Discussion Starters
1. Who are refugees? Why did Sangoel and his family leave Sudan?
2. How did your parents or caregivers decide on your name? How would/did you feel when having to change it?
3. What does Sangoel's name mean to him? Why does he consider it so special that he insists on keeping it?

4. How do Sangoel's classmates treat him? How can you make someone from a different culture feel welcome?

Quotes for Interpretation

1. "America was big and open and free. There was no barbed wire to keep them in."
2. "Sangoel remembered the words of the Wise One: 'Education is your mother and your father.'"
3. "'In America I have lost my name.'"

MULTIPLE AFRICAN/MIDDLE EASTERN (AND OTHER) COUNTRIES

Outcasts United: The Story of a Refugee Soccer Team That Changed a Town. **Warren St. John. Delacorte Press, 2012. 978-0-385-74194-1. 226 pp. Nonfiction. Gr. 7–12.**

Selected Awards: Christopher Award 2013; Notable Social Studies Trade Books for Young People 2013.

In this successful young-adult adaptation of the bestseller *Outcasts United: An American Town, a Refugee Team, and One Woman's Quest to Make a Difference* (2009), journalist Warren St. John offers an inspiring story of the Fugees, a youth refugee soccer team based in Clarkson, Georgia. The author skillfully intertwines accounts of the team's pivotal matches with stories of the hardships faced by its dedicated Jordan-born female coach Luma Mufleh as she strives to keep the underprivileged group together. The hardships faced by the team's individual war-traumatized members as they attempt to acculturate to the conservative, white, "sleepy little town" are also covered (25). Special attention is given to several Burundian, Kosovar, Liberian, and Sudanese players and their homeland conflicts, with brief mentions of team members of Afghani, Bosnian, Congolese, Ethiopian, Gambian, Iraqi, Somali, and Turkish backgrounds. The narrative persuasively demonstrates the far-reaching benefits of the boys' involvement in the sports team, with the Fugees serving simultaneously as a tutoring center and a second family to the many who struggle with inadequate schooling, stinging prejudice, and the dangerous lure of gangs. While concluding on an optimistic note by listing the academic successes of the players, the book also reminds its audience that socioeconomic challenges continue to plague refugees, and it indirectly encourages readers to donate to the still-active multi-cultural soccer team.

Discussion Starters
1. Discuss the benefits of refugee youth joining the Fugees.
2. Reread the contract Luma makes the soccer players sign (76–77). How and why does it differ from the usual sports team contracts?
3. Why are the refugee boys at a relatively high risk of becoming gang members? How does Luma try to keep them away? How would you approach the problem in her situation?
4. List examples of prejudice against immigrants and refugees in Clarkson. How could a little homogeneous town become better pre-pared to integrate refugees of diverse backgrounds?

Quotes for Interpretation
1. "'[Luma] said we're all foreigners, and this is a team where every-body unites . . . And she told us she was going to kick us off the team if we didn't'" (58).
2. "The boys on the Under Fifteens felt the conflict between the two worlds more strongly than their younger siblings, if only because they had spent more time in their home countries" (74).

UNIDENTIFIED AFRICAN COUNTRY

The Orange Houses. Paul Griffin. Dial Books, 2009. 978-0-8037-3346-6. 147 pp. Fiction. Gr. 9–12.

Selected Awards: ALA Best Books for Young Adults 2010; ALA Top Ten Best Books for Young Adults 2010.

Griffin's intense yet lyrical novel, set in the Orange Houses projects of the Bronx, traces the tragedy-prone friendship of three teens of different backgrounds who connect emotionally as outcasts and creatively as gifted artists attempting to transcend their depressing reality through creativity. Jimmi, an eighteen-year-old psychotic war veteran turned junkie, drafts original street poetry; Tamika, a fifteen-year-old hearing-impaired, self-doubting high schooler, draws impressive people-less cityscapes, and Fatima, a sixteen-year-old illegal refugee smuggled to New York on an oil tanker from an unspecified war-torn African country, creates beautiful objects out of unsold newspapers. While the book's tragic tone initially seems to peak in Jimmi's apparent hanging, it ultimately culminates in Fatima's deportation after an immigration lawyer was paid multiple families' lifetime savings to file her emergency asylum petition. Fatima thus ironically gets to see the Statue of Liberty she has always yearned to visit only through the windows of the detention center and the Africa-bound plane she is put on. In spite of such a crushing turn of events, the book is moving but not overtly sentimental, showing that while all odds are stacked against the three teens, they still encounter glimpses of hope and beauty. Griffin's mastery of street dialogue, deft characterization, and his courage to raise tough questions about immigration laws, the school system, and health care make this slim book one not to be overlooked.

Discussion Starters
1. What connects Jimmi, Tamika, and Fatima?
2. Whom do you see as the villain in the story? Who is the hero? Why?
3. Discuss the path to legalization for refugees such as Fatima as presented in the book.
4. What is Fatima's first impression of the Orange Houses? What does it imply about U.S. living standards?
5. Analyze Fatima's fascination with the Statue of Liberty. Why does the national monument sometimes seem to have more significance for those outside of the country?

Quotes for Interpretation
1. "In the dim light and over the gang graffiti they painted the statue, adding six ultraviolet wings to Liberty as she looked over an expressionist cityscape" (82).

2. "'The project Jimmi said we were working on? The most beautiful thing in the world? He meant friendship. Sister, this is a lovely country. You have peace here. One needs only a little food, a warm place to sleep and dream, and someone with whom she can share a laugh'" (141).

Notes

1. Monica Anderson, "African Immigrant Population in U.S. Steadily Climbs," Pew Research Center, last modified February 14, 2017, www.pewresearch.org/fact -tank/2017/02/14/african-immigrant-population-in-u-s-steadily-climbs/.

2. Ibid.

3. Kristen McCabe, "African Immigrants in the United States," *Migration Information Source*, July 21, 2011, www.migrationpolicy.org/article/african-immigrants -united-states.

4. Randy Capps, Kristen McCabe, and Michael Fix, *Diverse Streams: African Migration to the United States* (Washington, DC: Migration Policy Institute, 2012), 8.

5. Capps, McCabe, and Fix, *Diverse Streams*, 8; Irma T. Elo et al., "Africans in the American Labor Market," *Demography* 52, no. 5 (2015): 1516.

6. Elo et al., "Africans in the American Labor Market," 1515.

7. Capps, McCabe, and Fix, *Diverse Streams*, 2.

8. McCabe, "African Immigrants in the United States."

9. Ibid.

10. Anderson, "African Immigrant Population in U.S. Steadily Climbs"; McCabe, "African Immigrants in the United States."

11. McCabe, "African Immigrants in the United States."

12. Kevin J. A. Thomas, "What Explains the Increasing Trend in African Emigration to the U.S.?" *The International Migration Review* 45, no. 1 (2011): 3, 22.

13. Ibid., 22.

14. Capps, McCabe, and Fix, *Diverse Streams*, 1.

15. Capps, McCabe, and Fix, *Diverse Streams*, 1, 10; McCabe, "African Immigrants in the United States."

16. McCabe, "African Immigrants in the United States;" Jie Zong and Jeanne Batalova, "Sub-Saharan African Immigrants in the United States," *Migration Information Source*, October 30, 2014, www.migrationpolicy.org/article/sub-saharan-african -immigrants-united-states-2.

17. Capps, McCabe, and Fix, *Diverse Streams*, 1; McCabe, "African Immigrants in the United States"; Zong and Batalova, "Sub-Saharan African Immigrants in the United States."

18. Capps, McCabe, and Fix, *Diverse Streams*, 1.

19. McCabe, "African Immigrants in the United States"; Zong and Batalova, "Sub-Saharan African Immigrants in the United States."

20. Capps, McCabe, and Fix, *Diverse Streams*, 1.

21. Jie Zong and Jeanne Batalova, "Middle Eastern and North African Immigrants in the United States," *Migration Information Source*, June 3, 2015, www.migrationpolicy.org/article/middle-eastern-and-north-african-immigrants-united-states.

22. Ibid.

23. Ibid.

24. Jie Zong and Jeanne Batalova, "Syrian Refugees in the United States," *Migration Information Source*, January 12, 2017, www.migrationpolicy.org/article/syrian-refugees-united-states.

25. Hisham S. Foad, "Waves of Immigration from the Middle East to the United States," last modified December 20, 2013, https://papers.ssrn.com/sol3/papers.cfm?abstract_id=2383505; Zong and Batalova, "Middle Eastern and North African Immigrants in the United States."

26. Foad, "Waves of Immigration."

27. Zong and Batalova, "Middle Eastern and North African Immigrants in the United States."

28. Foad, "Waves of Immigration"; Zong and Batalova, "Middle Eastern and North African Immigrants in the United States."

29. Foad, "Waves of Immigration."

30. Jamil Al Wekhian, "Acculturation Process of Arab-Muslim Immigrants in the United States," *Asian Culture and History* 8, no. 1 (2016): 93.

31. Charles Jaret, "Troubled by Newcomers: Anti-Immigrant Attitudes and Action during Two Eras of Mass Immigration to the United States," *Journal of American Ethnic History* 18, no. 3 (1999): 22.

32. Al Wekhian, "Acculturation Process of Arab-Muslim Immigrants," 93, 96.

33. Ibid., 93.

34. Ibid., 89, 93.

35. Ibid., 91; Foad, "Waves of Immigration"; Zong and Batalova, "Middle Eastern and North African Immigrants in the United States."

36. Faye Hipsman and Doris Meissner, "Immigration in the United States: New Economic, Social, Political Landscapes with Legislative Reform on the Horizon," *Migration Information Source*, April 16, 2013, www.migrationpolicy.org/article/ immigration-united-states-new-economic-social-political-landscapes -legislative-reform.

37. Foad, "Waves of Immigration."

38. Ibid.

39. Roger Daniels, "United States Policy towards Asian Immigrants: Contemporary Developments in Historical Perspective," *International Journal* 48, no. 2 (1993): 315.

40. Muzaffar Chishti, Faye Hipsman, and Isabel Ball, "Fifty Years On, the 1965 Immigration and Nationality Act Continues to Reshape the United States," *Migration Information Source*, October 15, 2015, www.migrationpolicy.org/article/fifty-years-1965-immigration-and-nationality-act-continues-reshape-united-states.

41. Capps, McCabe, and Fix, *Diverse Streams*, 2.

42. Capps, McCabe, and Fix, *Diverse Streams*, 2; Zong and Batalova, "Sub-Saharan African Immigrants in the United States."

43. Capps, McCabe, and Fix, *Diverse Streams*, 2; Zong and Batalova, "Sub-Saharan African Immigrants in the United States."

44. Thomas, "What Explains the Increasing Trend," 5.

45. Chishti, Hipsman, and Ball, "Fifty Years On;" Thomas, "What Explains the Increasing Trend," 5.

46. Thomas, "What Explains the Increasing Trend," 5–6.

47. Hipsman and Meissner, "Immigration in the United States."

48. Chishti, Hipsman, and Ball, "Fifty Years On."

49. Thomas, "What Explains the Increasing Trend," 6.

50. Anderson, "African Immigrant Population in U.S. Steadily Climbs."

51. Thomas, "What Explains the Increasing Trend," 6.

52. Foad, "Waves of Immigration."

53. Ibid.

54. Zong and Batalova, "Middle Eastern and North African Immigrants in the United States."

55. Ibid.

56. Foad, "Waves of Immigration."

57. Hipsman and Meissner, "Immigration in the United States."

58. White House Office of the Press Secretary, "Executive Order: Protecting the Nation from Foreign Terrorist Entry into the United States," last modified January 27, 2017, https://www.whitehouse.gov/the-press-office/2017/01/27/executive-order-protecting-nation-foreign-terrorist-entry-united-states.

BIBLIOGRAPHY

Al-Hazza, Tami Craft. "Motivating Disengaged Readers through Multicultural Children's Literature." *New England Reading Association Journal* 45, no. 2 (2010): 63–68.

Al-Hazza, Tami Craft, and Katherine T. Bucher. "Building Arab Americans' Cultural Identity and Acceptance with Children's Literature." *The Reading Teacher* 62, no. 3 (2008): 210–19.

Al Wekhian, Jamil. "Acculturation Process of Arab-Muslim Immigrants in the United States." *Asian Culture and History* 8, no. 1 (2016): 89–99.

American Library Association. "ALA News: ALA Opposes New Administration Policies that Contradict Core Values." Last modified January 30, 2017. www.ala.org/news/press-releases/2017/01/ala-opposes-new -administration-policies-contradict-core-values.

Anderson, Monica. "African Immigrant Population in U.S. Steadily Climbs." Pew Research Center. Last modified February 14, 2017. www .pewresearch.org/fact-tank/2017/02/14/african-immigrant-population -in-u-s-steadily-climbs/.

APA Presidential Task Force on Immigration. "Crossroads: The Psychology of Immigration in the New Century." *Journal of Latino/a Psychology* 1, no. 3 (2013): 133–48.

Aronowitz, Michael. "The Social and Emotional Adjustment of Immigrant Children: A Review of the Literature." *International Migration Review* 18, no. 2 (1984): 237–57.

Bal, Matthijs P., and Martijn Veltkamp. "How Does Fiction Reading Influence Empathy? An Experimental Investigation on the Role of Emotional
Transportation." *PLoS ONE* 8, no. 1 (2013): 1–12.

Balderrama, Francisco E. "The Emergence of Unconstitutional Deportation and Repatriation of Mexicans and Mexican Americans as a Public
Issue." *Radical History Review* 93 (2005): 107–10.

Bartle, Lisa R. *Database of Award-Winning Children's Literature.* www
.dawcl.com/.

Bersh, Luz Carime. "The Curricular Value of Teaching about Immigration
through Picture Book Thematic Text Sets." *Social Studies* 104, no. 2
(2013): 47–56.

Bicha, Karel D. "Hunkies: Stereotyping the Slavic Immigrants, 1890–1920."
Journal of American Ethnic History 2, no. 1 (1982): 16–38.

Bishop, Rudine Sims. "Mirrors, Windows, and Sliding Glass Doors." *Perspectives: Choosing and Using Books for the Classroom* 6, no. 3 (1990). https://
scenicregional.org/wp-content/uploads/2017/08/Mirrors-Windows
-and-Sliding-Glass-Doors.pdf.

Branca-Santos, Paula. "Injustice Ignored: The Internment of Italian-
Americans during World War II." *Pace International Law Review* 13,
no. 1 (2001): 150–82.

Cameron, Lindsey, Adam Rutland, Rupert Brown, and Rebecca Douch.
"Changing Children's Intergroup Attitudes toward Refugees: Testing
Different Models of Extended Contact." *Child Development* 77, no. 5
(2006): 1208–19.

Capps, Randy, Kristen McCabe, and Michael Fix. *Diverse Streams: African Migration to the United States.* Washington, DC: Migration Policy Institute, 2012.

Central Intelligence Agency. "Armenia." In *The World Factbook 2017.* Washington, DC: Central Intelligence Agency, 2017. https://www.cia.gov/
library/publications/the-world-factbook/geos/am.html.

———. "Kosovo." In *The World Factbook 2017.* Washington, DC: Central
Intelligence Agency, 2017. https://www.cia.gov/library/publications/
the-world-factbook/geos/kv.html.

———. "Taiwan." In *The World Factbook 2017.* Washington, DC: Central
Intelligence Agency, 2017. https://www.cia.gov/library/publications/
the-world-factbook/geos/tw.html.

Children's Literature Comprehensive Database. www.clcd.com.

Chishti, Muzaffar, Faye Hipsman, and Isabel Ball. "Fifty Years On, the 1965 Immigration and Nationality Act Continues to Reshape the United States." *Migration Information Source*, October 15, 2015. www.migration policy.org/article/fifty-years-1965-immigration-and-nationality-act -continues-reshape-united-states.

Colby, Susan A., and Anna F. Lyon. "Heightening Awarness [sic] about the Importance of Using Multicultural Literature." *Multicultural Education* 11, no. 3 (2004): 24–28.

Cooper, Patricia M. "Teaching Young Children Self-Regulation through Children's Books." *Early Childhood Education Journal* 34, no. 5 (2007): 315–22.

Cress, Susan W., and Daniel T. Holm. "Developing Empathy through Children's Literature." *ERIC Document* 427 316 (1998): 1–9.

Daniels, Roger. "United States Policy towards Asian Immigrants: Contemporary Developments in Historical Perspective." *International Journal* 48, no. 2 (1993): 310–34.

Durand, Jorge, Douglas S. Massey, and Rene M. Zenteno. "Mexican Immigration to the United States: Continuities and Changes." *Latin American Research Review* 36, no. 1 (2001): 107–27.

Elo, Irma T., Elizabeth Frankenberg, Romeo Gansey, and Duncan Thomas. "Africans in the American Labor Market." *Demography* 52, no. 5 (2015): 1513–42.

Foad, Hisham S. "Waves of Immigration from the Middle East to the United States." Last modified December 20, 2013. https://papers.ssrn.com/sol3/ papers.cfm?abstract_id=2383505.

Gall, Meredith Damien, and Maxwell Gillett. "The Discussion Method in Classroom Teaching." *Theory into Practice* 19, no. 2 (1980): 98–103.

Gilman, Sander L. *Difference and Pathology: Stereotypes of Sexuality, Race, and Madness*. Ithaca, NY: Cornell University Press, 1985.

Graseck, Susan. "Teaching with Controversy." *Educational Leadership* 67, no. 1 (2009): 45–49.

Gutiérrez, David G. "A Historic Overview of Latino Immigration and the Demographic Transformation of the United States." In *The New Latino Studies Reader: A Twenty-First-Century Perspective*, edited by Ramón A.

Gutiérrez and Tomás Almaguer, 108–25. Oakland: University of California Press, 2016.

Hainmueller, Jens, and Michael J. Hiscox. "Attitudes toward Highly Skilled and Low-Skilled Immigration: Evidence from a Survey Experiment." *American Political Science Review* 104, no. 1 (2010): 61–84.

Hainmueller, Jens, and Daniel J. Hopkins. "Public Attitudes toward Immigration." *Annual Review of Political Science* 17 (2014): 225–49.

Hefflin, Bena R., and Mary Alice Barksdale-Ladd. "African American Children's Literature That Helps Students Find Themselves: Selection Guidelines for Grades K-3." *The Reading Teacher* 54, no. 8 (2001): 810–19.

Heinze, Andrew R. "The Critical Period: Ethnic Emergence and Reaction, 1901–1929." In *Race and Ethnicity in America: A Concise History*, edited by Ronald H. Bayor, 131–66. New York: Columbia University Press, 2003.

Hipsman, Faye, and Doris Meissner. "Immigration in the United States: New Economic, Social, Political Landscapes with Legislative Reform on the Horizon." *Migration Information Source*, April 16, 2013. www.migration policy.org/article/immigration-united-states-new-economic-social -political-landscapes-legislative-reform.

Huang, Qiaoya. "Multicultural Children's Literature: Through the Eyes of Many Children." *International Journal of Bilingual Education and Bilingualism* 17, no. 6 (2014): 748–52.

Hwang, Wei-Chin. "Acculturative Family Distancing: Theory, Research, and Clinical Practice." P*sychotherapy: Theory, Research, Practice, Training* 43, no. 4 (2006): 397–409.

Jaret, Charles. "Troubled by Newcomers: Anti-Immigrant Attitudes and Action during Two Eras of Mass Immigration to the United States." *Journal of American Ethnic History* 18, no. 3 (1999): 9–39.

Katz, Michael B., Mark J. Stern, and Jamie J. Fader. "The Mexican Immigration Debate: The View from History." *Social Science History* 31, no. 2 (2007): 157–89.

Khailova, Ladislava. *The Stories We Share: Database of PreK-12 Books on the Experience of Immigrant Children/Teens in the U.S.* http://library.niu .edu/ulib/projects/stories/index.html.

Kitano, Harry H. L. *Race Relations*. Upper Saddle River, NJ: Prentice Hall, 1997.

Kramer, Paul A. "Not Who We Are." *Slate*, February 3, 2017. www.slate.com/
    articles/news_and_politics/history/2017/02/trump_s_muslim_ban_and
    _the_long_history_of_american_nativism.html.

Lempke, Susan Dove. "The Faces in the Picture Books." *Horn Book Magazine*
    75, no. 2 (1999): 141–47.

Lesser, Gabriel, and Jeanne Batalova. "Central American Immigrants in
    the United States." *Migration Information Source,* April 5, 2017. www
    .migrationpolicy.org/article/central-american-immigrants-united
    -states.

Levin, Fran. "Encouraging Ethical Respect through Multicultural Litera-
    ture." *Reading Teacher* 61, no. 1 (2007): 101–4.

Lifshitz, Jessica. "Curating Empathy." *Literacy Today* 33, no. 6 (2016): 24–26.

Lin, Grace. "The Windows and Mirrors of Your Child's Bookshelf: TEDx
    Talk." Filmed January 2016, Natick, MA. http://mirrorswindows
    doors.org/wp/ted-talk-by-grace-lin/.

Manderson, Desmond. "From Hunger to Love: Myths of the Source, Inter-
    pretation, and Constitution of Law in Children's Literature." *Law and
    Literature* 15, no. 1 (2003): 87–141.

Manross Guilfoyle, Brooke. "Colorblind Ideology Expressed through Chil-
    dren's Picture Books: A Social Justice Issue." *Jesuit Higher Education: A
    Journal* 4, no. 2 (2015): 37–56.

Mar, Raymond A., Colin G. DeYoung, Daniel M. Higgins, and Jordan B. Peter-
    son. "Self-Liking and Self-Competence Separate Self-Evaluation from
    Self-Deception: Associations with Personality, Ability, and Achieve-
    ment." *Journal of Personality* 74, no. 4 (2006): 1047–78.

Mar, Raymond A., Keith Oatley, and Jordan B. Peterson. "Exploring the Link
    between Reading Fiction and Empathy: Ruling Out Individual Differ-
    ences and Examining Outcomes." *Communications* 34, no. 4 (2009):
    407–28.

Massey, Douglas S. "The New Immigration and Ethnicity in the United
    States." *Population and Development Review* 21, no. 3 (1995): 631–52.

McCabe, Kristen. "African Immigrants in the United States." *Migration
    Information Source,* July 21, 2011. www.migrationpolicy.org/article/
    african-immigrants-united-states.

"Middle East." In *Encyclopedia Britannica.* Last modified August 20, 2014. https://www.britannica.com/place/Middle-East.

Murphy, Jim. *Pick & Shovel Poet: The Journeys of Pascal D'Angelo.* New York: Clarion Books, 2000.

Nee, Victor, and Hilary Holbrow. "Why Asian Americans Are Becoming Mainstream." *Daedalus* 142, no. 3 (2013): 65–75.

Pew Research Center. "Latinos and the New Trump Administration." Last modified February 23, 2017. www.pewhispanic.org/2017/02/23/latinos -and-the-new-trump-administration.

———. "Modern Immigration Wave Brings 59 Million to U.S., Driving Population Growth and Change through 2065." Last modified September 28, 2015. www.pewhispanic.org/2015/09/28/modern-immigration-wave -brings-59-million-to-u-s-driving-population-growth-and-change -through-2065.

———. "The Rise of Asian Americans." Last modified April 4, 2013. www .pewsocialtrends.org/2012/06/19/the-rise-of-asian-americans/.

Ross, Edward Alsworth. *The Old World in the New: The Significance of Past and Present Immigration to the American People.* New York: Century, 1914.

Ryan, Pam Muñoz. "From the Author: Learn about Pam Muñoz Ryan." https://www.scholastic.com/esperanza/popups/authornote.htm.

Thomas, Kevin J. A. "What Explains the Increasing Trend in African Emigration to the U.S.?" *The International Migration Review* 45, no. 1 (2011): 3–28.

Ting, Renee I. "Accessibility of Diverse Literature for Children in Libraries: A Literature Review." *SLIS Student Research Journal* 6, no. 2 (2017): 1–8.

Topp, Michael Miller. "Racial and Ethnic Identity in the United States, 1837–1877." In *Race and Ethnicity in America: A Concise History,* edited by Ronald H. Bayor, 63–95. New York: Columbia University Press, 2003.

Tschida, Christina M., Caitlin L. Ryan, and Anne Swenson Ticknor. "Building on Windows and Mirrors: Encouraging the Disruption of 'Single Stories' through Children's Literature." *Journal of Children's Literature* 40, no. 1 (2014): 28–39.

U.S. Census Bureau. "The Foreign-Born Population in the United States." www.census.gov/newsroom/pdf/cspan_fb_slides.pdf.

———. "Nativity, Citizenship, Year of Entry, and Region of Birth: 2000." https://factfinder.census.gov/faces/tableservices/jsf/pages/product view.xhtml?pid=DEC_00_SF3_QTP14&prodType=table.

———. "Selected Social Characteristics in the United States: 2009." http://factfinder2.census.gov/faces/tableservices/jsf/pages/productview .xhtml?pid=ACS_09_1YR_CP2&prodType=table.

———. "Selected Social Characteristics in the United States: 2009–2013 American Community Survey 5-Year Estimates." https://factfinder .census.gov/bkmk/table/1.0/en/ACS/13_5YR/DP02/330M200US422.

———. "Table 1.1. Population by Sex, Age, Nativity, and U.S. Citizenship Status: 2013." www.census.gov/data/tables/2013/demo/foreign-born/ cps-2013.html.

U.S. Department of Homeland Security. "INS Records for 1930s Mexican Repatriations." Last modified February 11, 2016. https://www.uscis .gov/history-and-genealogy/our-history/historians-mailbox/ins -records-1930s-mexican-repatriations.

U.S. Department of State. "U.S. Relations with Kosovo." Last modified March 17, 2016. https://www.state.gov/r/pa/ei/bgn/100931.htm.

———. "U.S. Relations with Taiwan." Last modified September 13, 2016. https://www.state.gov/r/pa/ei/bgn/35855.htm.

Vezzali, Loris, Sofia Stathi, and Dino Giovannini. "Indirect Contact through Book Reading: Improving Adolescents' Attitudes and Behavioral Intentions toward Immigrants." *Psychology in the Schools* 49, no. 2 (2012): 148–62.

White House Office of the Press Secretary. "Executive Order: Border Security and Immigration Enforcement Improvements." Last modified January 25, 2017. https://www.whitehouse.gov/the-press-office/2017/01/25/ executive-order-border-security-and-immigration-enforcement -improvements.

———. "Executive Order: Protecting the Nation from Foreign Terrorist Entry into the United States." Last modified January 27, 2017. https:// www.whitehouse.gov/the-press-office/2017/01/27/executive-order -protecting-nation-foreign-terrorist-entry-united-states.

Williams, Virginia Kay, and Nancy Deyoe. "Diverse Population, Diverse Collection? Youth Collections in the United States." *Technical Services Quarterly* 31, no. 2 (2014): 97–121.

Zhou, Min. "Growing Up American: The Challenge Confronting Immigrant Children and Children of Immigrants." *Annual Review of Sociology* 23 (1997): 63–95.

Zong, Jie, and Jeanne Batalova. "Asian Immigrants in the United States." *Migration Information Source*, January 6, 2016. www.migrationpolicy .org/article/asian-immigrants-united-states.

———. "Caribbean Immigrants in the United States." *Migration Information Source*, September 14, 2016. www.migrationpolicy.org/article/caribbean -immigrants-united-states.

———. "European Immigrants in the United States." *Migration Information Source*, December 1, 2015. www.migrationpolicy.org/article/european -immigrants-united-states.

———. "Mexican Immigrants in the United States." *Migration Information Source*, March 17, 2016. www.migrationpolicy.org/article/mexican -immigrants-united-states.

———. "Middle Eastern and North African Immigrants in the United States." *Migration Information Source*, June 3, 2015. www.migrationpolicy.org/ article/middle-eastern-and-north-african-immigrants-united-states.

———. "South American Immigrants in the United States." *Migration Information Source*, March 1, 2016. www.migrationpolicy.org/article/ south-american-immigrants-united-states.

———. "Sub-Saharan African Immigrants in the United States." *Migration Information Source*, October 30, 2014. www.migrationpolicy.org/article/ sub-saharan-african-immigrants-united-states-2.

———. "Syrian Refugees in the United States." *Migration Information Source*, January 12, 2017. www.migrationpolicy.org/article/syrian-refugees -united-states.

Zygmunt, Eva, Patricia Clark, Susan Tancock, Wilfridah Mucherah, and Jon Clausen. "Books like Me: Engaging the Community in the Intentional Selection of Culturally Relevant Children's Literature." *Childhood Education* 91, no. 1 (2015): 24–34.

INDEX

A

Act to Limit the Immigration of Aliens into the United States, 150, 189
adoption
  All the Broken Pieces: A Novel in Verse (Burg), 77–78
  Dogtag Summer (Partridge), 79–80
  Escape from Saigon: How a Vietnam War Orphan Became an American Boy (Warren), 80–81
  Mommy Far, Mommy Near: An Adoption Story (Peacock), 46–47
  Rebecca's Journey Home (Sugarman), 83–84
Afghanistan
  classification of, 26
  Come Back to Afghanistan: A California Teenager's Story (Akbar & Burton), 192–193
  Shooting Kabul (Senzai), 194–195
Africa/Middle East
  Afghanistan, 192–195
  characteristics of African immigrants, 185–187
  characteristics of Middle Eastern immigrants, 187–188
  Egypt, 195–196
  Ethiopia, 196–199
  immigration laws, impact on migrants, 188–191
  Iran, 199–201
  Israel, 201–202
  multiple African/Middle Eastern countries, 208–209
  Nigeria, 202–203
  recent migration from, 26
  scholarly resources, 191–192
  Sierra Leone, 204–205
  Sudan, 205–208
  unidentified African country, 209–211
African & American: West Africans in Post-Civil Rights America (Halter & Johnson), 192
African Americans, 149
African immigrants
  characteristics of, 185–187
  impact of immigration laws on, 188–191
Agosín, Marjorie, 100–102
Akbar, Said Hyder, 192–193
Al Wekhian, Jamil, 188
ALA (American Library Association), 15
Alegría, Malín, 139–140
Al-Hazza, Tami Craft, 13
Aliki, 157–158
All the Broken Pieces: A Novel in Verse (Burg), 77–78
Almaguer, Tomás, 98
Alvarez, Julia, 134–136
The Always Prayer Shawl (Oberman), 168–170
American Born Chinese (Yang), 40–41
American Library Association (ALA), 15
amnesty, 96
Anderson, Monica, 185
annotations, 24
Any Small Goodness: A Novel of the Barrio (Johnston), 118–119

Anya's Ghost (Brosgol), 170–171
APA Presidential Task Force on Immigration, 12, 26
Applegate, Katherine, 205–206
Arab-Israeli War, 190
Are Italians White?: How Race Is Made in America (Guglielmo & Salerno), 152
Argentina, 99–100
Armenia
    classification of, 26–27
    At Ellis Island: A History in Many Voices (Peacock), 153–154
Aronowitz, Michael, 12
Asgedom, Mawi, 198–199
Ashes of Roses (Auch), 160–161
Asia
    Asian immigration to U.S., 33–36
    Bangladesh, 37–39
    Cambodia, 39–40
    China/Taiwan, 40–55
    India, 55–61
    Japan, 61–66
    Korea, 66–77
    multiple Asian (and other) countries, 86–89
    recent migration from, 26
    scholarly resources, 36–37
    unidentified Asian country, 89–90
    Vietnam, 77–86
Asian American Dreams: The Emergence of an American People (Zia), 37
Asian immigrants
    discrimination against, 34–36
    increase in, 33
    success of, 33–34
Asian Immigration to the United States (Yang), 37
Asiatic Barred Zone Act, 188–189
Ask Me No Questions (Budhos), 37–39
At Ellis Island: A History in Many Voices (Peacock), 153–154
At the Edge of a Dream: The Story of Jewish Immigrants on New York's Lower East Side 1880–1920 (Epstein), 152
Auch, Mary Jane, 160–161

B
Backlash 9/11: Middle Eastern and Muslim Americans Respond (Bakalian & Bozorgmehr), 191
Bakalian, Anny P., 191
Bal, P. Matthijs, 9

Balderrama, Francisco E.
    Decade of Betrayal: Mexican Repatriation in the 1930s, 98
    on repatriation of Mexican immigrants, 96
Bangladesh, 37–39
Bartle, Lisa R., 21–22
Bartone, Elisa, 163–164
Batalova, Jeanne
    on Asian immigrants, 33, 34
    on European immigrants, 147
    on Middle Eastern immigrants, 187
Bayoumi, Moustafa, 191
Becoming American: The Early Arab Immigrant Experience (Naff), 192
Becoming Naomi León (Ryan), 119–120
Bercaw, Edna Coe, 67–68
Between Arab and White: Race and Ethnicity in the Early Syrian American Diaspora (Gualtieri), 191
Beyond Smoke and Mirrors: Mexican Immigration in an Era of Economic Integration (Massey, Durand, & Malone), 98
Bishop, Rudine Sims
    on books as mirrors/windows, 13, 15
    on multicultural literature, 8
Black Ethnics: Race, Immigration, and the Pursuit of the American Dream (Greer), 191
Bolshevik Revolution of 1917, 149
books
    on child/teen immigration as confidence-boosting mirrors, 11–14
    selection of literary texts, 21–24
    as tolerance-promoting windows into worlds of young immigrants, 8–11
Borderline (Stratton), 199–201
Born Confused (Hidier), 55–57
Bozorgmehr, Mehdi, 191
Bracero Program, 95
Brave Girl: Clara and the Shirtwaist Makers' Strike of 1909 (Markel), 178–179
Brooklyn Bridge (Hesse), 171–172
Brosgol, Vera, 170–171
Brown, Monica, 142–143
Brown v. Board of Education, 136
Broyles, Anne, 175–176
Bucher, Katherine T., 13
Budhos, Marina, 37–39
bullying
    All the Broken Pieces: A Novel in Verse (Burg), 77–78
    Borderline (Stratton), 199–200
    Drita, My Homegirl (Lombard), 166–167

90 Miles to Havana (Flores-Galbis), 102–103
Shooting Kabul (Senzai), 194–195
Yoon and the Jade Bracelet (Recorvits), 76–77
Bunting, Eve, 89–90
Burg, Ann E., 77–78
Burning Beethoven: The Eradication of German Culture in the United States during World War I (Kirschbaum & Stupp), 153
Burton, Susan, 192–193
Burundi, 186
Buss, Fran Leeper, 108–109

C

California Gold Rush, 34
Cambodia, 39–40
Cameron, Lindsey, 10
Caribbean
    immigrants from, 93–94, 97
    recent migration from, 26
    See also Latin America/Caribbean
Carter, Alden R., 86
Central America
    immigrants from, 93–94, 97
    Journey of Dreams (Pellegrino), 109–110
    See also Latin America/Caribbean
Cervantes, Angela, 115–116
Chang, Iris, 36
Charlton-Trujillo, E., 132–133
child labor
    Brave Girl: Clara and the Shirtwaist Makers' Strike of 1909 (Markel), 178–179
    Peppe the Lamplighter (Bartone), 163–164
children
    books as tolerance-promoting windows into worlds of young immigrants, 8–11
    books on child/teen immigration as confidence-boosting mirrors, 11–14
    immigrant status of, 3
    multicultural literature, benefits of, 4
Children's Literature Comprehensive Database, 21–22
Chile, 100–102
China/Taiwan
    American Born Chinese (Yang), 40–41
    as country of origin for Asian immigrants, 33
    Good Fortune: My Journey to Gold Mountain (Wong), 42–43
    Hannah Is My Name (Yang), 43–44
    Landed (Lee), 44–46
    Mommy Far, Mommy Near: An Adoption Story (Peacock), 46–47

My Chinatown: One Year in Poems (Mak), 47–48
Ruby Lu, Brave and True (Look), 48–50
Ruby Lu, Empress of Everything (Look), 50–51
Split Image: A Story in Poems (Glenn), 51–52
Yang the Youngest and His Terrible Ear (Namioka), 53–54
The Year of the Dog: A Novel (Lin), 54–55
Chinese Exclusion Act, 5, 34–35
Chinese immigrants, 5, 34–35
The Chinese in America: A Narrative History (Chang), 36
Choi, Yangsook, 44, 45
Choy, Catherine Ceniza, 36
The Circuit: Stories from the Life of a Migrant Child (Jiménez), 120–122
Cohn, Diana, 137–139
The Columbia Guide to Asian American History (Okihiro), 37
The Columbia History of Latinos in the United States since 1960 (Gutiérrez), 98
Come Back to Afghanistan: A California Teenager's Story (Akbar & Burton), 192–193
Coming to America: A History of Immigration and Ethnicity in American Life (Daniels), 152
Coming to America: A Muslim Family's Story (Wolf), 195–196
confidence, 11–14
Cooney, Caroline B., 204–205
CrashBoomLove: A Novel in Verse (Herrera), 122–123
Cress, Susan W., 9
Cuba
    Cuba 15 (Osa), 103–105
    Flight to Freedom (Veciana-Suarez), 105–106
    Heat (Lupica), 106–107
    immigrants from, 97
    90 Miles to Havana (Flores-Galbis), 102–103
    Cuba 15 (Osa), 103–105
Cuban Adjustment Act of 1966, 97
Cubias, Daisy, 108–109
cultural authenticity, 23–24
Czech Republic, 155–156

D

Daniels, Roger, 152
database
    for selection of literary texts, 21–22
    The Stories We Share database, 27
Database of Award-Winning Children's Literature, 21–22
De León, Arnoldo, 98

Dear Juno (Pak), 66–67
*Decade of Betrayal: Mexican Repatriation in the
    1930s* (Balderrama & Rodríguez), 98
Delgado, Francisco, 137
Democratic Republic of Congo, 186
DeSipio, Louis, 191
Deyoe, Nancy, 15, 23
Diamonds in the Shadow (Cooney), 204–205
difference, 6–7
Difference and Pathology (Gilman), 6–7
discrimination
    against Asian immigrants, 34–36
    books as tolerance-promoting windows, 8–11
    Borderline (Stratton), 199–201
    against European immigrants, 148–152
    against immigrant Other, theories of, 5–7
    impact of immigration laws on Middle
        Eastern/African immigrants, 188–191
    against Italian immigrants, 162–163
    against Japanese Americans, 63–64
    against Latin American immigrants, 94
    against Mexican immigrants, 95–97
    against Middle Eastern immigrants, 188
    against Sammy Lee, 72
    *Separate Is Never Equal: Sylvia Mendez & Her
        Family's Fight for Desegregation*, 136–137
    Shooting Kabul (Senzai), 194–195
    Stormwitch (Vaught), 112–113
    Weedflower (Kadohata), 65–66
Diversity Visa Program, 186, 190
Dogtag Summer (Partridge), 79–80
Dolan, Jay P., 152
Dominican Republic, 97
Drita, My Homegirl (Lombard), 166–167
*Driven Out: The Forgotten War against Chinese
    Americans* (Pfaelzer), 37
Durand, Jorge
    *Beyond Smoke and Mirrors: Mexican
        Immigration in an Era of Economic
        Integration*, 98
    on Bracero Program, 95

E

Eastern Europe
    discrimination against Eastern European
        immigrants, 149–150
    immigration from, 147–148
    See also Europe
economic concerns, 6

education
    of African immigrants, 186–187
    of Asian immigrants, 33–34
    books as confidence-boosting mirrors, 11–14
    books as tolerance-promoting windows, 8–11
    of European immigrants, 148
    of Latin American immigrants, 94
    of Middle Eastern immigrants, 187
    multicultural literature for, 4
    stereotypes and, 7
Egypt
    classification of, 26
    Coming to America: A Muslim Family's Story
        (Wolf), 195–196
    immigrants from, 187
El Salvador
    immigrants from, 97
    Journey of the Sparrows (Buss & Cubias),
        108–109
Elya, Susan Middleton, 125–126
emotional transportation, 9–10
empathy, 9–10
employment
    of Mexican immigrants, 96–97
    role in Mexican immigration patterns, 94–95
English language
    Home at Last (Elya), 125–126
    immigrant children and, 12
    proficiency of African immigrants, 186–187
    proficiency of Asian immigrants, 34
    proficiency of European immigrants, 148
    proficiency of Middle Eastern immigrants,
        187
Epstein, Lawrence J., 152
Eritrea, 186
*Escape from Saigon: How a Vietnam War Orphan
    Became an American Boy* (Warren), 80–81
Esperanza Rising (Ryan), 123–125
Ethiopia
    *Of Beetles & Angels: A Boy's Remarkable
        Journey from a Refugee Camp to Harvard*
        (Asgedom), 198–199
    Faraway Home (Kurtz), 196–198
    immigrants from, 186
eugenics, 149–150
Europe
    Armenia, 153–154
    Czech Republic, 155–156
    European immigration to U.S., 147–152
    Germany, 156–157

Greece, 157–158
Hungary, 159–160
Ireland, 160–161
Italy, 162–165
Kosovo, 166–167
Poland, 167–168
Russia, 168–176
scholarly resources, 152–153
Scotland (United Kingdom), 177–178
Ukraine, 178–179
unidentified European country, 180–181
Every Time a Rainbow Dies (Williams-Garcia),
116–117

F
Fader, Jamie J., 97
Faraway Home (Kurtz), 196–198
Felin, M. Sindy, 113–114
females
Brave Girl: Clara and the Shirtwaist Makers'
Strike of 1909 (Markel), 178–179
female genital mutilation, 202–203
Yell-Oh Girls!: Emerging Voices Explore Culture,
Identity, and Growing Up Asian American,
87–89
fiction, 9
Filipinos, 35
"First Crossing" (Ryan), 86
First Crossing: Stories about Teen Immigrants
(Gallo), 86–87
First Quota Act, 150, 189
Flores-Galbis, Enrique, 102–103
Foad, Hisham S., 190
Fresh Girl (Placide), 110–112
Friedman, Robin, 201–202
Full Cicada Moon (Hilton), 61–63

G
Gaby, Lost and Found (Cervantes), 115–116
Gall, Meredith Damien, 11
Gallo, Donald R., 86–87
gangs
Any Small Goodness: A Novel of the Barrio
(Johnston), 118–119
Illegal (Restrepo), 126–127
Shadow of the Dragon (Garland), 84–85
Garland, Sherry, 84–86
Garza, Rodolfo O. de la, 191

Gentlemen's Agreement, 35
Germany
discrimination against German immigrants,
150–152
How I Became an American (Gündisch),
156–157
Ghana, 186
Gillett, Maxwell, 11
Gilman, Sander, 6–7
Giovannini, Dino, 10
Glenn, Mel, 51–52
Global Families: A History of Asian International
Adoption in America (Choy), 36
Gonzales, Manuel G., 98
González, Juan, 98
Good Fortune: My Journey to Gold Mountain
(Wong), 42–43
grade reading levels, 22
Grant, Madison, 150
Graseck, Susan, 10
The Great Departure: Mass Migration from Eastern
Europe and the Making of the Free World (Zahra),
153
Great Depression, 96
Greece, 157–158
"The Green Armchair" (Ho), 86
Greer, Christina M., 191
Griffin, Paul, 209–211
Griswold del Castillo, Richard, 98
Gualtieri, Sarah M. A., 191
Guatemala
immigrants from, 97
Journey of Dreams (Pellegrino), 109–110
Guglielmo, Jennifer, 152
Gündisch, Karin, 156–157
Gutiérrez, David, 98
Gutiérrez, Ramón A., 98

H
Haines, David W., 191
Hainmueller, Jens, 6
Haiti
Fresh Girl (Placide), 110–112
immigrants from, 97
Stormwitch (Vaught), 112–113
Touching Snow (Felin), 113–114
Half and Half (Namioka), 177–178
Halloween, 175–176
Halmoni's Day (Bercaw), 67–68

Halter, Marilyn, 192
Hannah Is My Name (Yang), 43–44
Harris, Carol Flynn, 164–165
Harvest of Empire: A History of Latinos in America
  (González), 98
Heat (Lupica), 106–107
Heinze, Andrew R., 149
Hernández-León, Rubén, 98
Herrera, Juan Felipe, 122–123
Hesse, Karen
  Brooklyn Bridge, 171–172
  Letters from Rifka, 174–175
Hest, Amy, 180–181
Hidier, Tanuja Desai, 55–57
Hilton, Marilyn, 61–63
Hispanic Americans
  immigration to U.S., 94–98
  percentage of U.S. population, 93–94
  See also Mexico
Ho, Minfong, 86
Holm, Daniel T., 9
Holm, Jennifer L., 162–163
Home at Last (Elya), 125–126
Home of the Brave (Applegate), 205–206
Honduras
  Gaby, Lost and Found (Cervantes), 115–116
  immigrants from, 97
Hopkins, Daniel J., 6
*How Does It Feel to Be a Problem?: Being Young and
  Arab in America* (Bayoumi), 191
How I Became an American (Gündisch), 156–157
How the Irish Became White (Ignatiev), 153
Hungary, 159–160
Hwang, Wei-Chin, 12

I

I Lived on Butterfly Hill (Agosín), 100–102
identity
  of immigrant children/teens, 11–12, 13
  national identity, 6–7
  See also self
Ignatiev, Noel, 153
Illegal (Restrepo), 126–127
illegal immigrants
  Illegal (Restrepo), 126–127
  La Línea (Jaramillo), 128–129
  Return to Sender (Alvarez), 134–136
  Sofi Mendoza's Guide to Getting Lost in Mexico
    (Alegría), 139–140

immigrant Other
  Asian immigrants as, 34–36
  European immigrants as, 148–152
  Irish immigrants as, 148–149
  Mexican immigrants as, 95–96
  Middle Eastern immigrants as, 188
  multicultural literature as window, 8–9
  theories of discrimination against, 5–7
immigrants
  books as confidence-boosting mirrors, 11–14
  books as tolerance-promoting windows, 8–11
  limited availability of literature on, 14–15
  multicultural literature, benefits of, 4
  number of, 3
immigration
  African immigrants, characteristics of, 185–187
  Asian immigration to U.S., 33–36
  European immigration to U.S., 147–152
  immigration laws, impact on Middle Eastern/
    African migrants, 188–191
  Latin American/Caribbean immigration to
    U.S., 93–98
  selection of literary texts about, 21–24
Immigration Act of 1917, 35
Immigration Act of 1924
  immigration ban on Asians, 35
  Mexican immigrants and, 95
  quota-based restrictions with, 6
Immigration and Nationality Act of 1965
  European immigration and, 147
  impact on African immigrants, 189–190
  impact on Asian immigration, 36
  impact on Middle Eastern immigrants, 190
Immigration Reform and Control Act (IRCA),
  96–97
The Importance of Wings (Friedman), 201–202
income
  of Asian immigrants, 34
  of European immigrants, 148
  of Latin American/Caribbean immigrants, 94
  of Middle Eastern immigrants, 187
India
  Born Confused (Hidier), 55–57
  as country of origin for Asian immigrants, 33
  Monsoon Summer (Perkins), 57–58
  Motherland: A Novel (Vijayaraghavan), 58–60
  Shine, Coconut Moon (Meminger), 60–61
individuation, 6–7
*Infamy: The Shocking Story of the Japanese American
  Internment in World War II* (Reeves), 37

Inside Out & Back Again (Lai), 81–83
internment camps
    Italian Americans in, 151
    Japanese Americans in, 35
    Weedflower (Kadohata), 65–66
Iran, 199–201
Iraq, 187
IRCA (Immigration Reform and Control Act), 96–97
Ireland, 160–161
The Irish Americans: A History (Dolan), 152
Irish immigrants
    discrimination against, 148–149
    as immigrant Other, 5, 7
Islam
    Borderline (Stratton), 199–201
    Coming to America: A Muslim Family's Story
        (Wolf), 195–196
    perception of Middle Eastern immigrants in
        U.S., 188
Islamophobia
    Shooting Kabul (Senzai), 194–195
    in U.S., 188
Israel, 201–202
Italians
    discrimination against, 151–152
    immigration to U.S., 149–150
Italy
    Penny from Heaven (Holm), 162–163
    Peppe the Lamplighter (Bartone), 163–164
    A Place for Joey (Harris), 164–165

J

Jacobs, Linda K., 192
Jacobson, Matthew Frye, 153
Jamaica
    Every Time a Rainbow Dies (Williams-Garcia),
        116–117
    immigrants from, 97
Japan
    Under the Blood-Red Sun (Salisbury), 63–64
    as country of origin for Asian immigrants, 33
    Full Cicada Moon (Hilton), 61–63
    Weedflower (Kadohata), 65–66
Japanese immigrants, 35
Jaramillo, Ann, 128–129
Jaret, Charles, 152, 188
Jewish immigrants
    The Always Prayer Shawl (Oberman), 168–170
    discrimination against, 5

immigration to U.S., 149–152
    Letters from Rifka (Hesse), 174–175
    Rivka's First Thanksgiving (Rael), 167–168
    When Jessie Came Across the Sea (Hest), 180–181
Jiménez, Francisco, 120–122
Johnson, Lyndon B., 36
Johnson, Violet Showers, 192
Johnston, Tony, 118–119
Journey of Dreams (Pellegrino), 109–110
Journey of the Sparrows (Buss & Cubias), 108–109
Journey to the Golden Land (Rosenblum), 172–174

K

Kadohata, Cynthia, 65–66
Karr, Kathleen, 159–160
Karzai, Hamid, 192
Katz, Michael B., 96–97
Kenya, 186
Kirschbaum, Erik, 153
Kitano, Harry H. L., 35, 95–96
Korea
    as country of origin for Asian immigrants, 33
    Dear Juno (Pak), 66–67
    Halmoni's Day (Bercaw), 67–68
    My Name Is Yoon (Recorvits), 69–70
    Necessary Roughness (Lee), 70–71
    *Sixteen Years in Sixteen Seconds: The Sammy
        Lee Story* (Yoo), 71–73
    A Step from Heaven (Na), 73–74
    Wait for Me (Na), 74–76
    Yoon and the Jade Bracelet (Recorvits), 76–77
Kosovo, 166–167
Kovalski, Maryann, 167
Kramer, Paul A., 4
Krudop, Walter Lyon, 153
Kurtz, Jane, 196–198

L

La Línea (Jaramillo), 128–129
Lai, Thanhha, 81–83
Landed (Lee), 44–46
Latin America/Caribbean
    Argentina, 99–100
    Chile, 100–102
    Cuba, 102–107
    El Salvador, 108–109
    Guatemala, 109–110
    Haiti, 110–114

Latin America/Caribbean (continued)
    Honduras, 115–116
    immigration to U.S., 93–98
    Jamaica, 116–117
    Mexico, 118–142
    Peru, 142–143
    recent migration from, 26
    scholarly resources, 98–99
Latinos: Remaking America (Suárez-Orozco &
    Páez), 98
laws, immigration, 188–191
Lebanon, 187
Lee, Erika, 37
Lee, Marie G.
    Necessary Roughness, 70–71
    "The Rose of Sharon," 86
Lee, Milly, 44–46
Lee, Sammy, 71–73
Lempke, Susan Dove, 14
Letters from Rifka (Hesse), 174–175
Lewin, Ted
    illustrations for Peppe the Lamplighter
        (Bartone), 163, 164
    illustrations for The Always Prayer Shawl
        (Oberman), 168, 169
Lewis, E. B., 196
Liberia, 186
libraries, 14–15
Life, After (Littman), 99–100
Lifshitz, Jessica, 13
Lin, Grace
    on lack of multicultural literature, 14
    The Year of the Dog: A Novel, 54–55
"Lines of Scrimmage" (Marston), 86
literature, 8–11
    See also multicultural literature
Littman, Sarah Darer, 99–100
Lombard, Jenny, 166–167
Look, Lenore
    Ruby Lu, Brave and True, 48–50
    Ruby Lu, Empress of Everything, 50–51
Los Angeles Justice for Janitors Campaign, 137
Lubar, David, 86
Lupica, Mike, 106–107
Lynch, Patrick James, 180

M

Madlenka (Sís), 155–156
Maine Humanities Council, 39
Mak, Kam, 47–48

"Make Maddie Mad" (Williams-Garcia), 86
Malone, Nolan J., 98
Man of the Family (Karr), 159–160
Manderson, Desmond, 9
Mar, Raymond A., 9
Marianthe's Story: Painted Words and Spoken
    Memories (Aliki), 157–158
Marisol McDonald Doesn't Match/Marisol
    McDonald No Combina (Brown), 142–143
Markel, Michelle, 178–179
Marshall Plan, 147
Marston, Elsa, 86
Massey, Douglas S.
    Beyond Smoke and Mirrors: Mexican
        Immigration in an Era of Economic
        Integration, 98
    on Bracero Program, 95
    New Faces in New Places: The Changing
        Geography of American Immigration, 98
McCall, Guadalupe Garcia, 140–142
Medina, Jane, 130–132
Meminger, Neesha, 60–61
MENA (Middle East and North Africa), 187, 190
Mexicanos: A History of Mexicans in the United
    States (Gonzales), 98
Mexico
    Any Small Goodness: A Novel of the Barrio
        (Johnston), 118–119
    Becoming Naomi León (Ryan), 119–120
    The Circuit: Stories from the Life of a Migrant
        Child (Jiménez), 120–122
    CrashBoomLove: A Novel in Verse (Herrera),
        122–123
    Esperanza Rising (Ryan), 123–125
    history of migration to U.S. from, 94–97
    Home at Last (Elya), 125–126
    Illegal (Restrepo), 126–127
    immigrants from, 93–94
    La Línea (Jaramillo), 128–129
    Under the Mesquite (McCall), 140–142
    My Diary from Here to There/Mi Diario de Aquí
        Hasta Allá (Pérez), 129–130
    My Name Is Jorge: On Both Sides of the River
        (Medina), 130–132
    Prizefighter en Mi Casa (Charlton-Trujillo),
        132–133
    The Quiet Place (Stewart), 133–134
    Return to Sender (Alvarez), 134–136
    Separate Is Never Equal: Sylvia Mendez & Her
        Family's Fight for Desegregation (Tonatiuh),
        136–137

¡Sí, Se Puede!/Yes, We Can!: Janitor Strike in L.A. (Cohn), 137–139
Sofi Mendoza's Guide to Getting Lost in Mexico (Alegría), 139–140
Michalikova, Nina, 153
Middle East
    See Africa/Middle East
Middle East and North Africa (MENA), 187, 190
Middle Eastern immigrants
    characteristics of, 187–188
    impact of immigration laws on, 188–191
    self-validation through reading, 13
migrant workers, 120–122
Migration Policy Institute, 190
minorities
    Asian Americans as racial minority in U.S., 33
    books on child/teen immigration as confidence-boosting mirrors, 11–14
    lack of multicultural literature, 14–15
Mohammed, Khadra, 207–208
Mommy Far, Mommy Near: An Adoption Story (Peacock), 46–47
Monsoon Summer (Perkins), 57–58
Morin, Leane, 175
Morocco, 186
Motherland: A Novel (Vijayaraghavan), 58–60
multicultural literature
    books as tolerance-promoting windows into worlds of young immigrants, 8–11
    books on child/teen immigration as confidence-boosting mirrors, 11–14
    limited availability of, 14–15
    selection of literary texts, 21–24
Muslims
    Borderline (Stratton), 199–201
    Coming to America: A Muslim Family's Story (Wolf), 195–196
    perception of Middle Eastern immigrants in U.S., 188
My Chinatown: One Year in Poems (Mak), 47–48
My Diary from Here to There/Mi Diario de Aquí Hasta Allá (Pérez), 129–130
"My Favorite Chaperone" (Okimoto), 86
My Name Is Jorge: On Both Sides of the River (Medina), 130–132
My Name Is Sangoel (Williams & Mohammed), 207–208
My Name Is Yoon (Recorvits), 69–70

N
Na, An
    A Step from Heaven, 73–74
    Wait for Me, 74–76
Naff, Alixa, 192
Nam, Vickie, 87–89
Namioka, Lensey
    Half and Half, 177–178
    "They Don't Mean It!," 86
    Yang the Youngest and His Terrible Ear, 53–54
national identity, 6–7
nationalism, U.S., 98
national-origins quota system
    European immigration and, 150
    Middle Eastern immigrants and, 189
    removal of, 147
nativism, 149–151
Naturalization Act of 1790, 149
Necessary Roughness (Lee), 70–71
New Destinations: Mexican Immigration in the United States (Zúñiga & Hernández-León), 98
New Eastern European Immigrants in the United States (Michalikova), 153
New Faces in New Places: The Changing Geography of American Immigration (Massey), 98
The New Latino Studies Reader: A Twenty-First-Century Perspective (Gutiérrez & Almaguer), 98
Nicaragua, 97
Nigeria
    immigrants from, 186
    No Laughter Here (Williams-Garcia), 202–203
90 Miles to Havana (Flores-Galbis), 102–103
No Laughter Here (Williams-Garcia), 202–203
North to Aztlán: A History of Mexican Americans in the United States (De León & Griswold del Castillo), 98

O
Oatley, Keith, 9
Obama, Barack, 187
Oberman, Sheldon, 168–170
O'Brien, Anne Sibley, 39–40
Of Beetles & Angels: A Boy's Remarkable Journey from a Refugee Camp to Harvard (Asgedom), 198–199
Okihiro, Gary Y., 37
Okimoto, Jean Davies, 86
The Old World in the New (Ross), 5–6

One Green Apple (Bunting), 89–90
The Orange Houses (Griffin), 209–211
Osa, Nancy, 103–105
Other
    See immigrant Other
The Other African Americans: Contemporary African and Caribbean Immigrants in the United States (Shaw-Taylor & Tuch), 192
Outcasts United: An American Town, a Refugee Team, and One Woman's Quest to Make a Difference (St. John), 208
Outcasts United: The Story of a Refugee Soccer Team That Changed a Town (St. John), 208–209

P

Páez, Mariela, 98
Page Law, 34
Pak, Soyung, 66–67
Palacios, Sara, 142–143
Palestinian immigrants, 190
parents, 12
Partridge, Elizabeth, 79–80
A Path of Stars (O'Brien), 39–40
Peacock, Antoinette, 46–47
Peacock, Louise, 153–154
Pellegrino, Marge, 109–110
Penny from Heaven (Holm), 162–163
Peppe the Lamplighter (Bartone), 163–164
Pérez, Amanda Irma, 129–130
Perkins, Mitali, 57–58
Peru, 142–143
Peterson, Jordan B., 9
Pew Research Center
    on Asian immigrants, 34
    on Latin American immigrants, 94
    on views of European immigrants, 148
Pfaelzer, Jean, 37
Philippines, 33
A Place for Joey (Harris), 164–165
Placide, Jaïra, 110–112
poetry
    CrashBoomLove: A Novel in Verse (Herrera), 122–123
    My Name Is Jorge: On Both Sides of the River (Medina), 130–132
    Split Image: A Story in Poems (Glenn), 51–52
Poland, 167–168
post-reading discussions, 10–11
poverty, 187

prejudice
    See discrimination
Prizefighter en Mi Casa (Charlton-Trujillo), 132–133
public opinion
    on European immigrants, 148
    on Latin American immigrants, 94
"Pulling Up Stakes" (Lubar), 86

Q

quality, of literary texts, 23
questions, 23–25
The Quiet Place (Stewart), 133–134
quota
    See national-origins quota system

R

race/ethnicity
    books as confidence-boosting mirrors, 11–14
    books as tolerance-promoting windows, 8–11
    immigrant Other, theories of discrimination against, 5–7
    See also discrimination
Rael, Elsa Okon, 167–168
Rebecca's Journey Home (Sugarman), 83–84
Recorvits, Helen
    My Name Is Yoon, 69–70
    Yoon and the Jade Bracelet, 76–77
Reeves, Richard, 37
Refugee Act of 1980, 190
refugees
    African immigrants as, 186–187
    All the Broken Pieces: A Novel in Verse (Burg), 77–78
    from Asia, 36
    Of Beetles & Angels: A Boy's Remarkable Journey from a Refugee Camp to Harvard (Asgedom), 198–199
    Diamonds in the Shadow (Cooney), 204–205
    Drita, My Homegirl (Lombard), 166–167
    Home of the Brave (Applegate), 205–206
    Inside Out & Back Again (Lai), 81–83
    Journey of the Sparrows (Buss & Cubias), 108–109
    from Latin America/Caribbean, 97
    from Middle East, 187–188
    Middle Eastern/African immigrants as, 190
    Muslim ban in U.S., 191
    My Name Is Sangoel (Williams & Mohammed), 207

Outcasts United: The Story of a Refugee Soccer Team That Changed a Town (St. John), 208–209
Shadow of the Dragon (Garland), 84–86
story reading, impact of, 10
Regan, Dian Curtis, 86
religion
    Borderline (Stratton), 199–201
    Coming to America: A Muslim Family's Story (Wolf), 195–196
    Islamophobia in U.S., 188
    Muslim ban in U.S., 191
    See also Jewish immigrants
repatriation, 96
Republic of Kosovo, 27
resources, 27
    See also scholarly resources
Restrepo, Bettina, 126–127
Return to Sender (Alvarez), 134–136
Rivka's First Thanksgiving (Rael), 167–168
Roberts, Kenneth, 150
Rodríguez, Raymond, 98
Roediger, David R., 153
"The Rose of Sharon" (Lee), 86
Rosenblum, Richard, 172–174
Ross, Edward A., 5–6
Ruby Lu, Brave and True (Look), 48–50
Ruby Lu, Empress of Everything (Look), 50–51
Russia
    The Always Prayer Shawl (Oberman), 168–170
    Anya's Ghost (Brosgol), 170–171
    Brooklyn Bridge (Hesse), 171–172
    immigrants from, 149
    Journey to the Golden Land (Rosenblum), 172–174
    Letters from Rifka (Hesse), 174–175
    Shy Mama's Halloween (Broyles), 175–176
Ryan, Caitlin L., 14
Ryan, Pam Muñoz
    Becoming Naomi León, 119–120
    Esperanza Rising, 123–125
    "First Crossing," 86
    on repatriation of Mexican immigrants, 96

S

Safe Haven?: A History of Refugees in America (Haines), 191
Salerno, Salvatore, 152
Salisbury, Graham, 63–64
Saudi Arabia, 187

scholarly resources
    on Africa/Middle East immigration, 191–192
    on Asian immigration, 36–37
    on European immigration, 152–153
    on Latin America/Caribbean immigration, 98–99
Scotland (United Kingdom), 177–178
"Second Culture Kids" (Regan), 86
segregation, 136–137
selection/organization principles
    chapter organization, 26–27
    selection of literary texts, 21–24
    The Stories We Share database, 27
    style, discussion, recommendations for use, 24–25
self
    books on child/teen immigration as confidence-boosting mirrors, 11–14
    fear of difference, 6–7
    See also identity
self-reflection, 8
Senzai, N. H., 194–195
Separate Is Never Equal: Sylvia Mendez & Her Family's Fight for Desegregation (Tonatiuh), 136–137
Shadow of the Dragon (Garland), 84–86
Shapiro, Michelle, 83
Shaw-Taylor, Yoku, 192
Shine, Coconut Moon (Meminger), 60–61
Shooting Kabul (Senzai), 194–195
Shy Mama's Halloween (Broyles), 175–176
¡Sí, Se Puede! /Yes, We Can!: Janitor Strike in L.A. (Cohn), 137–139
Sierra Leone
    Diamonds in the Shadow (Cooney), 204–205
    immigrants from, 186
Sís, Peter, 155–156
slavery, 189
Slavs, 149–152
Small, David, 133–134
Sofi Mendoza's Guide to Getting Lost in Mexico (Alegría), 139–140
Somalia, 186
South Africa, 186
South America, 93–94, 97
    See also Latin America/Caribbean
Southern Europe, 149–150
Split Image: A Story in Poems (Glenn), 51–52
St. John, Warren, 208–209
Stathi, Sofia, 10

Steiner, Matt, 80–81
stereotypes
    in *American Born Chinese* (Yang), 40–41
    individuation and, 6–7
    of Irish immigrants, 149
Stern, Mark J., 97
Stewart, Sarah, 133–134
Stock, Catherine, 207
Stoddard, Lothrop, 150
The Stories We Share database, 27
Strangers from a Different Shore: A History of Asian
    Americans (Takaki), 37
Strangers in the West: The Syrian Colony of New
    York City, 1880–1900 (Jacobs), 192
Stratton, Allan, 199–201
Stupp, Herbert W., 153
Suárez-Orozco, Marcelo M., 98
Sudan
    Home of the Brave (Applegate), 205–206
    immigrants from, 186
    My Name Is Sangoel (Williams & Mohammed),
        207–208
Sugarman, Brynn Olenberg, 83–84
suicide, 51–52
"The Swede" (Carter), 86
Sweet, Melissa, 178, 179
Syria, 187, 188–189

T
Taiwan, 27
    See also China/Taiwan
Takaki, Ronald T., 37
terrorism
    Borderline (Stratton), 199–201
    discrimination against Middle Eastern
        immigrants, 188
    immigration laws, impact on immigrants, 191
    Shooting Kabul (Senzai), 194–195
Thanksgiving, 167
"They Don't Mean It!" (Namioka), 86
This American Life (NPR), 192
Thomas, Kevin J. A., 186, 190
Ticknor, Anne Swenson, 14
tolerance, 8–11
Tonatiuh, Duncan, 136–137
Topp, Michael Miller, 5
Touching Snow (Felin), 113–114

Trump, Donald
    executive order on immigration, 4
    Muslim ban, 191
    stance towards Latinos, 98
Tschida, Christina M., 14
Tuch, Steven A., 192

U
Ukraine, 178–179
Under the Blood-Red Sun (Salisbury), 63–64
Under the Mesquite (McCall), 140–142
United States
    African immigrants in, 185–187
    Asian immigration to, 33–36
    discrimination against immigrant Other,
        theories of, 5–7
    European immigration to, 147–152
    impact of immigration laws on Middle
        Eastern/African immigrants, 188–191
    Latin American/Caribbean immigration to
        U.S., 93–98
    Middle Eastern immigrants in, 187–188
U.S. Census Bureau, 3, 14
U.S. Department of Homeland Security, 96
US Immigration in the Twenty-First Century:
    Making Americans, Remaking America (DeSipio
    & Garza), 191
U.S.-Cuba Migration Accords, 97
U.S.-Mexico border wall, 98

V
Vaught, Susan, 112–113
Veciana-Suarez, Ana, 105–106
Veltkamp, Martijn, 9
Vezzali, Loris, 10
Vietnam
    All the Broken Pieces: A Novel in Verse (Burg),
        77–78
    as country of origin for Asian immigrants, 33
    Dogtag Summer (Partridge), 79–80
    Escape from Saigon: How a Vietnam War
        Orphan Became an American Boy
        (Warren), 80–81
    Inside Out & Back Again (Lai), 81–83
    Rebecca's Journey Home (Sugarman), 83–84
    Shadow of the Dragon (Garland), 84–86

The Vietnamese Boat People, 1954 and 1975–1992
    (Vo), 37
Vijayaraghavan, Vineeta, 58–60
Vo, Nghia M., 37

W

Wait for Me (Na), 74–76
Warren, Andrea, 80–81
Weedflower (Kadohata), 65–66
When Jessie Came Across the Sea (Hest), 180–181
whiteness
    European immigrants and, 149–150, 152
    Middle Eastern immigrants and, 189
    theories of discrimination against immigrant
        Other, 5–6
*Whiteness of a Different Color: European Immigrants
    and the Alchemy of Race* (Jacobson), 153
whites
    discrimination against European immigrants,
        148–152
    percentage of U.S. population, 93
Williams, Karen Lynn, 207–208
Williams, Virginia Kay, 15, 23
Williams-Garcia, Rita
    Every Time a Rainbow Dies, 116–117
    "Make Maddie Mad," 86
    No Laughter Here, 202–203
Wilsdorf, Anne, 48, 50
Wolf, Barnard, 195–196
Wong, Li Keng, 42–43
*Working Toward Whiteness: How America's
    Immigrants Became White: The Strange Journey
    from Ellis Island to the Suburbs* (Roediger), 153
World War I
    discrimination against European immigrants
        during, 150–151
    Mexican immigration during, 95

World War II
    Under the Blood-Red Sun (Salisbury), 63–64
    discrimination against European immigrants
        during, 150–151
    discrimination against Japanese Americans
        during, 35
    European immigration and, 147
    Mexican immigration during, 95
    Weedflower (Kadohata), 65–66

Y

Yang, Belle, 43–44
Yang, Gene Luen, 40–41
Yang, Philip Q., 37
Yang the Youngest and His Terrible Ear (Namioka),
    53–54
The Year of the Dog: A Novel (Lin), 54–55
*Yell-Oh Girls!: Emerging Voices Explore Culture,
    Identity, and Growing Up Asian American* (Nam),
    87–89
Yoo, Paula, 71–73
Yoon and the Jade Bracelet (Recorvits), 76–77

Z

Zahra, Tara, 153
Zenteno, Rene M., 95
Zia, Helen, 37
Zong, Jie
    on Asian immigrants, 33, 34
    on European immigrants, 147
    on Middle Eastern immigrants, 187
Zúñiga, Víctor, 98